Just Postmode

Postmodern Studies 23

Series
edited by
Theo D'haen
and
Hans Bertens

Postmodern Studies 23

Just Postmodernism

Edited by
Steven Earnshaw

Rodopi

Amsterdam - Atlanta, GA 1997

⊗ The paper on which this book is printed meets the requirements of "ISO 9706:1994, Information and documentation - Paper for documents - Requirements for permanence".

ISBN: 90-420-0276-X (bound)
ISBN: 90-420-0233-6 (paper)
Editions Rodopi B.V., Amsterdam - Atlanta, GA 1997
Printed in The Netherlands

Table of Contents

ABSTRACTS
iii-viii

STEVEN EARNSHAW
'Just Postmodernism: Introduction'
ix-xxv

STELLA SWAIN
'Postmodern Narratives and the Absurdity of Law'
1-28

JOHN PHILLIPS
'Just Sentences: The Incalculable in Postmodern Justice'
29-50

GARY DAY
'Totalling Up Postmodernism'
51-66

EDWARD FULLBROOK
'Postmodernising *Homo Economicus*'
67-87

GERALDINE STONEHAM
'Mastering Timespace: Virtual Reality and Post-colonial Time Travel'
89-106

JOHN McLEOD
'Living In-Between:
Interstitial Spaces of Possibility in Timothy Mo's *Sour Sweet*'
107-128

DEBORAH MADSEN
'The Racial Dominant:
Postmodernism and American Ethnic Women's Fiction'
129-155

PAULINA PALMER
'Lesbian Fiction and the Postmodern:
Genre, Narrativity, Sexual Politics'
157-180

KATE FULLBROOK
'The Godfather:
Borges and the Ethics of the Labyrinth'
181-196

LUIGI CAZZATO
'From Elitist Modernism to Populist Postmodernism?'
197-219

MARGHERITA GANERI
'The Postmodern Revival of the Historical Novel in Italy:
Aesthetic and Cultural Implications'
221-235

KEVIN DONNELLY
'Postmodern Cinema? La Cinéma Postmoderne Expliquée Aux Enfants'
237-259

ESTHER SONNET
'Desire and Delusion: Allegories of Postmodern Heterosexuality'
261-277

JAMIE BRASSETT
'Become-Cyborg! (A Pierced-Tongued Call to Prosthetic Arms)'
279-300

ABSTRACTS

STEVEN EARNSHAW

'Just Postmodernism: Introduction' *ix-xxv*

The introduction identifies the move towards new notions of justice across a range of current debates in postmodernism. It traces the incommensurability between traditional conceptualisations of 'justice' and the more recent 'postmodern' versions (Derrida, Lyotard) where justice is often configured via a gaming motif. The latter analysis undermines frameworks for (distributive) justice based on either utilitarianism or social contract philosophy, yet ultimately must fall back upon this reasoning and humanism to salvage its own ostensible objectives.

STELLA SWAIN

'Postmodern Narratives and the Absurdity of Law' *1-28*

The essay discusses 'law' as a product of narrative discourses evolving historically within politically and geographically defined spaces. This is of particular significance where 'English' law is characterised as 'imperial' law. Colonial, postcolonial, and immigrant nations, indigenous peoples which have been under the dominion of English law and whose fight for autonomy is still to be formulated within the 'phrase regimens' of the English legal system, find that the 'modern' identities that it constructs are ultimately legitimated and confined by history and tradition – the antithesis of modernity. It is argued that postmodern critique emanating from what was the 'imperial centre' actually disables the empowerment offered by modern ideology.

JOHN PHILLIPS

'Just Sentences: The Incalculable in Postmodern Justice' *29-50*

This essay analyses a range of arguments about the idea of justice in order to set up enabling distinctions between what might be called classical, modern and postmodern conceptions. Aristotle, Immanuel Kant and Jean-François Lyotard are provisionally taken as exemplifying these respective positions. The essay then goes on to assess the complex and often paradoxical relations between logic and mathematics, on the one hand, and ethics and politics on the other, with an aesthetics of judgement playing an irreducible role on the other (third) hand each time.

GARY DAY

'Totalling Up Postmodernism' *51-66*

This essay argues that postmodernism's antipathy to the notion of totality masks its complicity with capitalism. The essay examines the work of Jean-François Lyotard and the management guru Tom Peters. It shows that there are distinct parallels between them. Both, for example, reject the ideas of truth, totality and hierarchy. It is further argued that the postmodern aesthetic of the sublime functions to aestheticise the market and to provide a rationale that prevents it from being conceived as a whole. These and other arguments illustrate that as a cultural expression of free market logic, postmodernism is part of a totality whose existence it denies.

EDWARD FULLBROOK

'Postmodernising *Homo Economicus*' *67-87*

In recent years, a postmodern conception of the economic subject, one around which a new research paradigm is developing, has appeared in France. It has emerged out of a collaboration between René Girard and economists at the *École Polytechnique*. Known as the Intersubjectivists, the new group bases itself on a conception of the economic subject as decentred and fragmented. It conceives of the self as an ongoing project of self-creation in a manner based on Girard's concept of mimetic desire. In place of the autonomous, well-defined subjects of Neoclassical economics, Intersubjectivist selves are individuals whose economic identities are interdependent, who are driven by a lack of being, and whose demands are in constant flux. This essay discusses these developments and their historical underpinnings.

GERALDINE STONEHAM

'Mastering Timespace: Virtual Reality and Post-colonial Time Travel' *89-106*

Cosmologist Frank Tipler, in his book *The Physics of Immortality*, suggested that '"Life" is a form of information processing, and the human mind – and the human soul – is a very complex computer program'. In his theoretical model the resurrection of the dead at the Last Judgement will be a matter of data retrieval and virtual experience. For the postmodernist and postcolonial writer and critic, concerned above all with the interface between simulation and reality, and with deconstructing borders between self and other, them and us, here and there, then and now, the imaginative potential of this marriage between theory and technology is immense. Such ideas are explored by the essay in relation to Bharati Mukherjee's novel, *The Holder of the World* (1993).

JOHN McLEOD

'Living In-Between:

Interstitial Spaces of Possibility in Timothy Mo's *Sour Sweet*' *107-128*

Timothy Mo's *Sour Sweet* (1982) is considered in the context of Homi Bhabha's work on the relationship between the postmodern and the postcolonial, focusing in particular upon his theory of interstitiality. The essay seizes upon Bhabha's argument that there exists a space of possibility in between holistic discourses of cultural identity where new forms of identity can be negotiated vital to the survival of the migrant. It is a space opened, in Bhabha's terms, by the confluence of postmodernism and postcolonialism. By focusing upon the descriptions of landscape in *Sour Sweet*, the essay demonstrates how Mo seeks to open this space in the novel. Mo's novel also facilitates a critique of Bhabha's work, and suggests that Bhabha's optimism for such spaces of possibility is premature.

DEBORAH MADSEN

'The Racial Dominant:

Postmodernism and American Ethnic Women's Fiction' *129-155*

This essay focuses upon the concept of postmodernist 'antimodels' – strategic points of difference from, or active antagonism towards, a dominant postmodernist model of fiction that is perceived to have failed in crucial ways to engage with America's most pressing social and cultural problems. Using as examples of this antimodel Amy Tan's *The Joy Luck Club*, Maxine Hong Kingston's *The Woman Warrior,* Sandra Cisneros's *The House on Mango Street*, and Louis Erdrich's *Love Medicine*, the essay questions the ways in which postmodernism can be deemed a patriarchal discourse by considering what are the similarities and what the differences between these texts and the opposed stances of feminism and postmodernism?

PAULINA PALMER

'Lesbian Fiction and the Postmodern:

Genre, Narrativity, Sexual Politics' *157-180*

This essay investigates the connections and tensions between 'the lesbian' and 'the postmodern', as reflected in theory and fiction. For example, the representation of the individual as the product of culture and psychic drives and the emphasis on subjectivity as fractured and decentred, associated with postmodernism, conflict with the focus on individual agency and collective political action which are key principles of lesbian and gay liberation.

Such theoretical perspectives inform a number of works of fiction produced in the 1980s and 1990s, and the major part of the essay concentrates on exploring their influence on lesbian fictional representation in the work of writers such as Fiona Cooper, Ellen Galford, Jeanette Winterson, Mary Wings and Sarah Schulman.

KATE FULLBROOK

'The Godfather:

Borges and the Ethics of the Labyrinth' *181-196*

Recent studies of Borges's impact on the shaping of postmodern fictional practice tend to concentrate on the metafictional dimensions of his work, on the aspects of Borges's writing which open sympathetically to narratives of poststructuralist theory and to concentrate on the reflexivity and self-referentiality of language and texts. The argument in this essay takes a different direction and concentrates on the ethical obsession in Borges's work. It outlines the key ethical questions posed by Borges and looks at the ways in which these interests have formed a significant, yet insufficiently analysed, inheritance in the work of those postmodern writers for whom Borges serves as the most significant godfather.

LUIGI CAZZATO

'From Elitist Modernism to Populist Postmodernism?' *197-219*

The essay is concerned with the question of the postmodern literary trend of *genre* fiction and the question of elite/mass literature. Most of the debate on postmodernism has been dedicated to the continuity/discontinuity issue. This essay demonstrates that if, in textual terms, there is any real discontinuity between modernism and postmodernism, it is exactly the collapsing of the hierarchical division between high and low literature.

The essay begins with a brief historical account of the 'poetics of the New' or the 'poetics of the *écart*', which culminates in the fetishist defence of the use-value of modernism, and then analyses the postmodern return of fabulation or 'narrativity' with the adoption of popular genres.

MARGHERITA GANERI

'The Postmodern Revival of the Historical Novel in Italy:

Aesthetic and Cultural Implications' *221-235*

This essay looks at the renewed interest in history as subject matter for the novel. With particular reference to the scene in Italy, it discusses contemporary literary theory and the need to re-establish categories of historical inquiry. It argues that this urgency is a cultural phenomenon, where the desire for critical perspectives that can make sense of history is one of the reasons for the flowering of the 'neo-historical novel'. Eco's *Il nome della rosa* is located as one of the key texts – in terms of marketing and consumption as much as its treatment of history – to understanding this phenomenon.

KEVIN DONNELLY

'Postmodern Cinema? La Cinéma Postmoderne Expliquée Aux Enfants' *237-259*

Many of the theorisations of postmodern culture have readily pointed to cinema as furnishing prime examples of the postmodern. Oddly though, the term 'postmodernism' has never been systematically utilised by established film historians and theorists.

The essay contends that postmodernism is a valuable term for film studies and not only demonstrates as much, but goes some way toward setting out an approach for the discussion of certain modes of contemporary cinema in the light of postmodern culture. After summarising attitudes to postmodern cinema, the essay provides a matrix with which contemporary mainstream cinema can be set in a postmodern perspective, a perspective which is fruitful, allowing insights that are unavailable to the dominant paradigms in film scholarship.

ESTHER SONNET

'Desire and Delusion: Allegories of Postmodern Heterosexuality' *261-277*

Hal Hartley's *Amateur* (1994) is a construction and textual deconstruction of heterosexuality. For a postmodernist feminist analysis, the film is particularly interesting for the 'knowingness' with which it poses a commonality in the visual registers of pornography and dominant cinema. In the context of the film's preoccupations with issues of sex, Otherness and desire, this reading of the film addresses questions around 'lack', patriarchal power and the acquisition of sexual identities, but, however, with a view to challenging the standard Lacanian formulation. This analysis focuses instead on the theoretical spaces opened up when the knots conventionally tying 'self-hood', gender and sexuality are *loosened.*

JAMIE BRASSETT

'Become-Cyborg! (A Pierced-Tongued Call to Prosthetic Arms)' *279-300*

One of the favourite images that Body Modifiers use to describe their personal/cultural practice is that of the 'Modern Primitive'. This desire to reinscribe an ancient, spiritual dimension within contemporary life could not only be seen as a consequence of postmodernity, but is evident in many current leisure activities and political actions (compare the tribalism surrounding underground party and rave culture and the paganism of the road protests).

But the primitive has already been absorbed and surpassed, chewed up and spat out by the capitalist machine. So where do the (post)modern Primitives go wrong? Deleuze and Guattari show us again (though David Harvey does not like the answer): take the line of flight of the schizo, or, Become-Cyborg. Disorganise the body surface with piercings, tattoos, scars and prosthetics. Overscribe the so-called sanctity of The Face through cosmetic surgery.

Just Postmodernism

Introduction

I'll have my bond! Speak not against my bond!
I have sworn an oath that I will have my bond.
Thou call'dst me dog before thou hadst a cause,
But since I am a dog, beware my fangs.
The Duke shall grant me justice.
(Shylock, *Merchant of Venice* III.3)

Someone must have been telling lies about Joseph K.,
for without having done anything wrong he was
arrested one fine morning.
(Franz Kafka, *The Trial*)

Just Postmodernism offers essays on a wide variety of topics that continue to inform postmodernism, as well as taking up more recent concerns. The most noticeable of the latter is the attention paid to the question of justice, and it is this which I shall focus upon in the introduction.

If for much of the eighties and early nineties Lyotard's *The Postmodern Condition* (1979) provided the reference point for understanding and constructing what postmodernism might be, 'an incredulity toward metanarratives', it is now Lyotard's dialogue with Jean-Loup Thébaud in *Just Gaming* (also 1979) which is increasingly the new touchstone. The English title of Lyotard's book suggests that we are players in the tricky game of justice, but the pun also suggests that there is a triviality to such an exercise and that justice is nothing more than 'mere gaming'. As to the French title, *Au Juste,* it is difficult to give an adequate translation. In normal context it could mean 'by the way', or 'to be more precise', or 'exact', but it might also bring to mind 'être juste', 'to be fair', especially in the context of the book. There might be a pun on 'mot juste', and it might also mean 'to the just man'.[1] The underlying ambiguity in both languages (the suggestion of serious justice alongside a frivolous [word] play), possibly masking an ambivalence, is typical of the poststructural approach. It is indicative of how difficult it is for the so-called 'linguistic turn' of poststructuralist thought to achieve any kind of rapprochement with discourses on justice in areas of philosophy other than poststructuralism, or in the kind of legal theory where there is a commitment to clear, unambiguous language.

Yet it is the case that some sense of justice has underwritten many projects deemed postmodern, including postmodernity itself, even if it has not been until recent years that this foundation has received something more than lip service in the postmodern debate.[2] The reason for this is that, for philosophers of the postmodern, justice is nothing other than an old-fashioned metanarrative. Hence postmodern commentary on justice scrupulously circumvents defining a postmodern understanding by consigning this metanarrative to the past.

> Jean-Loup Thébaud: Let us return now, if you will, to the answer that modernity gives to the question of justice, namely, the answer of autonomy.
>
> Jean-François Lyotard: In modernity, let us say since Rousseau, the answer to the question of justice in relation to theoretical discourse, is displaced,

1 Thanks to Sylvia Brondex, Phil Cox and Lisa Hopkins for this. Of course, there is a further irony in trying to achieve precision with translation of a phrase that means 'to be more precise'.

2 It has also involved some hasty revisionism: Derrida in his essay 'Force of Law' claims that much of his previous work is about justice, even if those texts identified as deconstructionist do not seem 'to foreground the theme of justice (as theme, precisely), or the theme of ethics or politics' (Derrida 1992:7).

> because it has been thought that the just will be that which can be prescribed by the set of the utterers of the statements. (Lyotard and Thébaud 1985:29)

Thus the very idea of justice as something that can be prescribed is consistently gainsaid in postmodern discourse, since such a justice requires language and authority, neither of which comes to us untainted. Throughout *Just Gaming*, justice is subjected to the deconstructive scalpel. It becomes a language game that for some (many) others would disable any usable notion of justice. Further, the inherent antagonism in postmodern thought to epistemological groundings forecloses the use of ingredients that many find necessary for a conception of justice, essentials such as 'freedom' and 'rights'. Regardless of this, the championing by postmodern writers of disadvantaged and wronged groups has proceeded apace, with little detailed analysis when this does occur of what constitutes just behaviour and just deserts (if, in fact, desert has anything to do with justice[3]). It is sustained by a dogged belief that justice, whatever that is, is to be demanded and to be had. That certain groups have been wronged appears self-evident – our sense of injustice is finely tuned – but the putting in place of justice, or even understanding what it could consist of, has remained vague.

It is a notion of justice that is at stake in the confrontation between postmodern thought and feminist activity. This was under discussion in Kate Fullbrook's 'Whose Postmodernism?' in *Postmodern Subjects/Postmodern Texts* (Rodopi, 1995). There she argued that strong versions of postmodernism and strong versions of feminism are incompatible, and that 'post' has become a designer label in the 'postmodern language game' that can even save something like fascism by turning it into 'postfascism', as some extreme right-wing groups have been prone to do. Such 'easy co-optation' runs 'counter to the notion of

3 Howard Caygill suggests that Kant's design of 'retributive justice' – castrating rapists and pederasts for example – is making a comeback (1995:272).

justice which we most patently need' (84). The conclusion is that it is postmodernism itself which presents a problem for justice and feminism. In contradistinction in the same volume, Leslie Moran discussed 'The Legal Subject of Sado-Masochism' using postmodern/poststructural work on subjectivity and sexuality as a positive force in order to counter prevailing discriminations. It looked at the 'Spanner Case' whereby consenting sado-masochists had been prosecuted and jailed in what is the injustice of the criminal justice system. In both essays it is this underlying sense of justice which drives the writing on postmodern issues, understandably troubled as to whether a postmodern environment can provide justice or not.

It might be objected that here, and with the postmodern attention to justice and the law as a whole, postmodernism has stuck with its own particular discursive worldview. Although both postmodern and more traditional strands of thinking on justice might begin with Aristotle, Plato and Kant, the postmodernists usually end up with Lyotard and Derrida whereas the 'traditionalists' end up with John Rawls and his critics. There would probably be some justification to a charge that neither side can hear the other: the language of poststructuralist critical theory undoubtedly sits uneasily with theories of (distributive) justice. Some contact has been made between jurisprudence and critical theory, for example, Ronald Dworkin's 'Law as Interpretation' (1982-3) and Stanley Fish's 'Working on the Chain Gang: Interpretation in the Law and Literary Criticism' (1982-3), and the work of the Critical Legal Studies project in America has been vital. The latter's critique of the claims of law to be 'based in reason' clashes head-on with those wishing to maintain the law as a rational process (Swain, p.12, this volume). As to neither side truly listening, *Just Gaming* has no discussion of modern theories of justice whatsoever. Derrida mentions Rawls and Hart in a roll-call of those involved in discussions of justice, but it soon becomes clear that they are not involved in his particular mode of discourse (Derrida 1992:14). It is also probably true to say that it is the language of economics that has been dominant in discourses on justice in recent years, a fact that for most would run counter to the received ideal of justice as beyond pecuniary consideration.[4]

Current mainstream discussion of justice is discussion of 'distributive justice' which wrestles with the difficulty of putting into practice a system that would ensure some kind of equity, whereas justice in the postmodern battlefield is subject to a more deconstructive assessment of an abstracted justice with much less awareness of, or concern for, the practicalities, other than to throw into question the role of authority and interpretation.

John Rawls has been the major figure in 'distributive justice' since his seminal *A Theory of Justice* (1972). He has two principles for the organisation of society:

> first, each person engaged in an institution or affected by it has an equal right to the most extensive liberty compatible with a like liberty for all; and second, inequalities as defined by the institutional structure or fostered by it are arbitrary unless it is reasonable to expect that they will work out to everyone's advantage and provided that the positions and offices to which they attach or from which they may be gained are open to all. (1993:76)

However, this latter view is somewhat modified by his later claim that 'since we cannot maximize with respect to more than one point of view, it is natural, given the ethos of a democratic society, to single out that of the least advantaged and maximize their long-term prospects consistent with the liberties of equal citizenship' (93-4). In other words, when it comes to distribution of justice, the

4 For a critique of this literature see White 1986. The danger of economics being the final arbiter is satirically criticised in Dickens's *Bleak House*: 'The one great principle of English law is, to make business for itself. . . . Viewed by this light it becomes a coherent scheme, and not the monstrous make the laity are apt to think it' (451).

point of view should be that of the least advantaged ('the difference principle'). I would argue that whilst we may feel it is just to look to the least advantaged, we can hardly accept that it is the natural ethos of democratic society, especially not as Rawls sees democratic society. The appeal is a *deus ex machina* (or should this be *ultra vires*?). But even before this there appears to be an assumption on Rawls's part that rational 'man' is self-interested at the expense of all else: 'A rational man would not accept an institution merely because it maximized the sum of advantages irrespective of its effect on his own interests' (1993:75). Here Rawls is repeating his earlier stance, taking the principle of society from 'social contract' philosophy rather than the alternative of 'utilitarianism' which would, contrary to his view, sacrifice the 'goods' (personal inviolability, liberty, opportunity, etc.) of the few for the greater good (1990 [1972]: esp.14). Either way (social contract or utilitarianism) it is taken for granted that self-interest is the bottom line for such thinking, and something that Rawls regards as an intuitive truth. Nor is it a contentious issue for two of his major critics, Nozick and Hayek. Both attack the concept of some central agent distributing justice, and in fact Hayek calls such thinking primitive since it could only be achieved by some absolute, totalitarian state: 'While an equality of rights under a limited government is possible and an essential condition of individual freedom, a claim for equality of material position can be met only by a government with totalitarian powers' (1993:141). As Hans Bertens describes it, this is actually splitting the question of justice into two issues, one where the problem is to guarantee an equality of rights, the other to guarantee material equality.[5] Hayek's manoeuvre is quite obviously politically motivated to discredit communism. This enables a non-totalitarian form of government to be introduced which ensures

5 Letter to the author, 03 July 1996. For this and other comments on an earlier draft as used here, my thanks to Hans Bertens.

that at least some rights are maintained, whilst handing over any arguments to do with economics to a free-market economy. The trick is to disengage material conditions from a consideration of rights. It would be hard to disagree with Hayek's point that perfect distribution of material wealth requires absolute power, yet it is hard to see why this does not apply equally to the distribution of rights (defined here simply as 'freedom'). Hayek makes a curious defence later on in the same article when deriding those who despise people who have accumulated wealth:

> What those who attack great private wealth do not understand is that it is neither by physical effort nor by their act of saving and investing, but by directing resources to the most productive uses that wealth is chiefly created. And there can be no doubt that most of those who have built up great fortunes in the form of new industrial plants and the like have thereby benefited more people through creating opportunities for more rewarding employment than if they had given their superfluity to the poor. (156-7)

The difficulty in administering distributive justice thus becomes a defence of the capitalist system. As Bertens comments, one of the main problems with Hayek's viewpoint is that 'the majority of the great fortunes he refers to have been built by way of criminal operations'.[6] Or, to take another angle, James Boyd White, in an essay that confronts the vast area of legal discourse that gives itself over to economics, states: 'the language of economics is blind to the differences of wealth among different actors in the real world and hence to what many of us would regard as the inherent unfairness of the transactions in which they engage' (1986:181). There is also an assumption on the part of many of those critics engaged in discussing distributive justice that everything is to be calculated solely in terms of gain accruing to individual selves. For example, employment is

6 Letter to the author.

usually calculated as an equivalent to foregone leisure ('the hedonistic calculus') and that those involved are necessarily and obviously acting as rational men purely for their own best long-term interests. However, it is possible to point to research elsewhere to show that the necessity for work is other than one of purely financial gain.[7] I also think that behind all this there is an assumption that human behaviour is underpinned by some version of 'the selfish gene', whereby, either conceived individually or as a group, humans act out of egotism. However, even this view is changing following on from work done by psychologists studying the behaviour of primates: 'It does not follow that our motives for co-operation are always "self-serving"; on the contrary, we may more usually be guided by affection, loyalty, or shame' (Clark 1996:25).

It is the case that the postmodern and poststructural discourse on justice begins from a viewpoint in opposition to the mainstream commentators on distributive justice because they use a different (twentieth-century) philosophical base-line. For the postmodernists it is the assimilation of Levinas's thought, where duty to the Other is primary (what Rawls would term a 'deontological' theory, yet which is obviously of a different type from his own), in the sense that such a duty is not conceived of as self-interested: no reward is to be expected at any time. This is clearly at odds with Rawls, who believes there is an 'absence of strong and lasting benevolent impulses' (1990:14). This could hardly be much further from Levinas's 'Other' calling us to account. In Rawls's theory democracy exists through self interest. I cannot see any way of reconciling the two standpoints. The value of Rawls et al. in discussions of justice is that they have a clarity of purpose which is not always the case in postmodern thought. However, their desire to be logically and practically aware of the problems of justice (Enlightenment reasoning) is usually undermined by other senses of

7 See, for example, Will Hutton, *The State We're In* (1995), esp. pp.99-105, and Edward Fullbrook in this volume.

justice they import that will not square with these, as in Hayek's defence of the extremely wealthy via a market argument and Rawls's foundation of individual rights (which undoubtedly conflicts with his 'difference principle'). Modern theories of justice believe that they can fix justice whereas postmodern philosophy sees only slippage and arbitrary authority.

The notion of 'gaming' in relation to justice is also worthy of comment. 'Play' and 'playfulness' have always been understood as characteristic of postmodernism, and to align this with the serious issue of justice might be taken to be at best in poor taste and at worst in bad faith. However, it appears that 'gaming', like 'just', is to have two meanings. Alongside 'playfulness' 'gaming' can also be understood as the selection of the best moves in given situations, and Lyotard does indeed talk about justice in such terms (see below). Although Alan Ryan in his introduction to the edited collection *Justice* (1993) notes that his book does not deal with theories tying in justice to game theory and theories of rational choice (16), the pervasiveness of the metaphor in *Justice* is still to be noted. For instance Hayek alludes to two writers who have looked on the question of justice as a serious game (127): Adam Smith in *The Theory of Moral Sentiments* (1801) and Adam Ferguson's *Principles of Moral and Political Science* (1792). Both these writers in turn refer back to the Stoics who considered life to be a game of skill, and Hayek himself starts discussing 'fairness' in terms of playing the rules of the game (152-3). Neither side, traditional or postmodern, appears able to avoid reliance upon game metaphors. Yet the language can often seem inappropriate:

> JFL: Absolute injustice would occur if the pragmatics of obligation, that is, the possibility of continuing to play the game of the just, were excluded. That is what is unjust. Not the opposite of the just, but that which prohibits that the question of the just and the unjust be, and remain, raised. Thus, obviously, all terror, annihilation, massacre, etc., or their threat, are, by

> definition, unjust. The people whom one massacres will no longer be able to play the game of the just and the unjust. (66-7)

Lyotard thus interprets 'injustice' as 'unfairness' rather than 'not justified'. To massacre is therefore unjust in that it is not playing by the rules, not because it in any sense lacks justification. But why anyone should feel obliged to play the game of justice in the first place is not explained. Nearer to the mark is Bertens' comment: 'What we have here, rather tortuously formulated in order to avoid all liberal-humanist connotations, is a rather classical argument for "free speech" and the right of free speech to shock us into new states of awareness and new conceptions of justice'.[8] Lyotard's comments, to me at least, do not seem too far removed from Kant's *deus ex machina* prescription to abide by the rational rules of 'grace', whereby we make ourselves happy if we play fair: 'To view ourselves . . . as in the kingdom of grace, in which all happiness awaits us, except in so far as we ourselves limit our participation in it by actions which render us unworthy of happiness, is a practically necessary idea of reason' (1934:461). If Lyotard corrals 'playing fair' without foundation, Derrida does a similar thing in another poststructural classic on justice, 'Force of Law'. At turns providing a brilliant critique of the notion of justice and its relationship to law, with some weaker defence of why we should be involved with justice despite its impossibility, Derrida's *deus ex machina* is provided by Levinas. For Derrida, the demand of justice is that it be a 'gift without exchange, without circulation, without recognition or gratitude, without economic circularity, without calculation and without rules, without reason and without rationality' (25).[9] Given the tradition that Levinas, and by extension Derrida, are working within, it is not surprising that this has religious resonance: 'Love is patient and

---

8 Letter to the author.

9 See John Phillips, this volume, for a discussion of Derrida's essay.

kind; love is not jealous or boastful; it is not arrogant or rude. Love does not insist on its own way; it is not irritable or resentful; it does not rejoice at wrong, but rejoices in the right. Love bears all things, believes all things, hopes all things, endures all things' (1 Corinthians 13). This infinite gift that Derrida claims true justice should be (in the abstract sense, of course) is nothing other than a mystical foundation of his own.

The constant weaving between a deconstructive dalliance with the notion of justice, and a drawing back from discrediting all notions of justice, is typical of the paradox justice and law provide for postmodern discourse. With 'game' we seem to have something more than a powerful metaphor at work and are unable to decide whether justice is a question of the rules of a (the) game, or whether in calling it a game we somehow trivialise justice. Once again, the title of Lyotard's book appears apt, and such thinking as his 'Justice . . consists in working at the limits of what the rules permit, in order to invent new moves, perhaps new rules and therefore new games' (Lyotard 1985:100) is certain to remain provocative.

Just Postmodernism

As with the previous two volumes I edited or co-edited in this series, *Postmodern Surroundings* and *Postmodern Subjects/Postmodern Texts*, the organisation of the essays has been somewhat difficult given the range of material involved. In those books it was decided to place them author-alphabetically and to pick out some common threads in the introduction. In this volume the essays have been ordered so that there is a common association between the essays if read in sequence. It will also quickly become evident that the vacillation between postmodernism as enabling and postmodernism as paralysing is played out in the various lines on postmodernism taken by the essays here. For example, putting forward postmodernism's positive side are the pieces by McLeod (postcolonial), Swain and Phillips (law), Palmer (lesbianism), Brassett (the body). Those giving a negative verdict on postmodernism tend to see it as collusive in commodification, of knowledge (Day), of cinema (Donnelly) and of marginal identities (Stoneham). Deborah Madsen berates male writers of postmodern fiction for their complicity with patriarchy.

The first two essays deal directly with postmodernism and law. Stella Swain gives a contemporary overview and then particularises the debate: we misread English Law if we take it purely as a product of Enlightenment ideology. In many ways Swain is reading against the postmodern grain (as she acknowledges) by tethering English law within its national context, although this crucial focus upon its own specific history rather than matching it solely with Enlightenment epistemology might be seen as a postmodern manoeuvre in itself through its granting of contingent difference. She notes that English Law is also postcolonial law, or the law of the postcolonialists. John Phillips in 'Just Sentences: The Incalculable in Postmodern Justice' tackles the problems of justice as encountered in the philosophical heritage, from Kant through to the poststructuralists. It provides us with 'provisional distinctions on what might be called classical, modern and postmodern conceptions' of justice. In doing so he brings together contemporary philosophy, ethics, politics and literature.

Gary Day's article is an attack on entrenched economic attitudes, specifically the market and the way it works (or is supposed to work): it is fuelled by a sense of injustice at the acceptance of harmful 1980s free-market economic doctrine, and again, like the previous two essays, uses Lyotard, especially *Just Gaming*. It analyses the collusion between postmodern thought and the prevailing economic system and argues that postmodernism continues to promote a position of particularity which makes it impossible to do otherwise, simultaneously advancing a professionalism that amounts to elitism. He matches up recent management theory (Tom Peters) with Lyotard's proclamations by way of their 'respective shattering of totality'. Edward Fullbrook's essay is likewise concerned with economic modelling. It scrutinises this classical version of 'homo economicus' and offers instead interdependent economic identities, a move which is counter to the arguments above on distributive justice and their 'hedonistic calculus'. It uses the work of the Intersubjectivists, which has emerged out of the collaboration between René Girard and economists at the *École Polytechnique*.

The position of the subject and its strategies to counter marginalisation (ethnic, female, lesbian, postcolonial) is the focus of the next cluster of essays. John McLeod's piece on Timothy Mo's *Sour Sweet* and Geraldine Stoneham's essay on Bharati Mukherjee, both address the postcolonial legacy (also tackled in Stella Swain's piece). The answer to how it is possible to cope with such subject-positioning is somewhere along the lines of 'living in-between' (McLeod) or a problematic 'virtual reality' (Stoneham). The search to find a way of living in the midst of an unjust heritage does not mean that a home in a postmodern fluid subjectivity is the easy option however. The conflict between the movement of the postmodern, and the identity crises of the postcolonial, entails a confrontation between the two in both essays. The antagonism between subject, agency and postmodernism is also encountered in Deborah Madsen's 'Postmodernism, Feminism and the Dissenting Ethnic Voice' where writers such as Toni Morrison and Maxine Hong Kingston have placed themselves outside what they consider to be the patriarchy of postmodernism. Their works often use the techniques and attitudes associated with postmodernism yet still present themselves as 'antimodels' to postmodernism, thereby making the term 'postmodernism' an extremely uncomfortable one with respect to the justice it can offer. There is a similar tension at work in contemporary lesbian fiction. Paulina Palmer looks at the work of, amongst others, Ellen Galford, Mary Wings and Sarah Schulman, writers of fiction that challenges essentialist notions of gender and sexuality through transgression.

An obvious connection between these and the next few essays is this dispute with the terminology of postmodernism itself. McLeod feels that the growing disparity between postmodernism and postcolonialism has now gone too far, to the detriment of both. For Luigi Cazzato it is narrativity and postmodernism, as well as the context of elitism and popular culture, that is under scrutiny. Kate Fullbrook is also within the arena of literature with the 'godfather' of postmodern fiction, Borges. Her focus is on the ethical aspects that have been overlooked and that might be traced in his successors, ethics clearly functioning as a close relative to the upsurge in interest in justice. As for Margherita Ganeri, the revival of the historical novel in Italy is symbolic of the oft-commented upon problem for the present age of what relationship is possible with the past: 'what is lost in this new conception of history is a certain faith in the documentability of truth'. The appropriation of genres by postmodern fiction is a theme of a number of these pieces: of science-fiction and detective (Cazzato); gothic and thriller (Palmer); historical (Ganeri).

Kevin Donnelly sets up his essay to explain postmodern film, to show how the terminology of postmodernism is necessary for an understanding of cinema. The spectre of commodification looms once again as he shows how films have become a means to selling the often more profitable tie-in products (children's toys, records) and in the very siting of cinemas within multiplexes. Esther Sonnett's links up both an interest in postmodern cinema and subjectivity by an examination of Hal Hartley's 1994 film *Amateur*. This is something of a celebration of the possibilities of fluid subjectivity, like Palmer's, an attitude not lost in Jamie Brassett's assessment of body art, where it is not just sense of self (selves) that is malleable, but flesh and bone. Taken together, what these essays illustrate is the ambivalence present in the title *Just Gaming*, a sense of possibilities available that have not been there before, coupled with an acute awareness of the difficulties encountered at every turn.

Steven EARNSHAW
Sheffield Hallam University

Works Cited

Caygill, Howard. *A Kant Dictionary*. Oxford: Blackwell, 1995.

Clark, Stephen R. L. 'The Moral Animals'. *TLS* 06 September 1996. 25-6.

Derrida, Jacques. 'Force of Law: The "Mystical Foundation of Authority"'. *Deconstruction and the Possibility of Justice.* Drucilla Cornell, Michael Rosen and David Gray Carlson, eds. New York: Routledge, 1992. 3-67.

Dickens, Charles. *Bleak House*. Ware, Herts: Wordsworth, 1993.

Dowson, Jane and Steven Earnshaw, eds. *Postmodern Subjects/Postmodern Texts*. Amsterdam: Rodopi, 1995.

Dworkin, Ronald. 'Law as Interpretation'. *Critical Inquiry* 9 (1982-3): 179-200.

Earnshaw, Steven, ed. *Postmodern Surroundings*. Amsterdam: Rodopi, 1994.

Fish, Stanley. 'Working on the Chain Gang: Interpretation in the Law and in Literary Criticism'. *Critical Inquiry* 9 (1982-3): 201-16.

Fullbrook, Kate. 'Whose Postmodernism?' in Dowson and Earnshaw, 71-87.

Hayek, F. A. von. '"Social" or Distributive Justice', in Ryan, 117-58.

Hutton, Will. *The State We're In*. London: Jonathan Cape, 1995.

Kafka, Franz. *The Trial*. Harmondsworth: Penguin, 1953.

Kant, Immanuel. *Critique of Pure Reason*. Trans. J. M. D. Meiklejohn. London: Dent, 1934.

Lyotard, Jean-François. (1979). *The Postmodern Condition: A Report on Knowledge*. Manchester: Manchester University Press, 1984.

Lyotard, Jean-François and Jean-Loup Thébaud. (1979). *Just Gaming*. Manchester: Manchester University Press, 1985.

Moran, Leslie J. 'The Legal Subject of Sado-Masochism' in Dowson and Earnshaw, 159-79.

Nozick, Robert. 'Distributive Justice', in Ryan, 95-116.

Rawls, John. (1972). *A Theory of Justice*. Oxford: Oxford University Press, 1990.

---. 'Distributive Justice', in Ryan, 73-94.

Ryan, Alan, ed. *Justice*. Oxford: Oxford University Press, 1993.

Shakespeare, William. *The Merchant of Venice*. Harmondsworth: Penguin, 1967.

White, James Boyd. 'Economics and Law: Two Cultures in Tension'. *Tennessee Law Review* 54 (1986): 161-202.

Postmodern Narratives and the Absurdity of Law

> We are caught in the stories of others, so we are protagonists in the stories we are told by others, and we have to assume for ourselves the stories that the others tell about us, which have their own founding events, their own strategies, their own plots.
>
> Paul Ricoeur

1. Story-Tellers in Post-Imperial Nations

Postmodernist thought positions law as a product of modernity, and seeks to establish a critical distance from legal discourse. In a recent critique by Ann Barron, for example, it is argued that as a 'system of thought and a practice of social regulation' legal discourse is 'a model of the kind of approach to social relations which postmodernism denies: "vengeance against the law", broadly conceived, is . . . the characteristic strategy of postmodern thought and politics' (Barron 1989:121). I will look here at aspects of this denial, and at some of the ways in which it can tend, conversely, to isolate law from constructive critique and its social and historical contexts. Ultimately I wish to emphasise the case for keeping routes open for border traffic between postmodern thought and legal discourse, and for finding ways through the oppositional relation of these categories.

The widespread institutional use of the term 'postmodern' in what might be termed the post-imperial west displays a consensus that the concept of the 'postmodern' is a legitimate apparatus for inquiring into our present condition and preoccupations. Yet a dominant concern of much contemporary thought is that consensus be challenged, that 'all that has been received if only yesterday . . . must be suspected' (Lyotard 1986:79). As Barron says, in presenting a critique of law, 'postmodernity demands that dissensus be given a voice' (Barron 1989:134-5). She refers to the fact that postmodernism 'is characterised by a preoccupation with the processes of exclusion and marginalisation which produce truth, rationality, sameness – whilst suppressing difference' (Barron 1989:121). This being the case, the consensus accumulated around versions of postmodernism should also provoke a reflexive, interrogative awareness as regards its currency as a critical conceit. As Renato Rosaldo argues, we should always be ready to ask who was not in the room when consensus was achieved (Rosaldo 1994:245).

Those non-participants have been identified in various ways by postcolonial theorists. The 'postmodern' meets the 'postcolonial' if we take, as Stuart Hall does, 'the whole process of expansion, exploration, conquest, colonisation and imperial hegemonisation' to be the 'outer face, the constitutive outside, of European and then Western capitalist modernity' (Hall 1996:249). Any chronological or ideological distance which is achieved in relation to the modern imperial and colonial projects may be asserted under the rubric of 'post-'ness, designating the abjuration of these projects, the 'end' of history and of the grand narrative. Yet this distance is equivocal: as Gayatri Spivak points out (1993:66), it is possible to identify ways in which current schools of thought disguise a move to bring the history of western modernity back into focus in a way that is inappropriate to a decentred, 'postcolonial' world. She suggests that 'some of the most radical criticism coming out of the West today is the result of an interested desire to conserve the subject of the West or the West as Subject'. Those 'not in the room' when these debates take shape include minority communities in what Homi Bhabha has termed that 'third space', where the 'negotiation of incommensurable differences creates a tension peculiar to borderline existences' (Bhabha 1994:218). In situations where peoples dispossessed in 'modernity' campaign for their rights, a postmodern disidentification with 'the law' on the grounds of incommensurability is unlikely to be strategically effective or appropriate; they are engaged, as Bhabha says, in a process of negotiation.

A less antithetical mode of interrogating the law than that which arises from the sameness/difference nexus is perhaps needed. Spivak's view of postmodern critique suggests that despite its hostility to the law it shares common ground on the level of its conservatism. Postmodern thought can be found to use a repudiation of law to tell a story that folds multiplicity back into homogeneity, the 'rest' back into 'the west', as the most significant protagonist of global history. As Anne McClintock has argued, the term 'post-' reduces 'the world's multitudinous cultures' to 'a subordinate, retrospective relation to linear, European time' (McClintock 1994:255). The 'war on totality' (Lyotard 1986:82) that underlies suspicion of the law creates its own totalising agenda.

The postmodernist disidentification with the legal model of social relations does not allow for a dissenting view which asserts its continued viability in certain contexts, or take account of the ways in which the law regulates social relations on the level of its symbolic and narrative power rather than its rationality. Focusing on the conditions accompanying authoritative discourse, Pierre Bourdieu argues that language achieves maximum symbolic power when deployed by individuals in situations where they derive authority from ritual and tradition.[1] Regardless of the meaning or value of a particular enunciation to an audience in this situation, it will carry weight as a manifestation of convention. Bourdieu argues that 'by structuring the perception which social agents have of the social world, the act of naming helps to establish the structure of this world, and does so all the more significantly the more widely it is recognised, i.e. authorised'; the law maintains its capacity to structure reality through what Peter Goodrich (1990) terms its 'masks', its language, its theatre, its history, which it constantly reconstitutes through narrative performance. This 'theatre' of law is enhanced today via the dissemination of its languages through the media.

With particular regard to the English legal system, the law creates a 'disposition towards recognition in the sense of misrecognition and belief' (Bourdieu 1991:113) in large part through performance and recitation. As Goodrich has argued, the law provokes misrecognition by instituting a past 'both immediate and immemorial', a *memory*, and memory is narrational: 'the law maps that narrative in a story of origins or of the sources from which the law comes' (Goodrich 1990:36). The manner in which this past is constructed suggests that a postmodern focus upon the 'modernity' of law foregrounds its metanarrative foundations, claims to universality and unitary reason at the expense of its more mythopoeic processes. This becomes particularly marked in the context of postcolonial conflict.

Recently, theorists have worked upon creative connections between the *post*modern and the *post*colonial. The work of Bill Readings offers one example.

1 Bourdieu writes: 'The specificity of the discourse of authority . . . consists in the fact that it is not enough for it to be *understood* (in certain cases it may even fail to be understood without losing its power), and that it exercises its specific effect only when it is *recognised* as such. This recognition – whether accompanied by understanding or not – is granted, in the manner of something taken for granted, only under certain conditions, namely, those which define legitimate usage: it must be uttered by the person legitimately licensed to do so, the holder of the *skeptron,* known and recognised as being able and enabled to produce this particular class of discourse: a priest, a teacher, a poet. It must be uttered in a legitimate situation' (Bourdieu 1991:22).

In line with Lyotard's advocating of judgement 'without universal prescriptives', and the search for a 'plurality of reasons rather than one unitary reason', he suggests that postmodernity offers the opportunity of 'ceasing to think community in terms of a universal "we"'. Addressing a 'we' of western intellectuals Readings argues that this 'gives us the chance to relinquish our enslavement to our own power'. He remarks upon the need to 'think difference' and to '*tell another story*':

> To struggle against ourselves, to attempt to think the multiplicity and diversity of culture without recourse to totalitarian notions of the universal, may be the best hope for avoiding total destruction in a world where the dream of consensus stands revealed as the nightmare of mutual annihilation. (Readings 1992:186)

He proposes that becoming 'postmodern' does not necessarily mean attempting to atone for the racism of modernity by accepting the full humanity of colonised indigenous peoples (he refers here to Australian aboriginals) and allowing them their 'rights' with regard to ownership of the land. Instead, an incalculable difference and unrepresentable 'other' must be invoked. The '*post-*' in postmodernity involves the institution of a 'zero hour', where we abandon the representations that pull us back into the dialectics of modernity, and instead allow a situation to develop where we keep 'difference in question' and accept the limited truth of our own language games. 'We' (the white descendants of an imperial race, or more precisely in the case of Australia, the 'British') should instead accept that there can be no discussion, that indigenous claims, their language and their stories, are untranslatable. There is no just society, only a plurality of justices. We should not try to make our story their story, but allow them their own, while we attempt to liberate ourselves from history and begin again.

In a similar vein, Graham Huggan argues for the importance of generating a fictional genre which narrativises the 'provisionality of all cultures' (Huggan 1995:408). He discusses various examples of recent 'postcolonial' Australian fiction which attempt a 'reassessment of cartography'. They are shown to shift emphasis 'away from the desire for homogeneity towards an acceptance of diversity reflected in the interpretation of the map, not as a means of spatial containment or systematic organisation, but as a medium of spatial perception which allows for the reformulation of links both within and between cultures' (411). Huggan invokes the thought of the postmodern theorists, Gilles Deleuze and Felix Guattari to support this process of erasure and imaginative reconstruction as a revolutionary move, offering liberation from history and modernity. A 'pre-modern', 'nomadic' life is contemplated as an experiment in 'creativity and becoming'. The postmodern nomad attempts to free itself of all roots, bonds, and identities, and thereby 'resists the state and all normalising powers'. Huggan emphasises the revolutionary potential of the map, and of the tactics available to the nomad who may destroy, alter and recreate the map; it may be 'reworked by any individual, group, or social formation'. The revisualisation of the map, he suggests, 'permits a disidentification from the procedures of colonialism'.

These are versions of the idea of the postmodern which combine an awareness of its critical versatility and potential in providing a place from which to establish a historically disengaged perspective, with a perception of its utopian and (re-)visionary value for the reorganisation of social relations 'against the law'. Yet this reconstitutive deployment of the 'post-', involving the call to reject universality, the institution of the state, the power of the map, the idea of the nation and the force of history can, as Spivak implies, leave the west in place as the privileged narrator and holder of the *skeptron* of history. It also disempowers the subaltern appealing to the law to recognise the rights of 'first nations'. The innovation of the 'post-' works both to recentre and elegise the events and ideologies which were the basis of imperialist and colonial achievement. Further, in marginalising the continuing role of the law as a performative cartographer and historiciser, it is, in this continuing respect, permitted its autonomy. Affirming the untranslatability of histories does not take account of the ways in which the legal system nevertheless continues to attempt to 'translate' them. From the perspective of people enmeshed in struggles over the maps of modernity (from which, as Edward Said has said, 'none of us is completely free', Said 1993:6) the emancipatory *appeal* of abandoning the law is precluded. This is not only because of the apparent 'eurocentrism' of such critique, or because of any instrinsically impossible utopianism, but because it involves disidentification with a legal system which survives as a storyteller functioning with coercive powers.

The law requires the competition, as opposed to the disengagement, of other voices and stories in the public arena (which is where the law increasingly performs) to check the imposition of its authority on otherwise silenced minorites. By disidentifying with the law, and not addressing its role as a remaining procedural site of colonial initiative and subaltern resistance, postmodern speculation permits the postimperial world its priority in the making and telling of history. Wherever racial conflict occurs in postcolonial communities, it is brought 'before the law', articulated in the phrases of the law, and resolved in the language of a legal system which may be identified as having evolved as an instrument of western imperialism (Fitzpatrick 1992:107).

Peter Goodrich has called the law 'the only reality of postmodern culture' (Goodrich 1990:11). It as an absurd survivor of the ruptures, failures and discontinuities which have precipitated the discovery of 'postmodernity' in cultural commentary. Attention to the characteristics of law in a national rather than global context renders its survival less absurd, and also points to the homogenising power of accounts of the postmodern.

Goodrich points out that the British legal institution is 'in its most general sense an inscription of the past in the present' (1990:36). It is rooted in the past in its operation through ritual, convention, statute and precedent. The idea of law in legal discourse is presented as the principle by which a mythical national past connects with the present and directs our future. As authorised speakers, addressing an imagined national community, legal representatives have the power to manufacture accounts of the past which are indistinguishable from 'reality', accounts which enter into the narrative and semantic fabric of the cultural archive.[2] Bourdieu argues that 'legal discourse is a creative speech which brings into existence that which it utters' (1991:44). This narrative and constructive potential of law should be taken into account when assessing its modes of oppression and investigating the ways in which it can work against itself.

Paul Ricoeur explores the idea that human experience is always already mediated by different symbolic systems (Ricoeur 1991),[3] and foregrounds our entanglement in stories: 'we are caught in the stories of others, so we are protagonists in the stories we are told by others, and we have to assume for ourselves the stories that the others tell about us, which have their own founding events, their own strategies, their own plots' (Ricoeur 1995:38). The law is, in an important sense, a tool for catching people in stories. Through its power to organise cultural symbols it functions as a story-telling machine, a loom for the

---

2 I refer here to the concept elaborated by Michel Foucault (1972), which he defines at one point as 'a practice that causes a multiplicity of statements to emerge as regular events', and 'the general system of the formation and transformation of statements' (130). Edward Said brings this notion to bear when he addresses the problem of the relation of the individual to society (Said 1991:186-7).

3 Paul Ricoeur ascribes to human experience a 'virtual narrativity' or 'pre-narrative structure'; one occasion on which this virtual narrativity is exposed is when an individual comes before the law (1991:434-5).

production of organised entanglement. New maps and new stories can only be created when those circulated in law are exposed and challenged. The law remains what Said has termed an 'unquestioned reality' of our society, because it retains the power to self-create. Social relations in the (post)colonial world continue to be pervaded and regulated by western law, nationally and internationally. The concept of the 'postmodern' offers a version of the contemporary condition which describes and prescribes our liberation from the law's totalising project, from a corrosive belief in the narrow, conflictual groupings of race, nationality, ethnic origin. Against this it emphasises multiculturalism, globalism, the acceptance of fluid subjectivities, heterogeneity and the *differend* (cf. Lyotard 1988). Postcolonial and legal critics find grounds to resist this optimism,[4] and insist upon our bond to the past at sites of unresolved conflict.

Whilst postmodernist critiques of law tend to approach it in a way that renders its denial instrumental for a reconstruction of the present as a point of rupture and departure, it can miss the extent to which, rather than being an anachronism or absurdity, the legal system itself is a site for the *staging* of

4 For example, in his essay Lawrence Grossberg questions articulations of postmodernity that assume the demise of such 'modern' motivations as ethnocentrism and nationalism: he explores the ways in which 'the discourse of the local and the global is itself situated as a cultural practice of intellectuals'. He asks what legitimates the claim of criticism to such 'public representativeness': 'Is globalisation a general phenomenon or is it an experience that belongs only to a specific class fraction – of global intellectuals, or a new metropolitan elite or a new information class. In other words, whose reality, experience or imaginary is being described?' (1996:176). Touching on the issue of the possibility of freedom from history, Vron Ware also expresses anxieties about the wisdom of proclaiming the obsolescence of past groupings (1996). He argues that contemporary social relations 'have been formed and contested throughout centuries of racial slavery and colonisation' and questions whether 'whiteness, as a racialised category, can ever be redeemed from centuries of association with domination'. He acknowledges the extent to which law continues to structure our reality in a way that threads us back into the past, when he says that race is a matter of legal definition (142-4). Also emphasising the proximity of history in law Peter Fitzpatrick traces the ways in which in modern European law 'binds Europeans in their own being' (1992:66).

heterogeneity and the *differend*, for (despite itself) revealing the 'provisionality of all cultures'. The law may be thought of as a matrix for the genesis both of old and new realities. A dramatic dialogism arises from attempts to reinstitute the monologic voice of law against the grain of an emerging cultural relativity in multicultural domains.

In order to sustain misrecognition of its authority by such an audience the law must translate tyranny into narrative necessity. As one of the judges in the case discussed below says, it cannot appear to be 'frozen in an age of racial discrimination'; consequently it defrosts and is potentially dissolved in a display of storytelling that exposes its dependence upon a history which is one among others.

The idea of the postmodern has become, in a sense, an orthodox metastory. I will now elaborate on the issues raised above by first outlining some instances in which the law has been approached from a postmodern perspective, and then by suggesting departures from the presentation of the law as it accords with certain forms of critical orthodoxy. Ultimately, I will argue that an effect of casting the law as a delegitimated product of European Enlightenment rhetoric is that its continued performativity in the realm of post/colonial relations is not addressed, and that the public forum and critical focus it provides for the acknowledgement of historical and cultural relativism is not insisted upon.

2. Postmodern Critique and the Modernity of Law

The 'founding events, strategies, and plots' of law, which are posited as continuous with those of modernity help to persuade us of our 'post-'ness. Ricoeur argues that 'most cultures have some original happening or act which gives a basis of unity to the diversity within the culture' (Ricoeur 1995:37); the culture of postmodern critique has a founding moment, produced retroactively, at the inception of modernity. This moment is not always explicitly located within a linear historical narrative, but often emerges as an epistemological break tethered to a particular historical event, that of the French revolution. This event serves to initiate a persuasive narrativity. An example of this rhetorical move occurs in Anthony Carty's preface to *Post-Modern Law: Enlightenment, Revolution and the Death of Man*. Carty argues that modern law is the creation of modern political thought, the most significant founding event of which is the French Revolution, though, as he notes, other nations will find *less* consummated expressions of their modernity than this popular movement toward liberation from political absolutism and the '"darkness" of history, tradition and authority' (Carty 1990:2). Carty proposes that 'post-modernism' as 'a method of legal deconstruction can be as well applied to the English and other legal orders', but that 'its origin is clearest in this turning against the most complete modern legal project, that produced by the French Revolution' (1990:viii). Postmodernism is thereby rhetorically founded at the inception of modern law. Modern law is presented by Carty as the product of an emergent desire for rational government, given its fullest textual expression in Rousseau's invention of the 'social contract' which was inspirational in the process toward revolution. He gives an account of the part played by the law in the attempt to build a political utopia, and the failure, inherent at its beginning, which eventually became manifest.[5] The

5 The story begins hopefully, but 'it is not long before doubt enters into the modern legal project'. The Law begins its modern enterprise by an act of creation, it 'supposes a Grand Subject which must encompass or act upon something in the exercise of its grand project, and this something cannot any longer be taken to be simply itself, a reflection of itself, as it were. So the "Other" appears. The "Other" is that upon which the "law" acts, but which it never completely absorbs, that which remains when the "Law" has spent itself. The "Other" may be called society'. The Social Contract failed because it supposed that 'men are there before the laws they create'. Carty concludes that 'the "Society" which the "Law" creates is a simulated order dedicated to the sacred name of the public good in which the individual, whose chains were to be broken, simply never had a chance' (Carty 1990:7).

'end' of this story is now, the present instant of this critical narrative, where we exist in a condition of sceptical wariness. Though postmodernist critiques of law are generally articulated in the form of ongoing debates about the problem of foundationalism and the synchronic relationship between language, subjectivity, and 'reality', they can nevertheless find legitimation in an implicit diachronic orientation and a subtextual organising narrative trajectory.

The absurdity of law from a postmodern perspective involves its connection to the delegitimated project of modernity, denoting the period roughly since the eighteenth century throughout which there was an erroneous but 'prominent assumption that increasing rationality is conducive to the promotion of order and control, achievement of enhanced levels of social understanding, moral progress, justice and human happiness' (Smart 1993:91). The point of Anne Barron's article, mentioned above, is to critique Ronald Dworkin for his continued faith in the law's rationality, truth and justice. In doing so she adopts the position of the Critical Legal Studies project. This project, as Drucilla Cornell points out in her analysis of the relations between legal theory, deconstruction and postmodernity, is indebted for its postmodernist perspective to an interpretation of the work of Jacques Derrida which undercuts the claims of law to an authority based in reason, and forwards the 'irrationalist' view that 'there can be no *rational* limiting principle by which to judge competing interpretations of legal doctrine' (Cornell 1992:101). Barron questions Dworkin's subscription to the pretence to 'universal applicability' in the law on the basis that 'as rational subjects we are all the same and therefore all equally subject to the law'. Postmodernist thought indicts the law on the basis of its reliance upon the fraudulent fiction of the liberated modern subject: 'in opposing the Enlightenment vision of society as an ordered totality, unified by reference to an essential subjectivity, postmodernism insists upon the irreducible heterogeneity and multiplicity of human experience'. Western legal discourse is understood to make the individual a subject, first by 'creating his or her identity in terms of a category which can be universally recognised and controlled', and then by 'tying him or her to that identity'. The postmodernist endeavours to expose and depose the fictions of homogeneity, accountability and free-agency on which this is predicated.

Postcolonialists also seek to show how political notions of equality render inequalities and cultural differences invisible (Rosaldo 1994:240). Focus upon the impossibility of 'justice' in a postmodern world where faith in totalising narratives is lost has the function of accentuating incommensurable difference.[6] Yet part of positing the obsolescence of metanarratives and the fraudulent universalism of modern law is a substitution, in the space made by this delegitimation, of a universalist postmodernity which disables attempts to rectify inequality.

The position from which postmodern interrogations are addressed is a constructed 'present' which comes after history, as both continuation and end-point; it is the result of a narrative activity sustained both through consensus and the moral and imaginative force of key historical events in western states.[7]

6 This is Alan Wolfe's approach when he offers a postmodern perspective on the law. He opens with the question 'if there are no metanarratives, is justice possible?'. Wolfe here invokes the collectively legitimated version of our contemporary condition offered by Jean-François Lyotard, who asserts in *The Postmodern Condition* that 'incredulity toward metanarratives' *is* the postmodern condition (Wolfe 1992:361).

7 This Eurocentric story-telling may be viewed in the light of the point made by Steven Connor regarding the relation between the phenomenon of postmodernism and the academy. He notes that one of the most striking things about the postmodern debate is the authority with which the 'disappearance of final authority' is announced, and the simultaneous 'promotion and recirculation of a total and comprehensive narrative of a cultural condition in which totality is no longer thinkable' (1989:10). The case has been made by Connor and Zygmunt Bauman that narratives of postmodernity are a response to, and mode of managing, the crisis of authority in the humanities in western universities resulting from diminished social power and influence. Postmodern debate

Although Anthony Carty acknowledges the predominantly French location of the dominant postmodernist voices (listed as 'Derrida, Foucault, Baudrillard and Lyotard'), he asserts the much wider relevance of their attack upon 'natural reason, the self-evident rights of man, and the confidently expressed will of the collectivity capable of emancipating itself from superstition, tradition and blind acceptance of authority', by saying that it is of 'universal import' (Carty 1990:1). Its various interrogative projects are anchored to the primary conceptual shift involved in a national revolution, which is then internationalised into the secularisation of thought which was the European Enlightenment. The attempt by 'man' to make himself, by a conflicted and oppressive society to remanufacture itself through rational endeavour,[8] leads eventually to a totalised 'modernity', which in turn underwrites a global postmodernity.

This unificatory approach suppresses elements of particularity and provisionality that emerge in the context of national histories. The historical development of the rule of law in Britain demands at least a nuancing of this postmodern story. It is arguable that whatever the case in France, where British law is concerned, the 'self-evident rights of man', the 'confidently expressed will of the collectivity' and emancipation from 'superstition, tradition and blind acceptance of authority' were not essential components (other than in legitimating imperialist and colonial endeavour, bringing the light of civilisation to darkness, freeing foreigners of their superstition and their land). The dream of

represents on one level, as Connor has said, 'an important readjustment of power relations' (1989:12).

8 Critics of postmodernist thought have also located its origins at a later historical occasion in France, again expanding its ambit of significance to indefinably broad coordinates. Robert Paul Resch argues, for example, that postmodern critique emerges 'post-1968 in France'. For Resch, what he terms 'dissident postmodernism' is characterised by a passive nihilism and anti-rationalist stance triggered by political betrayal at this time, and has a 'seductively pseudoradical appearance', insofar as it 'rails against dominant discourses and social practices in the name of difference, desire, liberty, pluralism, and so forth' (Resch 1989:518).

a consensual and contractual rule of law has not played a significant role in the development of governmental forms in Britain (as Christopher Hill argues; Hill 1996). Though formulations of the rule of law in Britain have customarily emphasised the individual's freedom, radical social approbation of an 'emancipatory humanism' or rational subject was never given full political expression. British law produces historical not rational subjects. It remains distinct from most other nations and cultures of the world in its retention of a feudal framework, its dependence on precedent, ritual and tradition, and government via a form of unwritten (or diffracted) constitution.[9] In positing the inevitable 'modernity' of a ubiquitous law, it is probable that the ways in which 'English' law is both 'pre-modern', modern and 'postmodern' (or none of these) is elided. Crucial historical elements of the emergence of modernity, including the founding event of revolution to which the discussion of postmodernity

9 Neal Ascherson points out that 'Britain is . . . a very, very archaic state form. There is nothing else like it in Europe. Indeed, there is very little like it in the developed world at all' (1995:19). This focus upon its insularity and singularity accords with the still popularly held, traditional view of English law as emerging mysteriously and organically from a mythic past. The nineteenth-century constitutional commentator, Walter Bagehot, once imaginatively configured English law as existing in a liminal space between an 'urban', mapped modernity and an unmapped, 'uncivil' *pre*-modern hinterland:

> Our law very often reminds one of those outskirts of cities where you cannot for a long time tell how the streets come to wind about in so capricious and serpent-like a manner. At last it strikes you that they grew up, house by house, on the devious tracks of the old green lanes; and if you follow on to the existing fields, you may often find the change half complete. Just so the lines of our Constitution were framed in old eras of sparse population, few wants, and simple habits; and we adhere in seeming to their shape, though civilisation has come with its dangers, complications and enjoyments. These anomalies, in a hundred instances, mark the old boundaries of a constitutional struggle. The casual line was traced according to the strength of deceased combatants; succeeding generations fought elsewhere; and the hesitating line of a half-drawn battle was left to stand for a perpetual limit . . .' (Bagehot 1963:265-6).

The stories that create 'England', the language that creates English legality rhizomically follow the lines of desire and seams of conflict forged across time.

implicitly refers us, may be said to offer no more than a sporadic accompaniment to the archaic but adaptive, idiosyncratic development of British governmentality and sociality.

Points of divergence are most apparent in the peculiar discursive strategies in, and public perceptions of, the English legal system. As Tim Murphy argues, historically English law developed in a form substantially different from continental forms of law. The distinction is usually drawn in terms of common law and civil law, and resides in the notion that civil law 'hypostasized the claims of reason . . . into the state, into codes', whilst English common law resisted codification and depended instead upon the power of tradition, on cases of 'precedent, *stare decisis*' (Murphy 1994:71-2).[10] It is a system which bases its authority on the inaccessibility and mystical quality of its procedures; history is invoked rather than texts being interpreted. Although a great deal of writing is very much involved in transcripts of cases, writing always 'comes later on the scene' (79). As a result 'the law' is continuously and anonymously rewritten. To that extent English law is not, and has never acceded to 'government by the people for the people', there was never an occasion upon which the laws of the nation were purposively framed by 'man'; they are the expression of a transcendent legality, underwritten by history and providence. Legal discourse in

10 Murphy shows how English law borrowed the modern clothes of continental law, in the process of effecting the continuation of what is essentially a medieval jurisprudence. He argues that since modern law emerged in the age of print technology, this permitted the actualisation of its 'dominant image in Western thought' as of 'something written down and fixed', something civilised and rational which 'can be the object of informed interpretation, systematic (or at least orderly) exposition, explicit critique and purposive alteration' (1994:73). The codification of law in post-Napoleonic Europe was the result of the attempt to combine these factors to the theoretical advantage both of the law, which thereby augments its authority, and the people, who may have faith in the law's accessibility and the integrity of legislators bound by the text. In contrast, though the English common law world remained 'scribal', it was not textual, not 'fixed in place by printed texts'. Though it retained the idea of the law as an inscription to be interpreted and applied, it is, as Murphy suggests, as a pre-text, rather than a text.

English common law on the whole avoids (what for postmodernists is) the Enlightenment indignity of posing as the result of reason and consensus. The English common law is legitimated by that against which modern civil law defines itself, tradition.[11] It finds its guarantor in history, narrative, convention, repetition. The British cultural imagination does not enshrine a modern 'beginning' of history or rationalist teleology to be dwelt upon as delusory. It records instead an erratic process of disguise, supplementation, accretion and transformation.

3. Law, Stories and Histories

As regards Britain's former colonies, immigrant nations and indigenous peoples who have been under the dominion of 'the Crown', and whose fight for autonomy is still to be formulated within what Lyotard might term the 'phrase regimens' (Lyotard 1988:151) of the English legal system, find that English law is concerned with preserving the authority of history rather than issues of equality. Recent challenges in colonial settler nations to the possession of foreign territory by the Crown involve the invention of 'native title'. This is intended to deal with the aboriginal claim on territory taken from them by colonists. In Australia this question was central to the internationally scrutinised 'Mabo Case' in 1992,[12] the reverberations of which continue to unsettle the settled white

11 As Neal Ascherson points out, 'what happened in the seventeenth century was that the English parliament just took absolutism away from the kings, from the divine right of kings, and gave it to parliament, where it still is. So there is no concept of *popular sovereignty*. Instead, you have an elected parliament, but it is completely sovereign – it is not subject to the people as a concept, it is not subject to a constitution' (1995:19).

12 This case is given fuller consideration elsewhere (Swain and Clarke 1995). The Mabo case specifically concerns the ownership of a small group of islands to the north east of

community. The establishment of 'native title' is a narrative activity, instituting competition as to where history is found and who makes it. In the Mabo case, the only judge (Dawson J) not prepared to recognise aboriginal or 'native title', even in the limited sense in which it has been allowed, met the challenge by appeal to English colonial law's institutional status as what Goodrich terms an 'inscription of the past in the present'. He argued that 'it would be wrong to attempt to revise history or to fail to recognise its legal impact, however unpalatable it may now seem. To do so would be to impugn the foundations of the *very legal system* under which this case must be decided'. The other six high court judges, however, do openly and at length rehearse and revise history in an attempt not to appear (to a national and international audience) to be 'frozen in an age of racial discrimination' (Mabo 1992:409). Accordingly a very large part of the transcript of the case amounts to historical reconstruction, an arduous excavation of texts and pretexts, and a montage of narratives. They range from a long passage entitled 'Early Contact with Europeans', through 'The Feudal Basis of the Proposition of Absolute Crown Ownership', 'The Aborigines and the Land in

---

Queensland. It was the culmination of an eleven-year litigation. The native people, referred to as the Meriam people, have occupied the islands since before the arrival of the Europeans. Their case has played a crucial role in bringing aboriginal claims for land rights into a framework that would be 'recognised' by the Australian court. In the Mabo case the High Court of Australia came to a momentous decision which established a new form of land ownership in Australia, that of 'native' or 'aboriginal title', which means that the common law recognises for the first time in its history a form of land-ownership which 'reflects the entitlements of the indigenous inhabitants' (Mabo 1992:409). The case is the occasion of the public recognition of the particular importance of history to English colonial law.

> In discharging its duty to declare the common law of Australia, this Court is *not free to adopt rules that accord with contemporary notions of justice and human rights* if their adoption would fracture the skeleton principle which gives the body of our law its shape and internal consistency. Australian law is not only the historical successor of, but is an organic development from, the law of England. Although *our law is the prisoner of its history*, it is now bound by decisions of courts in the hierarchy of the Empire then concerned with the development of its colonies (emphasis added).

1788' to various accounts of traditional claims to land. The production of multiple accounts by the Crown, as defendant, becomes the basis of maintaining the rule of law, and the activity of narration the vehicle of the legal process.

The Mabo litigation involved not only the requirement that English colonial law raid its archives for stories, but that aboriginals produce a comparable wealth of accounts. Commensurable evidence was required of fixed inhabitancy and cultivation, over generations, of areas concerned. A nomadic lifestyle, an escape from the textualised and mapped terrain, a narrative hiatus occurring at any point, would lead to disinheritance. A postmodern nomadism and a liberation from 'all roots, bonds, and identities' may prove a doubtful strategy when the winning language game still involves an emphasis upon inscription and continuity. On the other hand, using the same language means collaborating in the law's version of history. However, in this case the law's authority rests on the achievement of narrative cohesion wrought from a non-cohesive multiplicity of stories which render it a vulnerable host at a fabulists' convention even before competing accounts are offered. The invention of 'native title' can be both a vehicle for containing claims and the occasion of the law's deconstruction of its own authority. Colonial law was designed to legitimate settlement in perpetuity, and any challenge to colonial ownership now amounts to an assault upon the posteriority of history. Though native title has been the focus of optimism on the part of indigenous peoples in settler nations it may ultimately prove most useful because the law is called upon to publicly defend its legitimacy, and as this depends upon displaying the binding narrative logic of history, the task is laborious and treacherous. Land-title cases (including those arising in Canada, America and New Zealand) are characterised by their extraordinary length. The Mabo case itself runs to around two hundred pages. The establishment of land rights involves the tracing of Ariadne's thread – the thread of narrative and sequential logic – through a labyrinth of historical and anthropological representations, in the knowledge that the end of the thread is held by the undead monster of illegitimate, and delegitimated settlement locatable in the legal fiction of *terra nullius*, or uninhabited land. The law finds itself on trial, liable, like Theseus, to be torn apart by the Minotaur.

Whilst the multiplicity of documents and accounts are referred to and offered by representatives who hold the *skeptron* of an institution which reveres history, they expose the jeopardy of claiming history as grounds for absolute authority and right. Litigations regarding the entitlement of indigenous peoples to national territory are public forums for the staging of stories, and can become the site of challenge and dialogue if the jeopardy in which the invocation and rewriting of history places the law is insisted upon. Its processes in the context of postcolonial conflict can reveal the constructedness of the realities it creates, and make space for a negotiation of its grounds toward a greater representativeness. Where Australia is concerned, the neglect and dismissal of pre-existing roots, bonds and identities, or 'cartographic erasure' was historically a means of empowering one group and disempowering, even destroying, another.[13] Instead of positing an imaginative repetition of this erasure, attention could be drawn to the strategies employed by the law for preserving them, and the ways in which they may be deconstructed or challenged.

As it confronts manifestations of a multicultural society, and is challenged to formulate concepts such as 'native title', the law can only wield, to labour the mythological analogy, Theseus's magic sword. This magic consists in manifestations of what Bourdieu termed liturgical authority, of simply being 'known and recognised' as able to produce an authoritative class of discourse. Faced with potential deconstruction when giving consideration to subaltern

[13] This aspect of the history of Australian settlement is explored by Simon Ryan (Ryan 1994).

rights, the law draws upon its symbolic power, its status as 'creative speech'. Its stories appear to cohere through the suspension of disbelief demanded by its status as narrator. In the process of reconstructing the past and acknowledging, as one judge in the Mabo case says, the 'national legacy of unutterable shame' (Mabo 1992:449) consequent upon imperial dispossession, the law asserts its role as narrator of a colonial history in which litigants are no more than protagonists. Litigation over the possession of territory between cultures provides instances of what Lyotard terms the emergence of the *differend*. The colonial arbitrating law attempts to resolve the *differend* through an appeal to history, since there is, as Lyotard asserts, no rational way of achieving resolution. It can only be effected in terms of narrative, or what Ricoeur calls the 'configurative act' (Ricoeur 1991:142). Lyotard argues in *The Differend* that

> narrative is perhaps the genre of discourse within which the heterogeneity of phrase regimens . . . have the easiest time passing unnoticed . . . . Wherever in diegetic time it stops, its term makes sense and retroactively organises the recounted events. The narrative function is redeeming in itself. It acts as if the occurrence, with its potentiality of differends, could come to completion, or as if there were a last word. (Lyotard 1988:12)

Ricoeur's discussion of the power of emplotment reaches a similar conclusion. Yet the very spectacle of the law attempting to reconstruct its authority via an exhumation and exposure of texts and stories from the venerated tomb of the past reveals the extent to which law and history is fiction and interpretation, text rather than truth, matter rather than spirit. The recognition, or license, that is extended to the law 'in the manner of something taken for granted' and the authority it carries as 'narrative necessity', is undermined by internal contradictions which emerge in its efforts to narrate.

Investigation of the law's runic mode of operating is a route to demonstrating the provisionality of its right. In postmodern critique the law appears as an absurd survivor of the generalised failure and consequent delegitimised 'unreality' of modernity, but this law remains constructive, perpetuating past conflictual social and political arrangements, and attempting revision and self-reinvention. The legal system retains a world-making function. An examination of the relation between power, authority, narrative and reality is *as* appropriate a way of understanding its role as an emphasis upon its roots in the conceptual aporias of modernity. There is a sense in which, despite the invitation to accept cultural heterogeneity, postmodernist critique displays the 'synthesis of the heterogenous' that Ricoeur remarks upon as intrinsic to narrativity (1991:433) in that it does not recognise the law as a product of discourses which evolve within politically, historically, socially and geographically defined spaces. In the postcolonial 'third space' the law is not as insulated, complete and universal as it presents itself to be, or as it appears when employed as an originary instance for narratives of postmodernity. It can perform as a compelling narrator and historiographer, but is also diminished by these activities where they involve publicly mapping its own past. Lyotard argues that modernity is characterised by the need for legitimation, by attempts at rational, scientific objectivity as opposed to (pre-modern) story-telling.[14] Against the law, postmodern scepticism approves a return to narrative, to the liberated proliferation of discrete stories, in combination with a toleration of dissent, and an escape from history and the map. The law is a story-teller, and it is our own disposition toward recognition that determines whether its stories are premodern, modern or postmodern. To preserve its authority the law is liable to make those for whom it does not speak recognise the 'roots, bonds and identities' established

14 'The scientist questions the validity of narrative statements and concludes that they are never subject to argumentation or proof. He classifies them as belonging to a different mentality: savage, primitive, underdeveloped, backward, alienated, composed of opinions, customs, authority, prejudice, ignorance, ideology. Narratives are fables, myths, legends, fit only for women and children' (Lyotard 1986:27).

by law in the past, to make its story their story. This is also where such representations may be reassessed, and where attention can be dramatically drawn to the law's attempts to achieve emplotment in a way that situates it as one fabulist amongst others, rather than as an antithetical absurdity.

Stella SWAIN
University of the West of England

Works Cited

Ascherson, Neal. 'Nations and Regions' in Kearney, 14-22.

Bagehot, Walter. *The English Constitution*. Glasgow: Fontana, 1963, from the Longman's edition of 1915, first published 1867.

Barron, Anne. 'Ronald Dworkin and the Challenge to Postmodernism'. *Oxford Literary Review* 11 (1989): 121-36.

Bauman, Zygmunt. *Life in Fragments: Essays in Postmodern Morality*. Oxford: Blackwell, 1995.

Bourdieu, Pierre. *Language and Symbolic Power*. Ed. John B. Thompson. Trans. Gino Raymond and Matthew Adamson. Oxford: Polity Press in association with Blackwell Publishers, 1991.

Carty, Anthony, ed. *Post-Modern Law: Enlightenment, Revolution and the Death of Man*. Edinburgh: Edinburgh University Press, 1990.

Chambers, Iain and Lidia Curti, eds. *The Post-Colonial Question: Common Skies Divided Horizons*. London: Routledge, 1996.

Connor, Steven. *Postmodernist Culture*. Oxford: Blackwell, 1989.

Cornell, Drucilla. *The Philosophy of the Limit*. London: Routledge, 1992.

Fitzpatrick, Peter. *The Mythology of Modern Law*. London: Routledge, 1992.

Foucault, Michel. *The Archaeology of Knowledge*. Trans. A. M. Sheridan Smith. London: Tavistock, 1972.

Goodrich, Peter. *Languages of Law: From Logics of Memory to Nomadic Masks*. London: Weidenfeld and Nicholson, 1990.

Grossberg, Lawrence. 'The Space of Culture, The Power of Space' in Chambers and Curti, 169-88.

Hall, Stuart. 'When Was '"The Post-Colonial"? Thinking at the Limit' in Chambers and Curti, 242-60.

Hill, Christopher. *Liberty Against the Law*. London: Allen Lane, 1996.

Huggan, Graeme. 'Decolonising the Map'. *The Post-Colonial Studies Reader*. Eds. Bill Ashcroft et al. London: Routledge, 1995. 407-11.

Kearney, Richard, ed. *States of Mind: Dialogues with Contemporary Thinkers on the European Mind.* Manchester: Manchester University Press, 1995.

Lyotard, Jean-François. *The Differend: Phrases in Dispute*. Trans. Georges Van Den Abbeele. Minnesota: University of Minnesota Press, 1988.

---. *The Postmodern Condition: A Report on Knowledge*. Trans. Geoff Bennington and Brian Massumi. Manchester: Manchester University Press, 1984.

Mabo v. Queensland. *Commonwealth Law Reports* and *Australian Law Journal Report* 175/66 (1992): 408-99.

McClintock, Anne. 'The Angel of Progress: Pitfalls of the Term Postcolonialism'. *Colonial Discourse/Postcolonial Theory*. Eds. Francis Barker, Peter Hulme and Margaret Iversen. Manchester: Manchester University Press, 1994. 253-66.

Murphy, Tim. 'As If: *Camera juridica*'. *Politics, Postmodernity and Criticial Legal Studies*. Eds. Costas Douzinos, Peter Goodrich and Yifat Hachamovitch. London: Routledge, 1994. 69-106.

Readings, Bill. 'Pagans, Perverts or Primitives?' *Judging Lyotard*. Ed. Andrew Benjamin. London: Routledge, 1992. 168-91.

Resch, Robert Paul. 'Modernism, Postmodernism, and Social Theory: A Comparison of Althusser and Foucault'. *Poetics Today* 10 (1989): 511-49.

Ricoeur, Paul. 'Life: A Story in Search of a Narrative'. *Reflection and Imagination*. Ed. Mario J. Valdes. London: Harvester Wheatsheaf, 1991. 425-40.

---. 'Universality and the Power of Difference' in Kearney, 33-8.

Rosaldo, Renato. 'Social Justice and the Crisis of National Communities'. *Colonial Discourse/Postcolonial Theory*. Eds. Francis Barker, Peter Hulme, and Margaret Iversen. Manchester: Manchester University Press, 1994. 239-52.

Ryan, Simon. 'Inscribing the Emptiness: Cartography, Exploration and the Construction of Australia'. *De-Scribing Empire: Postcolonialism and Textuality*. Eds. Chris Tiffin and Alan Lawson. London: Routledge, 1994. 115-30.

Said, Edward. *Culture and Imperialism*. London: Chatto and Windus, 1993.

---. 'Criticism Between Culture and System'. *The World, the Text and the Critic*. London: Vintage, 1991. 178-225.

Smart, Barry. *Postmodernity*. Routledge: London, 1993.

Spivak, Gayatri Chakravorty. 'Can the Subaltern Speak?' *Colonial Discourse and Postcolonial Theory*. Eds. Patrick Williams and Laura Chrisman. Hemel Hempstead: Harvester Wheatsheaf, 1993. 66-111.

Swain, Stella and Andrew Clarke. 'Negotiating Postmodernity: Narratives of Law and Imperialism'. *Law and Critique* 6 (1995): 229-56.

Ware, Vron. 'Defining Forces: "Race", Gender and Memories of Empire' in Chambers and Curti, 142-56.

Wolfe, Alan. 'Algorithmic Justice'. *Deconstruction and the Possibility of Justice*. Eds. Drucilla Cornell, Michel Rosenfeld, and David Gray Carlson. London: Routledge, 1992. 361-86.

Just Sentences:

The Incalculable in Postmodern Justice

> This is the way to start a sentence about startling a sentence. (Bernstein)

> The sentence (*phrase*) is hierarchical: it implies subjections, subordinations, internal reactions. Whence its completion: how can a hierarchy remain open? The sentence is complete: it is precisely that language which is complete. (Barthes)

> Not every sentence (*logos*) has truth or falsity in it: a prayer (*euche*) is a sentence but it is neither true nor false. The present investigation deals with the *apophantic* [statement-making] sentence. The others we can dismiss, since consideration of them belongs rather to the study of rhetoric or poetry. (Aristotle)

Part One: Modernity and the Postmodern

To speak of 'postmodern justice' could be to imply that there are different types of justice corresponding to different situations; and that the different types are characterised by different forms of decision, embodied by differing modes of action. In that case to speak of 'postmodern justice' implies perhaps that there are also types of justice, forms of decision, modes of action, that are proper to say enlightenment, or to modernity. By extension this might also imply that justice must be characterised in terms of its historical specificity – a just action would then be one that is considered just only with reference to the specific historical context in which it is executed. But that of course would lead to a kind of idealisation of the concept of a justice whose reach is unlimited, and whose changing finite embodiments ensure only its mysterious ideality. To say that an action is 'just' is to call on a *generic* justice, the sense of which transcends the historical specificities of the action itself.

On the other hand, to speak of 'postmodern justice' might imply that there are different accounts of justice, that the postmodern account competes with or contests the modern account, that 'justice' is perhaps not what the moderns say it is but rather it is what 'we' postmoderns say it is. This way of speaking assumes an advance perhaps on previous thinking, the advantage maybe of hindsight (even though the problem of justice will necessarily be one of foresight). Or it may simply assume an *other* way of thinking, an alternative. Then, of course, a modernist or a rationalist (for the moment nothing more than parodic names) would undoubtedly contest 'postmodern justice' claiming that it is false, mistaken, wrong. Or perhaps, with more tolerance, that it may be alright for you postmoderns but it will not do for us. One could always anyway add that even the site and situation of the controversy is historically specific, so that justice between competing accounts of justice would have to be found in its actual embodiment in specific social relationships, modes of interpretation and evaluative practices.

Apparently then we cannot arrive at a characterisation of 'postmodern justice' without either falling into the contingency of a particular conception (whether 'postmodern' or not), or calling on a more general conception within which the postmodern perspective contends with others. For while the problem of how justice is itself to be situated remains prior to any of its individual characterisations any attempt to so situate it immediately becomes just such an individual characterisation.

But perhaps 'postmodern justice' precisely rebels against this law, according to which any attempt to situate the problem of justice involves a rationalisation, an account, a *logos* of justice, a concept legitimating decisions and actions that fall under its domain. On that basis the controversies over justice become questions about the relationship between sentences that concern the truth (apophantic sentences) and sentences that prescribe actions (prescriptive sentences). Perhaps 'postmodern justice' indicates a form of decision or action, a type of sentence or sentencing, that is radically independent of legislating rationalities. Then 'postmodern justice' would not be a determination but it would be that which always escapes all determinations. It would be the enigma and evanescence of a justice that is both necessary and impossible. And it would therefore promise a fecund politics, to the extent that its impossibility would constitute the necessity of nonetheless moving towards justice in the interminable response to an inevitably unjust law.

Justice and Rationality

Alasdair Macintyre's *Whose Justice? Which Rationality?* embodies a perspective from which it is necessary to assume 'that each particular conception of justice requires as its counterpart some particular conception of practical rationality and vice versa', and that such conceptions 'give expression to traditions of rational enquiry which are at one and the same time traditions embodied in particular types of social relationship' (Macintyre 1988:389). Macintyre's readings must thus assume that the texts he reads are anchored in determined ways, 'that Aristotle, Aquinas and Hume [and others] . . . were historically situated in the way that they were, themselves members of just such forms of community, who were inescapably involved in the conflicts central to the historically developing life of those communities at those times and places', and that these are not 'accidental or peripheral' facts about the philosophies of each (389). This inevitably calls for selective reading. According to Macintyre's argument Aristotle's theory of justice, and the schema of practical reasoning that informs it, is relevant in 'one's own life' only to the extent that it fits those conditions of life in the Athenian *polis* that are still relevant to 'modern communities' (391).

For instance there are 'Aristotelian practice-based enterprises and communities in which a justice of desert is the social virtue of those who recognise the ordered goods which they pursue as specifying what for them in their circumstances is required for and of those whose telos is the good as such' (391-2). So in Macintyre's reading Aristotelian justice involves a situation in which all the members of a community practise a system of exchange (of actions and goods) where the relative values of each exchange are governed by a general overdetermining value (good as such). Perhaps Macintyre's argument for Aristotle could be applied to a large industry in which each employee has his or her specific status valued in terms of specific contributions made to the economic growth of the company itself (rewarded by salary, office space, etc.). The example, although slightly parodic, is a tribute to the absurdity of some of Macintyre's conclusions. On the one hand, the idea that modernity is filled with relatively autonomous, tradition-centred communities seems a basic starting point given the antagonism, conflict and need for negotiation that lies at the basis of all experiences of cultural difference. On the other hand, the assertion that there are communities which each resemble the structure of some historically verifiable past community and its correlative philosophy (Thomistic educational communities, communities who embody Humean modes of social existence, etc.) seems inadequate. At the very least 'justice' in each of his readings is the term that is *called for* by the facts of cultural difference – even, and perhaps especially, *within* communities, but also crucially *between* them. But furthermore Macintyre operates on a covert concept of justice, not one he defends but one he practises and prescribes, a reading practice, a practice of philosophising. It works through a severe narrowing down (rationalising) of the philosophical and social 'text'. It asserts that a present day Aristotelianism could be just only within the confines of a situation commensurable with the situation that Aristotle (the man) found himself. Now Aristotle's concept of justice, at its most basic level, is an attempt to show how incommensurable parties can be made commensurable in the interests of community (the possibility of justice as precondition of community). Against this Macintyre thus seems to want to say that individuals can be made commensurable, but only if they already are. That is, justice is possible only where there is no need of justice.[1] This is not simply a paradox of Macintyre's text. It seems to occur whenever any attempt is made to fit a concept of justice (a system that could determine prescriptive sentences) to a rational schema (a system of apophantic sentences). What concept of justice emerges when such an attempt is avoided?

1 There is not enough space here to provide a reading of Macintyre's influential book but it is worth pointing out that Macintyre consistently limits the range of each of the theories in his enquiry to the situation within the communities to which each of the authors belonged. It is then easy for him to show that each theory reaches its limit beyond those confines. That is, his readings constitute the limitations. He for instance 'proves' that Aristotle's conception of justice could not have been designed to operate between Greek states owing to the Spartans' historical refusal to accept an Athenian offer of arbitration (51).

Justice and Postmodernism

In *The Postmodern Condition* Jean-François Lyotard famously argues that 'grand narratives' of human progress and liberation, rooted in Enlightenment thought, have lost credibility. So the term 'postmodernism' often comes to describe a variety of responses to the suggestion that both legitimation and knowledge are simultaneously in crisis. The relationship that this felt loss of credibility has brought about between concepts of legitimation and knowledge comes to a head at the level of the sentence, which traditionally carries out their work: a deontic sentence *prescribes* in the case of legitimation and an apophantic one *describes* in the case of knowledge. The former is tested by justice, the latter by truth. In the slightly later *Au Juste* Lyotard writes that 'justice consists in working at the limits of what the rules permit, in order to invent new moves, perhaps new rules and therefore new games' (Lyotard 1985:97). And in writing this he is, of course, describing a form of prescription that prescribes an antidote to any informing concepts or rules of prescription. Justice would consist in actions or decisions not yet permitted by the rules. But in that case it is a form of prescription that is tied with intricate complexity not only to the ancient and modern texts whose limits make it possible, but also to the limits of those protocols, the rules and moves of philosophy, criticism and theory, that constitute our axiomatics of reading and interpretation.

Lyotard's texts are not radically severed from the 'great' texts of the past (any attempt at such a severance would describe a canonically more modern gesture) but are often developed out of instances or moments in those texts that seem to offer an opening into unpredictability. In *Au Juste*, Lyotard draws on Kant's *Groundwork of the Metaphysics of Morals* as well as Aristotle's *Nicomachean Ethics* as texts which articulate theories of a justice that has no content in apophantic sentences. Kant's 'universal imperative of duty' states (in the interesting second formulation): 'Act as if the maxim of your action were to become through your will a universal law of nature' (52). The analogy of 'as if' (or 'in such a way that') is all important here for it reveals the use of an Idea that *necessarily* overruns its own limits. On the one hand 'nature' here refers to 'the universality of the law . . . the existence of things so far as determined by universal laws' (52). The imperative demands only that my maxim conforms to such a law. But on the other hand the concept of nature, as the analogue for universal legislation amongst free human beings, only makes possible a concept, an Idea of reason. This has no function but regulation. Reason can work with the *Idea* of a totality of free and reasonable (thus obligated) beings without the need for there to be such a totality empirically. As Lyotard argues, it is the maximisation of a concept of reason in order to regulate action. A just action is possible when reason thus transgresses its limit. Lyotard argues that this Idea is like a 'negative teleology': 'Do whatever ("do whatever" because it is not known what is just) with, as the only regulator of the "whatever", that what you do not be incompatible with a total society of reasonable beings . . . that they themselves may be obligated precisely because they are free' (Lyotard 1985:47). What is important for Lyotard here is that the finality (the realm of ends) is not a determinant concept but one which regulates judgements that are in no way derivable from or explainable by a pre-given justice: 'It is not known what is just . . . we have to judge case by case' (47). But for Lyotard it is doubtful that a judge could do without a finality of some kind – and most promising is this pseudo-finality, which is not a metaphysical finality at all, but 'it is simply one of reason's Ideas' (47).

So for Lyotard justice can only be understood from the point of view of prescriptions with no reference to rational models, possible constitutions etc. (the Kantian realm of ends is a regulative Idea based on the maximisation of the concept of freedom). He turns to Aristotle for the sense of what kind of judge can make prescriptions independently of the order of knowledge (*episteme*):

> Aristotle . . . recognises . . . that a judge worthy of the name has no true model to guide his judgments, and that the true nature of the judge is to pronounce judgments, and therefore prescriptions, just so, without criteria. This is, after all, what Aristotle calls prudence [*phronesis*]. It consists in dispensing justice without models. It is not possible to produce a learned discourse on what justice is. (Lyotard 1985:26)

So what Lyotard is interested in here in Aristotle as well as in Kant is the unfathomability of the ability to judge, which 'does not hang upon the observance of criteria' (17). Whether as Aristotle's *phronesis*, or as the will in Kant (or as will to power in Nietzsche), this ability involves being able to invent criteria case by case. It is a power that can create the terms of a law that does not exist as such, neither as a discourse of knowledge nor as a set of prescriptive criteria.

Lyotard gives this power and its observance the title 'paganism', indicating in a quite straightforward way any situation in which there can be no reference to or presumption of a metalanguage. Such a situation deserves the name 'pagan' when the judge, or the just person, is accountable within the same sphere of language as are those who will be the recipients of the judge's prescriptions (28-9), and who will thus in turn be able to judge the judge. This therefore means that judges must be accountable for their actions without relying on any legislating or authoritative discourse that might be represented as being beyond or above the evolving sphere of actions in any given social formation. But, in a way that is not quite so straightforward, paganism is also postmodernism in so far as the judge operates in a sphere analogous to 'the condition of the literatures and arts that have no assigned addressee and no regulating ideal, yet in which value is regularly measured on the stick of experimentation' (16). A postmodern or pagan condition is one in which a society is constantly forced to redraw its code, just as a postmodern art 'is measured by the distortion that is inflicted upon the materials, the forms and the structures of sensibility and thought' (16). 'Postmodern justice' thus denotes the ability to cope with society as radical contingency, to be just in a sphere of violent changes, unexpected arrivals, where accident is the law, and the tradition just is whatever is new. It is the exact opposite of what Macintyre says it is.

Justice is Deconstruction

So although postmodernism is not, for Lyotard at least, a periodising term,[2] it can be seen as a term that addresses a particular and increasingly urgent problem of modernity, that is, the apparent impossibility of justice. Kant's attempt to reconcile the unchanging laws of understanding (the mode of knowledge) and the freedom of the will (practical reason) in aesthetic judgement characterises modernity's essential aporia. The critical impulse that is enlightenment for Kant, reason's will to knowledge freed of all guidance, is an impulse towards the impossible: the infinite totality of things as they are, the unbridgeable space between knowledge and freedom crossed only in the creativity of the aesthetic judgement. Between the critical impulse, which is unregulated reason, and reason's certain knowledge of its own interminable limits, lies the modern aporia of justice. Whenever the concept of justice is evoked (for example, under its collocational terms freedom and responsibility in Kant) its solution returns us each time to the undecidable, our inability to choose between a regulating principle (that is already therefore a decision) on the one hand and the need to

2 'Postmodern is not to be taken in a periodising sense' (Lyotard 16).

make a decision despite or against the law on the other. Jacques Derrida outlines the basic form of the aporia as follows:

> Each case is other, each decision is different and requires an absolutely unique interpretation, which no existing, coded rule can or ought to guarantee absolutely. At least, if the rule guarantees it in no uncertain terms, so that the judge is a calculating machine – which happens – we will not say that he is just, free and responsible. But we also won't say it if he doesn't refer to any law, to any rule or if, because he doesn't take any rule for granted beyond his own interpretation, he suspends his decision, stops short before the undecidable or if he improvises and leaves aside all rules, all principles. (Derrida 1992:23)

Derrida situates deconstruction between two poles of what turns out to be a false distinction, that between justice and *droit* (or law). The distinction is false because, as Derrida argues, 'it turns out that *droit* claims to exercise itself in the name of justice and that justice is required to establish itself in the name of a law that must be "enforced"' (22). Justice cannot simply be outside or beyond the legislations of the law and the law must operate in the name of justice. Yet the two seem forever divided. The three parts of the aporia of justice that Derrida describes are as follows: first, the judge must act on the law, but as if no law existed in advance; the judgement must be as if it were a free decision. Second, a decision needs to be more than 'the programmable application or unfolding of a calculable process' (24), it must operate beyond the order of the calculable, towards a justice that is directed (like all writing) to the absolute alterity of the other (the randomly determined and in principle infinite addressee). Thirdly, a decision must be made *now*; in what Derrida calls the 'urgency' of the demand for justice; one cannot wait for ideal conditions (the regulative idea, or the messianic promise). So one cannot simply enact the regulative calculability of the law in cases which are always absolutely singular; each case demands an assessment, an interpretation. And one cannot ignore the law and improvise a decision. Rather, justice involves a recasting of the law each time a decision is demanded; justice remains essentially *a-venir*, 'to come', not beyond a horizon towards which we gradually progress or for which we tirelessly wait; but essentially, in the demand for decision, justice as always to come structures the undecidability of the moment itself, and the singularity of the present moment is a function of that formal undecidability.[3] The 'idea of justice' is infinite, then, because it is 'owed to the other' and its demand is of a 'gift without exchange, without circulation, without recognition or gratitude, without economic circularity, without calculation and without rules, without reason and without rationality' (25). I now turn to Aristotle's text on justice, economic circularity and law, in an attempt to address the incalculable there.

Part Two: Aristotle's Law

Book V of *The Nicomachean Ethics* is devoted to δικαιοσυνη, translated via the Latin as justice. It is here that Aristotle provides a prolonged discussion of the law (*nomos*) of proportionate reciprocity:

> ταις κοινωνιαις ταις αλλακτικαις συμεχει το τοιουτον δικαιον, το αντιπεπονθος, κατ αναλογιαν και μη κατ ισοτητα. τω αντιποιει γαρ αναλογον συμμενει η πολις. [1132b 33-37]
>
> (In associations in which exchange occurs the unifying bond is a type of justice, in the sense of reciprocating incommensurables by analogy, and not through equality. In fact it is analogy that holds people together in the polis.)

---

3 See Drucilla Cornell, *The Philosophy of the Limit*, for a discussion of Derrida's argument. She writes: 'For Derrida, judgment begins where calculation ends' (1988:135).

Association (*koinoniai*) for exchange (*allaktikai*), or more literally 'interchange', implies in the Greek both joining and discussion, depending on the context. Joining may be implied in either mechanical or commercial senses (linking, coupling, crossing, conjunction, merger or juncture); and discussion implies a whole range of discursive activities, including idle chatter, conversation, all kinds of intercourse, a dialogue, a caucus, a colloquy and a conference, as well as an exchange of political views, a forum, in fact any meeting in general.

Aristotle devotes a number of paragraphs to describing justice on the model of the necessary conditions for what we recognise, perhaps too quickly, as something like 'commercial' exchange. In fact *allaktikai*, based as it is on the root *alla* meaning 'otherwise', already gives the notion of exchange an emphasis which marks out the alternating, interchanging, dialogical aspects of the process. Exchange here, as a kind of reciprocal-rendering-otherwise-through-linking-intercourse, involves change and alteration as much as exchange and repayment, for taking one thing for another means making those things other than what they are. Exchanging things is just changing things. The *allagma*, the value of that which is taken or given in exchange, its 'price', involves thinking of it in terms of its own possible otherness – the price is the designator of this difference, the crossing or jointure without which nothing would be exchanged at all. The classical conception of exchange is therefore understandable only on the possibility of a kind of a priori substitutability in which a thing is only what it is if it has this in principle infinite capacity for being changed for something else. The *alla* here is an indispensable part of Aristotle's teaching on political justice, where the dichotomy – *alla* ('on the one hand') and *alle* ('on the other') – introduces different parts to each other in a way that confronts each part with its own difference (see Aristotle's play on the words *dikaion* [just] and *dicha* [a bisection] at 1132a 31). This difference is spatial in so far as things are literally exchanged (they change places and each ends up in 'another place' or 'elsewhere'); it is temporal in so far as the notion of value or price allows a delay before any actual exchange needs to come about; and it is figurative in so far as it is the 'manner' or the 'quality' of a thing that is to be considered otherwise. It is not therefore by chance that the same root delivers us into an analogous rhetorical register in which a declaration (the 'to speak' of *agoreuo*) or proclamation to the assembled *agora* (the political forum in the Athenian constitution) meets the 'otherwise' of *alle* in *allegorio* or allegory, which, whether regarded as speaking *so as to imply* something other than what is said, or *interpreting* something other than what is said, presupposes a common condition underlying both economy, government and discourse – that is, the possibility of describing something 'under the image of another'. Aristotle's account of this condition, in which the possibility of substitution becomes generalisable, is given in the figure of proportion, an analogy of promised repayment for entry into the general system of exchange. Community in Aristotle's conception can thus be considered as growing out of the figure of proportion which allows entities that are otherwise different to be made analogous. The figure is itself just analogy.

Naming and Necessity

Aristotle says that analogical justice is secured and maintained through a notion of currency, which must be taken in both the economic sense and as that which 'holds people together in a polis' (1132b 30). *Nomisma* is at once the current coin of a polis and, more generally, anything sanctioned by usage, custom or institution. So the analogy that he draws out here is between the role played in exchange by money on the one hand and, on the other, the transient principle of unity to which associations of all kinds within and between communities belong.

Koinoniai has a very general sense in the Greek and designates any association or community in which sharing or 'having in common' plays a part, including common linguistic usage, intimate discourse, shared beliefs, fashions etc. Thus 'currency' is in analogy with whatever it is that holds people together and Aristotle uses the analogy to direct our attention towards phenomena of association and exchange between persons and things which have no obviously natural commensurability.

The law that governs the way in which singular disparate entities are rendered analogous must itself be both singular – 'everything must be calculated under a single measure' – and contingent, it must be a sliding measure that arises by convention:

> In reality (*aletheia*) this measure is need (*chreia*), which holds everything together (for if people required nothing, or needed things to different extents, there would either be no *allage* or it would always be different): but that which is exchanged (*hupallagma*) is a need by current convention (*tes chreias to nomisma*) and gets its name by common agreement (*gegone kata syntheken*); in fact it has its name (*nomisma*) because it is not nature but law (*oti ou phusei alla nomo*), in so far as it is within our power to alter it (*metabalein*) or produce it needlessly (*poiesai achreston*).
>
> (1133a 26-30)

This abyssal sentence, which circles around questions of naming and necessity, is endlessly productive and therefore needs some unfolding. To take naming first, we are already beyond the sphere of justice in its narrow senses, for the proposition is concerned with the nature of the law (*nomos*) itself. *Nomos* is the 'measure' that holds things together in so far as it governs *allagma*, not simply exchange in the narrow economic sense, but the conditions of substitutability under which discourse occurs as a linking of differences by analogy. The law is thus absolute necessity (*chreon*), because without it there would be no discourse – there would either be nothing or an irreducible multiplicity of differences, which amounts to the same thing. Necessity manifests itself in the practices of exchange (in all its senses), for example, a need is assumed for the things exchanged. Aristotle's examples are of buildings, shoes and loaves of bread which of course hint at a natural necessity but in truth they must be regarded as being *needed* by convention only, not so much surplus to nature in the strict sense but radically undercutting it in a *nomos* that governs all experience of community, in which any 'commodity' must in some sense be regarded as being needed by somebody at some time in order for it to have a price. Thus *nomos* is called necessity but only by the currency of the law (*nomisma*), for it is a law (*nomisma*) that comes into being (*gegone*, from *gig-nomai*, 'to become') by *syntheken*, conventional agreement, and its name (*nomisma*) is necessity by *nomos* and not by nature (*phusis*). *Nomos* is the necessary law by which the law becomes necessary.

As for necessity, *chreia* is conventionally translated either as 'need' or as 'demand' but there are connotations here which may not be obvious in the current English usages of 'need' and 'demand' and which Aristotle indicates, with characteristic economy, by putting its various senses to work. The dominant sense is 'use' but that ranges from its usage in contexts of business, employment and service (say at war), to contexts of intimacy, familiarity and intercourse, in each case designating what 'advantage' is to be had in the relationship, as well as what is to be given in return. Indispensable here though is the related sense of 'want' or 'poverty' – the need to use or to take advantage of exchange is not natural in so far as it is the result of an absolute absence of the kind of necessity one might have expected from *physis* (where the flower necessarily emerges from the seed). The need for exchange comes about through the want of there being a need for exchange. In that sense it is both less than natural and superfluous to nature. So exchange is not a natural necessity, a necessary law of nature, but it replaces the absence of such a law with a kind of discourse, a field that makes possible the business of exchange. The single measure that holds everything together is thus revealed as a response to the absence of a necessary bond, the construction after the fact of a binding of parts, joining fragments that are thus essentially fragmented, neither fallen from a once complete harmonious unity nor gathering towards completion at some telic end of the process. The end of exchange is not the end of exchange. So *nomos* governs a complex of fragments whose very separateness-with-others calls on further fragmentary actions in order to maintain that separateness. This law, each time manifested as part of a yet-to-be-fulfilled transaction, determines an apparently random process.

Finally, *chreia* combines necessity with obligation to the extent that without the 'pledge' that one gives (although this is hardly a matter of choice – 'to which one is given' would be better) there would be no currency. We use our currency in so far as we are used by it. But it is, as Aristotle remarks in one brief clause, within our power to alter it (*metablein*, 'to throw it into a different position', 'to displace' it) or *poiesai achreston*, to make it useless, produce it in a way that is unserviceable or serves no purpose, without advantage, unprofitably, unsociably. Now this possibility of *a-chresis* (needlessness, superfluity, excess), which is also the possibility of *catachresis* (ill treatment, mis-use, impropriety), lies at the very basis of Aristotle's account of the current law. The necessity of the law, based as it is on a radical absence of necessity, is that it may be used in an unnecessary way.

Analogical Schemata

So reciprocity, or social justice, will have been achieved once people are predicated analogically under the measure of exchange with one another. But such a formulation can be achieved practically only in performance of the current measure, contingent on the moments of participation, which each time re-enact the law itself in a response that produces a perhaps infinitesimal change, but one which might have unforeseen effects elsewhere. *Nomos* is not just some kind of enclosure (a prison house of language?) from which neither escape nor objective determination is possible. Rather, the possibilities for particular interactions (which are necessarily endless) require the endless delay of the moment when all *singular* particulars have been equalised. The currency of the law requires that a formula is available in advance of any exchange and thus it also requires the formal impossibility of its own completion. In the meantime the currency will have been used and inevitably altered by whatever finite multiplicity prevails at any given time:

> *Antipeponthos* (mutual benefit, or reciprocity) occurs when things are equal, so that the farmer is to the shoemaker as the farmer's ware is to the shoemaker's. However, they must be brought into the analogical schema not after the exchange (otherwise there will be two extremes, one of which possesses both excesses) but when they still possess their own ware: in this way they are equals (*isoi*) and associates (*koinonia*) because it is [still] possible to establish equality in them: (farmer B : food C :: shoemaker D : his product equated to the food D) if reciprocity could not be established in this way, there would be no association (*koinonia*). (1133a 22-30)

As long as there is a law, an example of which would be the currency that establishes the relative prices of food and shoes, community is possible. However, out of this proposition arise two specific complications. The first involves the temporal dimension of the future perfect (the 'will-have-been'); and the second involves the dimension of *achresis*.

In Aristotle's account the correct tense would be the future perfect ('If an item is not required at the moment, currency serves to guarantee us a future exchange' [10-11]); currency ensures that everything *will have been* just. Each participant must be introduced into the analogical schema before the exchange in which the figure occurs can come about at all. The figure precedes the exchange yet the exchange defines the figure. The law is constituted by the use made of it by any of its particulars, who are themselves constituted in community by the currency of the law itself. The way in which the particulars of a community participate in the processes derived from their own currency must allow for endless additions to their number – there is in principle no limit to and thus no 'whole' of a community understood on this model (there have been plenty of examples of communities who resolutely and violently attempt to enforce such a limit, and this may be the central aporia of the notion of the nation state). Yet, by the same rule, the schema in its generality is deficient in the parts that would complete it, calling endlessly on the need (*chreia*) for further instantiations. A community is *essentially* and *originally* deficient in participants and this is what allows its growth, development and permutation in iterations *ad infinitum*. If in some impossible hypothesis the fragments all came together and there were enough for a whole community (and they were the right parts) that would cancel their currency, because it would cancel the need for further exchange. This implies a radical disjunction between particular reciprocities and actual or ideal reciprocity.

Reciprocity must be represented before the act which embodies it and this means that a dimension emerges such that a narrative becomes possible in which the outcome of a transaction is anticipated. One of the essential strands with which a just community is to be woven thus depends on a possibility well known to narratologists, the possibility of anachrony, the doubling of one temporal milieu into another, different temporal milieu. One aspect of this possibility is called *prolepsis* – 'taking before' – in the sense of taking the outcome provisionally on the expectation of it coming about at a later time. This is more than a simple preparation, *prolepsis* confronts us with an event before its time. However, the existence, or our trust in the existence, of the analogical schema depends on another anachronic dimension, the taking up of a presumed past into the consolation of *analepsis*, in the Greek *analeptikos* – 'taking back'–, a restorative that provides the means of regaining or making good. The restorative is promised to those who pledge their use of the currency and lies in the possibility of narrating a past event in relation to current events; and it thus makes up for a 'fault' in the system in so far as it is never the case that all the conditions for one's *koinonias* can be made simultaneously present. The analogical schema is therefore the figuration of the differences between separate elements and the rectification of those differences, in advance, for the purposes of their continued interaction, their association in general, and any possible repetition of the figure of exchange, their currency. Aristotle claims that without this sort of reciprocity there would be no association (community, group, family, lover or friend).

The dimension of *achresis* enters as a necessary surplus in so far as *nomos* maintains the possibility of exchange in the repeatability of a schema that must be able to differ. The temporal illusion ensures 'use' at the cost each time of an infinite fall-out where difference is in fact sublated in the analogy, which forms the figure of a currency that is at any given moment not current but *anachronic*, in a doubling of justice that renders the justice of the law open to the judgement of its double.

Aristotle's current law can now be formulated as a series of diversions from the trajectory towards the equalisation of disjunct elements: a temporal diversion of the present allows a time lapse between the events of exchange, a lapse which is itself the condition of possibility for exchange; a spatial divergence or dislocation delays the immediate coincidence of elements in exchange, so that a space of exchange, of association and community, will have been allowed in the form of a response to that inaugurating disjunction (which is always just another version of the analogical schema anyway). These diversions must be considered primary, because any instantiation of the current law is a result of the potential for disjunction. There is a kind of blankness which replaces the coincidence of spatial and temporal presence, but which constitutes the possibility of proceeding towards that coincidence. Its delay constitutes its possibility.

Aristotle's Postmodernism

Macintyre's reading of Aristotle thus fails to take account of the conditions that Aristotle outlines, that is, those conditions that leave his text open to readings beyond the finite economy of his theory. It is this, the 'pagan' or the 'postmodern' in Aristotle, that allows us all to be Aristotelians. On the one hand, we cannot leave the field of circulation, but on the other, under the term *achresis* this time, an irreducible, incalculable, uneconomical element, we can demand an idea of justice that is infinite, an obligation to the other and an interminable critique of the law. Aristotle's sentences, the analogical schema which makes two apophantic sentences one (or one two), leaves an incalculable residue, always ready for a new sentence, an addition that sees no end . . .

John PHILLIPS
Nene College

Works Cited

Aristotle. *De Interpretatione*. Ed. L. Minio-Paluello. Oxford: Oxford Classical Texts, 1956.

---. *Nicomachean Ethics*. Ed. I. Bywater. Oxford: Oxford Classical Texts, 1894.

Barthes, Roland. *The Pleasure of the Text*. Trans. Richard Miller. Oxford: Blackwell, 1990.

Bernstein, Charles. *Rough Trades*. Los Angeles: Sun and Moon Press, 1991.

Cornell, Drucilla. *The Philosophy of the Limit*. London: Routledge, 1988.

Derrida, Jacques. 'Force of Law: The "Mystical Foundation of Authority"'. Trans. Mary Quaintance. *Deconstruction and the Possibility of Justice*. Eds. Drucilla Cornell, Michel Rosenfield and David Gray Carlson. London: Routledge, 1992.

Kant, Immanuel. *Critique of Judgment*. Trans. Werner S. Pluhar. Indianapolis: Hackett, 1987.

---. *The Groundwork of the Metaphysics of Morals*. Trans. H. J. Paton. London: Hutchinson, 1949.

Lyotard, Jean-François. *The Differend: Phrases in Dispute*. Trans. Georges Van Den Abbeele. Manchester: Manchester University Press, 1988.

---. *The Postmodern Condition: A Report on Knowledge*. Trans. Geoff Bennington and Brian Massumi. Manchester: Manchester University Press, 1984.

Lyotard, Jean-François and Jean-Loup Thébaud. *Just Gaming*. Trans. Wlad Godzich. Manchester: Manchester University Press, 1985.

Macintyre, Alasdair. *Whose Justice? Which Rationality?* London: Duckworth, 1988.

Totalling Up Postmodernism

There may be no such thing as postmodernism but there are distinct postmodern attitudes, one of which is a critique of totality. One form of this totality is what Lyotard calls 'metanarratives', such as Marxism, which purport to explain all manner of phenomena in terms of basic laws, in this instance the class struggle. The postmodern, claims Lyotard, represents an 'incredulity towards metanarratives' (1984:xxiv). In their place, he proposes a notion of 'language games' which testify to the existence of different orders of utterance, for example, the cognitive and the affective. Since each language game has its own properties and rules specifying the uses to which it can be put, it would be unjust or even, in Lyotard's vocabulary, 'terroristic' to judge the claims of one language game by the procedures of another. A clash between two language games gives rise to what Lyotard calls a 'differend': 'A case of differend between two parties takes place when the "regulation" of the conflict that opposes them is done in the idiom of one of the parties while the wrong suffered by the other is not signified in that idiom' (Lyotard 1988:9). This differend is the state of the language 'wherein something which must be able to be put into phrases cannot yet be' and it is the task of literature and philosophy, continues Lyotard, 'to bear witness to differends by finding idioms for them' (1988:13).

It can be seen from this that the postmodern antipathy to totality is bound up with a politics of resistance and liberation. It is a commitment to enabling those who have been silenced to speak. Hence postmodernism's association with progressive movements such as feminism, ecology groups and gay and lesbian formations, all of which arose in response to the oppressions of capitalist ideology. In short, postmodernism's assault on hierarchy, tradition and the exclusions wrought by the homogeneities of white middle class patriarchy, make it the natural ally of radical politics.

It is against this view that I wish to argue. My contention is that the attachment of postmodern theory to the part rather than the whole blinds it to its own complicity with the ideology of the market. This is apparent in two ways, the first being the affinities between aspects of postmodernism and ideas of management and the market while the second, more subtle, lies in an interpretation of postmodernism as a specialised discourse promoting the cult of expertise and professionalism.

The symmetry between postmodernism and the market is a product of the mutual interpenetration of capital and culture. Culture, says Fredric Jameson, has expanded throughout the social realm while capital has colonised the previously autonomous realm of culture. Aesthetic production, he continues, has become integrated into commodity production. The need to produce 'ever more novel seeming goods . . . now assigns an increasingly essential structural function and position to aesthetic innovation and experimentation' (Jameson 1991:4-5). One example of this is the 'extraordinary flowering' of postmodern architecture which is grounded in the patronage of multinational business (Jameson 1991:5). Another is advertising where, as Stephen Brown has pointed out, 'Benneton has effectively assumed the mantle of modern art disturb[ing] and unsettl[ing] the bourgeois sensibility' (Brown 1995:130). This fusion of capital and culture has been rendered all but invisible by the postmodern habit of 'analys[ing] phenomena mainly from cultural and discursive perspectives and often in terms of disconnected fragments without grasping systemic interrelationships such as exist between the capitalist state, economy and mass media' (Best and Kellner 1991:268). Lyotard's contempt for what he calls 'the nostalgia of the whole' (Lyotard 1984:81) is one example of this and it is singularly ironic given that elsewhere he acknowledges that there is 'a kind of collusion' between the postmodern aesthetic of the sublime and the capitalist economy (Lyotard 1989:209). His failure to develop this insight means that his work ultimately replicates rather than critiques existing social relations.

Criticism's complicity with the social order, unwitting or otherwise, is nothing new. F. R. Leavis sought a way of valuing literature that avoided notions of quantity and measurement, but his metaphor for sound judgements, the gold standard, made his work the ally of the orthodox financial policy of the day. Furthermore, there were distinct similarities between the discourses of literary criticism and scientific management. Frederic Winslow Taylor published *The Principles of Scientific Management* in 1911 and if the date is not sufficient to establish it as a modernist text its conception of the body as machine certainly is. Taylor's work had a major impact on British industry in the interwar years, the very time that Leavis was developing his conception of criticism in works such as *Mass Civilisation and Minority Culture* (1930), *New Bearings in English Poetry* (1932), *Culture and Environment* (1933) and *Revaluation* (1936).

The main object of scientific management was to increase production by substituting tradition for technique. The time and motion study was used to analyse how workers performed their tasks with a view to making them more efficient. At first, it seems highly improbable that scientific management should have anything in common with literary criticism but a closer inspection reveals that this is indeed the case. To begin with the idea of production lies at the heart of Leavisian criticism. One of his metaphors for the critic is the worker whose job it is to produce the poem from the black marks on the page. They are the raw material, the poem the finished product. Moreover, Leavis explicitly opposes this product to the dominant and, in his opinion, dangerous view, that language was merely a 'method of symbolising human thought' (Leavis 1930:42). Accordingly, the aim of literary criticism was to show that language was 'more than a means of expression' (Leavis 1972:184). Thus, not only does criticism produce the poem but does so as an example of how to maximise the productive capacities of language.

Training is as important to Leavis as it is to scientific management. The subtitle of *Culture and Environment* is *The Training of Critical Awareness* and the examples in the book are intended to enable the reader to appreciate the richness of literature and to recognise the reductions of mass culture. The purpose of training – which exists in some tension with Leavis's commitment to tradition – is to make the reader more 'efficient' so that he or she is better 'equipped to profit from literature' (Leavis 1932:42). The idiom of scientific management is unmistakable here: it too promotes efficiency to increase profit. The time and motion study is an important factor in this process and it is analogous to the 'surveying eye' of criticism (Leavis 1936:17). Both are informed by what may be called 'the principle of visibility' which was institutionalised in 1937 by the founding of Mass Observation. This principle assumed that everything could be seen in its entirety. The work process and the poem are equally on display, neither conceals a hidden meaning; the nature of the former is 'self evident' while that of the latter is 'obvious'. Here, as elsewhere, the vocabulary of Leavis and Taylor converge.

Of course there are differences between the two discourses. Taylor's scientific management is concerned with maximising prosperity, Leavis's literary criticism with what constitutes human significance. Nevertheless, it is the case that Leavis's writings, particularly in the 30s, are shaped, in part, by the imagery, logic and diction of scientific management. The effect of this is to inhibit the process of valuation, making it as much a matter of quantity as quality.

But if scientific management sabotages the critical project of fusing life and literature, it also facilitates the establishment of literary criticism as a profession. The importance attached to training and a specialised vocabulary, together with that sense of service which was the ethic of professional life helped to put the study of literature on a secure footing. Ironically, criticism's professional status is gained at the expense of its humanism. The very existence of professions, as Thomas Bender has argued, with their distinct terminology and formal entry requirements seem to imply that existential issues are the province of the expert rather than things which affect everyone (Bender 1987:187). In practical terms this means that literary criticism is no longer aimed at a diverse public but at a group of disciplinary peers who evaluate it not according to its insights into existence, but according to well defined criteria, for example, levels of research and referencing. In short, as Harold Perkin remarks, professionalism entailed a theory of organisation which was ultimately hostile to the 'human factor' (Perkin 1989:304).

This hostility is also a factor in poststructuralism where the individual is reduced to an effect of language and in postmodernism where he or she is dissolved into desires and intensities. This would suggest that far from being theories of opposition or resistance as they proclaim themselves to be, poststructuralism and postmodernism merely lend a cultural gloss to the wholesale professionalisation of society. In addition, postmodernism provides consumer culture with its ideal subject, the subject of desire. Lyotard's early work for example, *Discours, figure* (1971) and *Economie libidinale* (1974), dismantles traditional notions of personal identity and intersubjective relations in favour of the free flow of desire. His celebration of desire, ceaseless, restless, and endlessly self renewing endorses the fundamental operation of consumerism which is to stimulate desire without ever satisfying it. What is noticeable about not only Lyotard's but many postmodernists' descriptions of desire is that they are couched in the vocabulary of the market place. Desire 'circulates' within a 'libidinal economy'. It is modelled on the economy as is the economy on desire. Desire cannot therefore transcend the market but instead functions to make it 'sexy' (Jameson 1991:274). The market no longer exploits, it excites.

Excitement is a key term in the work of Tom Peters, one of the new management gurus. Business, he declares in a recent book, *The Pursuit of Wow: Every Person's Guide To Topsy Turvy Times* (1994), should be exciting. It should also be 'passionate' and the more 'unbridled' the passion the better (116). Peters is so passionate about what he does that he gets 'goose bumps' just talking about it (116). A sense of euphoria pervades his work. What seems to matter is the charge and intensity of a particular venture, rather than its success. In this respect Peters's work complements the early Lyotard where affect and sensation predominate over other considerations.

The intensities in Lyotard and Peters are the result of their respective shattering of totalities. Lyotard explodes the categories of thought that impede the flow of desire while Peters blasts the economic planners for constraining the energy of creative individuals. Each attacks the idea of truth. 'There is no possible discourse of truth' writes Lyotard (1985:43) a view echoed by Peters's assertion that '*[t]here are NO right answers*' (1994:46). With the withering of truth comes the waning of hierarchy. In Lyotard, this means that philosophy can no longer be regarded as having a privileged access to reality, which is, in any case, not a given but a series of 'referents' produced by the 'establishment procedures' of 'different genres of discourse' (1988:4 and 9). Peters would agree: 'There is no reality. There is only perceived reality' (1994:41). For him, the decline of hierarchies means 'the end of our mindless love affair with planning' (167) and the elimination of traditional management structures.

The rejection of universally applicable truths leads, in both writers, to an appreciation of difference. Lyotard claims that postmodernism 'refines our sensitivity to difference' (1984:xxv) while Peters, siding with the 'particularists' against the 'universalists' (1994:209), is 'sick of tools, letters, plans and presentations that all look alike' (129), and therefore recommends adding 10 'differentiators' to products or services 'every 60 days' (90).

Above all, truth gives way to performance. The goal of postmodern knowledge, Lyotard declares, 'is no longer truth, but performativity' (1984:46). Performativity depends on 'imagination', the ability 'to make a new move or change the rules' of a particular language game (52). The accent is similarly on performance in Peters. 'Perform' he exhorts managers and executives (1994:280). As in Lyotard, successful performance depends on imagination on which, says Peters, the new knowledge economy is based (65). And again, as in Lyotard, this translates into being able to bend and break the rules into being able to create new categories and rearrange established ones (172).

The emphasis on performance in Lyotard and Peters points to how the market is being aestheticised. On a general level, Peters uses the term 'aesthetic' to describe business practice and suggests that companies 'ought to have an artist or musician to head [their] reengineering team' (1994:194). More specifically, Peters deploys the vocabulary of theatre throughout his book. Terms such as 'script' 'stage' 'actors' and 'audience' all help to reinforce his view that 'retail is theater . . . is performance art' (12).

This vocabulary is one example of Peters's use of metaphor. Others are sport, religion, physics and biology. Metaphor plays an important role in postmodernist thought. Richard Rorty argues that, since language does not tell the truth about the world we should consider it to be a succession of increasingly useful metaphors (1989). The test of these is not whether they are right, but whether they help us to achieve what we want to achieve. Lyotard puts this succinctly when he remarks that it is not the job of books to tell the truth but to 'produce effects' (1985:3). An example of this can be found in Peters where he attributes the success of a plumbing company to its attention to rhetoric, using the word 'investment' instead of price in its estimates (Peters 1994:99). More generally, Peters's aim is to provoke the reader to action. Having listed his thoughts on the meaning of design, Peters throws out this challenge: 'What are you gonna do about the list above? Today?' (128).

The postmodern aesthetic is the sublime which, as mentioned earlier, Lyotard detects in the economy. It is composed of a number of different features. In the first place it is not governed by any rules (Lyotard 1989:201) and this makes it consonant with a decentralised, deregulated market where managers are encouraged to 'honour rule breaking' (Peters 1994:103). Secondly, as an aesthetic of intensity (Lyotard 1989:205), the sublime is in accord with an economy where the words 'tingle', 'thrill', 'dazzle' and 'delight' are offered as 'the primary bases for evaluating the quality of products and services' (298).

These two features are themselves an expression of what Lyotard regards as the essential nature of the sublime: the presentation of the unpresentable. The sublime, says Lyotard, 'takes place when the imagination fails to present an object which might match a concept' (1984:78). The intensity of the sublime derives from its transcendence of all the categories of representation since these deal with what is recognisable or known and therefore limit 'the power of emotive expression' (Lyotard 1989:205). The sublime effect in Peters comes from transcending conventional models of the market. Asia, 'vast, teeming and pulsing with raw entrepreneurial energy' is an economy in excess of its representations since it can never 'keep up with itself' (1994:198 and 200).

There, more than anywhere else, can one experience Peters's equivalent of the sublime, the 'wow' effect, an intensity which arises from driving beyond current understandings of commerce.

Lyotard's characterisation of the postmodern sublime as 'that which puts forward the unpresentable in presentation itself; that which denies itself the solace of good forms' (1984:81) is a fitting aesthetic for a free market which, says Peters, is 'far too complex to comprehend' (1994:7). This may be regarded as a more compressed version of Lyotard's claim that '[w]e have the Idea of the world (the totality of what is) but we do not have the capacity to show an example of it' (1984:78). The sublime's accent on the unpresentable is the artistic equivalent of Mrs Thatcher's notorious declaration that there is no such thing as society. Peter Lilley later evoked the spirit of this remark when he denied the existence of poverty in this country thereby excusing his party from having to do anything about it.[1]

The abandonment of a planned economy leads to uncertainty in a number of areas, but particularly in respect to employment. As Peters puts it, 'traditional job security is gone' (1994:248). In Britain, 1 in 26 employees could expect to pick up a redundancy cheque in 1996 and 1 in 10 who are in work now (1996) will lose their jobs over the next three years.[2] The resulting anxiety finds its complement in the sublime which can be kindled by the threat of 'nothing further happening' (Lyotard 1989:198). In other words, not being able to get another job. However, the sublime is a 'contradictory feeling' made up of pleasure as well as pain and the pleasure comes from 'welcoming the unknown', in economic terms, reinventing oneself and learning new skills.

---

1 See *The Guardian* 16 April 1996, p.1.

2 See 'Down and Out in Britain', Business Section, *The Observer*, 17 March, 1996.

It would seem, then, that there are parallels between postmodernism and the market and this is most apparent in the sublime. The existence of these parallels should come as no surprise. They reflect how universities have, in recent years, ceased to be guardians of a cultural tradition and become instead consumer-orientated corporations. As a report in *The Times Higher Education Supplement* stated: 'universities [are now] businesses run with a view to profit'.[3] An increasing proportion of their funds comes from private sources or from money raised through developing closer links with industry. Individual departments are becoming more financially autonomous and are adopting managerial approaches to such matters as staff training and appraisal. Most important of all, universities have to compete with one another to attract students on whom a large part of their funding still depends. This means developing new courses with a wide appeal. Postmodernism with its valorisation of 'popular' rather than 'high' culture, is one such course. The postmodern celebration of the popular is presented as democratic, but it is anything but. What it focuses on are the pleasures of the popular without examining either the nature of this pleasure or indeed the use of it. As Adorno noted: 'Pleasure always means not having to think about anything, to forget suffering even when it is shown. Basically it is helplessness. It is flight, not . . . from a wretched reality, but from the last remaining thought of resistance. The liberation which amusement offers is freedom from thought and negation' (Adorno and Horkheimer 1992:144). In short, what matters for postmodernism is *frisson*, not thinking. That is why it buffs up the idols of the market place instead of interrogating them.

Another equally important way in which postmodernism brings income to the university is through the number of publications it generates. Its contributions

---

3 See 'Pay May Depend on Profit', *The Times Higher Education Supplement*, 19 April 1996.

to departmental ratings in Research Assessment Exercises are not only a sign of its financial importance, they also establish it as a *bona fide* subject. Market appeal and income generation are the criteria which determine the academic respectability of postmodernism, not its alleged insights into how customising a pair of jeans constitutes an act of resistance to the dominant order. Postmodernism is not a means of thinking about the important issues of life, it is about getting bums on seats.

The move away from 'high' culture has precipitated a crisis in the role of the intellectual. He or she no longer has a privileged relation to canonical texts, hence their interpretations lack the authority they once had. This, together with the growing importance of vocational degrees, has forced intellectuals to rethink their function. Threatened with obsolescence they have, according to Best and Kellner, 'attempted to postulate a new postmodern era and discourse to legitimate their continuing relevance' (1991:297). Postmodernism, in other words, is the means by which intellectuals in the humanities have reinvented themselves as a professional body. A crucial part of this process is the creation of a distinct terminology, for example, 'difference', 'opposition', and 'simulation'. These terms find their meaning not in what Habermas calls the 'life world', that sphere of social existence where we encounter one another as ends not means, but in the institutional procedures of the university: the template, the handbook, the module, the assessment criteria and so forth. Postmodernism belongs to the discipline of higher education, not the improvisations of daily life nor the utopian visions to which they occasionally give rise.

As part of the university which is itself tied into the needs of the economy, postmodernism can be seen as a bright star in the firmament of capitalism. It is the cultural endorsement of the market imperative. Capitalism and culture are so closely identified in postmodernism that the differences between them seems to vanish. For Jameson, they constitute a totality where 'the libidinal energies of one suffuse the other' (1991:275). Postmodernism is thus very different to Leavisian literary criticism which stood out against the values of capitalism even though it was unconsciously complicit with them. Leavis was able to provide a potentially more effective critique of capitalism because he understood that the cultural sphere could not be divorced from the economic one. Postmodernism's refusal to analyse the economy certainly weakens its understanding of culture. But it is not just a question of showing that postmodernism is wrong to deny the principle of totality, specifically a relation between culture and the economy. What needs to be pointed out is that it actually denies this principle in order that the totality can function more effectively.

By failing to address the economy, postmodernism suppresses the fact that the whole force of the concept of the market 'lies in its capacity to afford a model of the social totality' (Jameson 1991:272). At its most basic this model is of individuals each pursuing their own private interests which will eventually maximise the wealth of the nation. But this is contradictory. On the one hand, there is the conscious action of individuals, on the other, there is a law which ensures the spread of wealth. The concept of the market both asserts and denies human freedom. Consistent with the operation of ideology, postmodernism defuses this contradiction by concerning itself with one half, freedom, while remaining silent about the other, which denies that freedom. The postmodern 'subject' is 'free' only because postmodernism has no conception of how he or she may be determined by their place in the economy. More importantly, postmodernism's rejection of the autonomous subject in favour of schizoid intensities means that it even lacks a conception of a subject who can be free.

Postmodern freedom is therefore more rhetorical than actual and this chimes with the nature of freedom in capitalism, where it is defined as consumer choice rather than as the opportunity to develop alternative forms of social organisation. Postmodernism perpetuates this hollow conception of freedom by presenting consumerism as a site of resistance to the dominant order. That is to say, we can change the meaning of consumer goods and so 'make [our] own culture out of the resources provided by the commodity system' (Fiske 1989:15). Such arguments not only ignore the pervasiveness and coerciveness of consumerism, they seek to make it something both desirable and *chic*.

Postmodernism can thus be said to coincide with the imperatives of capitalism. Consequently, it reveals itself as an instance of that totality whose existence it denies. Moreover, it protects this totality from criticism by denigrating reason – most notably in the guise of critical theory – as a form of oppression. Specifically, it presents critical theory as the enemy of difference because it defines people in terms of how far they conform to a model of rationality. This is a fair charge, but one which can be found within the Enlightenment tradition itself, most notably in Adorno who described how reason was deflected from its goal of establishing the conditions of a fulfilled life by becoming mired in the institutional frameworks and discursive formations of capitalism. Instead of being concerned with ends, it became obsessed with method. It therefore became the task of critical theory to understand the various determinations of reason in order that it might transcend them. In short, critical theory sought to comprehend reason's relation to the social order.

In this, it showed itself aware of a fundamental truth; that what happens in one part of the social formation affects or is affected by what happens in another – tax cuts have to be financed by reductions in spending elsewhere – for example health, education and welfare. This is very different to postmodernism which, in making a simplistic contrast between totality and plurality, avoids analysing its relation to the social order with the consequence that it reproduces it in its entirety. A single instance will have to suffice. By glamorising the idea of difference, postmodernism sustains class division and inequality.

Critical theory understands difference as a function of the totality, that is to say, it discriminates between those differences which reinforce it and those which resist it. Postmodernism's celebration of difference means that it connives with the exploitations and exclusions of capitalism. By contrast, critical theory is motivated by the principles of fulfilment and inclusion. It aims to bridge division without abolishing difference. It looks forward to a time when *everyone* has the opportunity to live a more satisfying and complete life than they are able to at present. Critical theory is therefore an ongoing process, continually challenging the distortions, constraints and limitations of capitalism, to which postmodernism would forever reconcile us.

Gary DAY
De Montfort University, Bedford

Works Cited

Adorno, T. W. and Max Horkheimer, *Dialectic of Enlightenment*. Trans. J. Cumming. London: Verso, 1992.

Bender, Thomas. 'The Cultures of Intellectual Life: The City and the Professions'. *New Directions in American Intellectual History*. Eds. J. Higham and P. K. Conkin. Baltimore: Johns Hopkins University Press, 1979. 181-95.

Best, Steven and Douglas Kellner. *Postmodern Theory: Critical Interrogations*. Basingstoke: Macmillan, 1991.

Brown, Stephen. *Postmodern Marketing*. London: Routledge, 1995.

Fiske, John. *Understanding Popular Culture*. London: Unwin Hyman, 1989.

Jameson, Fredric. *Postmodernism, or the Cultural Logic of Late Capitalism*. London: Verso, 1991.

Leavis, F. R. *Mass Civilisation and Minority Culture*. Cambridge: The Minority Press, 1930.

---. *How To Teach Reading: A Primer For Ezra Pound*. Cambridge: The Minority Press, 1932.

---. 'Pluralism, Compassion and Social Hope'. *Nor Shall My Sword: Discourses On Pluralism, Compassion and Social Hope*. London: Chatto and Windus, 1972. 163-98.

Lyotard, Jean-François Lyotard. 'The Sublime and the Avant Garde'. *The Lyotard Reader*. Ed. Andrew Benjamin. Oxford: Basil Blackwell, 1989. 198-211.

---. *The Differend: Phrases in Dispute*. Trans. Georges Van Den Abbeele. Manchester: Manchester University Press, 1988.

---. *The Postmodern Condition: A Report on Knowledge*. Trans. Geoff Bennington and Brian Massumi. Manchester: Manchester University Press, 1984.

Lyotard, Jean-François and Jean-Loup Thébaud. *Just Gaming*. Trans. Wlad Godzich. Manchester: Manchester University Press, 1985.

Peters, Tom. *The Pursuit of Wow: Every Person's Guide to Topsy Turvy Times*. Basingstoke: Macmillan, 1995.

Taylor, Frederic Winslow. *The Principles of Scientific Management*. New York: Harper Row, 1911.

Post-Modernising *Homo Economicus*

It is desire which creates the desirable, and the project which sets up the end.

Simone de Beauvoir

For non-economists, mere mention of the word 'economics' may induce drowsiness. So it is doubly unfortunate that this essay must begin by distinguishing between two different but equally common senses of this soporific term. Sometimes 'economics' refers to economic phenomena, sometimes to the systematic study of that phenomena. In the context of postmodernism, the first usage predominates. For example, Lyotard's thesis that time has become a commodity, and the alleged paradigm shift in economics from use-value to sign-value outlined by Baudrillard, refer to the nature of economic activity, not to the foundational beliefs of economists. These fundamental principles have not shifted significantly for over a century, and it is this persistent core of economic faith and the emerging postmodernist challenge to it which is the subject of this essay.

The thinkers most responsible for this challenge – René Girard, Jean-Pierre Dupuy and André Orléan – wear the label of 'postmodernism' somewhat uncomfortably – and the term itself, if applied casually in terms of its popular associations with modish parody, easy relativism and, paradoxically, doctrinairism, could, in the worst instance, lead to a misrepresentation or a false simplification of their thought – but there are undeniably postmodernist elements in their joint critique of the metaphysics of centuries of economic orthodoxy. And, equally, there are postmodern aspects to their suggestions for a revised understanding of the basis of thinking about economic phenomena. What I want to do here is to outline the most important aspects of this historical confrontation between the established order of the metaphysics of economics and the new and radical challenge which is being mounted against it. This essay divides quite naturally into two parts. The first will examine the traditional core presuppositions of economic explanation, paying special attention to their philosophical roots. The second part will address the emerging alternative of a new philosophical grounding for economics, an alternative which is becoming known as Intersubjective Economics, and which bears distinct and important affinities with the major outlines of the thought which is designated as postmodern (E. Fullbrook, 1996, [a], 1996, [b]).

Perhaps it would be useful to note here that there is nothing intrinsically objectionable in the fact that both the new and the traditional basis of economic discourse rest on metaphysical foundations. It is important to emphasise that not only is there nothing scandalous about the presence of a metaphysics in a scientific or, like economics, a quasi-scientific discourse (in the sense of that discourse possessing a set of unfalsifiable propositions), but that, in my view, it is a necessity. This is so because systematised thought about any class of phenomena requires presuppositions about the nature of what is being investigated. Although in terms of the final results it matters greatly what those assumptions are (for example, whether the physicist assumes that light is composed of particles or of waves, or whether the social theorist assumes that individuals compose society or visa versa), it matters even more that some framework of supposition be established so that a process of inquiry can begin. If lucky, that framework will, until its possibilities are exhausted, provide a fruitful basis for raising questions and for forming and testing hypotheses. But the presuppositions which frame the tests, questions, and inquiries of those working within any given area of investigation – and this is my key point here – remain forever outside the falsification process *which characterises a legitimate scientific investigation*, and, therefore, never lose their metaphysical nature. This impregnability of an inquiry's foundations poses a constant temptation to those who accept any given framework, to forget or deny the metaphysical nature of that frame. The illusion of certainty produced by the metaphysics may come to be preferred to the uncertainty of inquiry which recognises its unfalsifiable and therefore always doubtful basis. It may happen – and outside the natural sciences it often does – that a research programme, especially when it enters its degenerate stage, turns upside down. The 'inquiry' can easily become merely a ritualised process of justification for the metaphysics. This is a recognisable pattern especially in the social sciences. And the number of observers who believe that this, or something like it, has happened to economics is, at the moment, growing exponentially.

Homo Economicus 1

The basis for the current unease regarding the traditional metaphysical foundations of economics are discernible in even the simplest statements of its nature and range. For example, a common, widely-available text like *Everyman's Dictionary of Economics* displays a serene certainty about the fundamental basis of economic inquiry. For example, in its definition of economic theory it notes uncontentiously that: 'The main method [of economic theory] is *a priori* deduction by logic from assumptions made about the nature of human beings and the environment'. The metaphysical elements of this definition are not even registered. Precisely what is going on here is worth careful dissection. Two of the definition's three terms, deductive logic and assumptions specifying the environments of the objects being considered, are standard elements of most systematic inquiries and therefore do almost nothing to single out the specific nature of economic investigation. It is the middle term, 'the nature of the human being', which refers to economic theory's distinguishing conceptional foundations. Orthodox economics takes the meaning of 'the nature of the human being' for granted, as if it were something known in the same way that the chemical formula for water is known. The profession of economics even considers it bad form to discuss, except in rigidly dogmatic terms, the meaning of 'the nature of the human being'. For the non-economist, however, the phrase is distressingly unclear: it raises far more questions than it answers. For example (and this is only one of many different kinds of examples which could be given), a very wide spectrum of respected and useful theories about the nature of the human personality exists, and this spectrum is itself the source of constant adjustment and debate. The description of economics' method quoted above neither recognises the existence of such varied, but important, theories of the human personality, nor shows any sign of noting that for every different theory about 'the nature of the human being' there potentially also exists a different economics. Traditional economic theory begins with a usually unregistered reliance on a single, uncontested view of 'human being', which provides its most characteristic metaphysical grounding. And it is essential to understand the particular psychological persuasion from which 'economics'' deductions take place. This core metaphysic of mainstream economics is based on a view of the human personality and human behaviour usually vaguely invoked with the term '*homo economicus*'. It is economics' reliance on this impoverished theory of human being that is the starting point for the Intersubjectivist challenge to its metaphysics.

I have used the word 'impoverished' to characterise traditional economics' view of the nature of human being. This is a serious judgement which demands further explanation. The standard view which economics takes of 'the human being' breaks down into two parts, which should be considered separately. The first part has to do with the entirely atomised nature of individuals as economic agents, especially as consumers. Traditional economics assumes that every person's consumer desires exist independently of those of every other person and of the market process. The second set of assumptions about *homo economicus* links to the first, but is separate from it. This second aspect of the definition of human being assumes that every person enjoys a simple unity of experience, such that they find all their experiences comparable in terms of an attribute called utility, defined circularly as the power to give satisfaction, and make all their decisions on the basis of a ranking of all their possible experiences in terms of this attribute. Obviously, these views of the nature of human beings diverge wildly from most of those held in the twentieth century. The origins of the idea of *homo economicus* lie in the seventeenth and eighteenth centuries when a pattern of thought identified with Newtonian mechanics spread to other fields, especially to philosophy, and when modern economics grew out of philosophical empiricism. The idea of the person with which all traditional economics works remains stubbornly located in its seventeenth/eighteenth-century origins. At the time, the intellectual world was dazzled by the success of mechanics, and it was as part of this general trend that economics adopted the simplistic mechanistic view of the human which it retains at the centre of its metaphysics.

The reasons for this are not difficult to trace historically. In the opening pages of his *Essay Concerning Human Understanding* (1690), radical empiricism's founding text (and an essay which fed directly into the conceptional framework of modern economics), John Locke explains that he sees his essay as subordinate to a larger vision. 'The commonwealth of learning', he writes, 'is not at this time without master-builders, whose mighty designs, in advancing the sciences, will leave lasting monuments to the admiration of posterity . . .' (1993:7). Referring to 'the incomparable *Mr Newton*' and then to his own endeavours as a philosopher, Locke continues: 'it is ambition enough to be employed as an under-labourer in clearing ground a little, and removing some of the rubbish that lies in the way to knowledge' (1993:7). Locke's deference to the 'master-builders' took the form, as it did for Hume in the next generation, of conceiving some of his most important psycho-philosophical theories *by analogy to the design of Newton's mechanics.*

Central to Newton's vision of the material world is the doctrine of *atomism*, the idea that the world is made up of entities whose qualities are completely independent of their relations with other entities. Isaiah Berlin describes how, as Newton's 'under-labourer', Locke developed a concept of mind analogous to the atomism of the new physics. Locke, writes Berlin, treated the mind

> as if it were a box containing mental equivalents of the Newtonian particles . . . . These 'ideas' are distinct and separate entities . . . , literally atomic, having their origin somewhere in the external world, dropping into the mind like so many grains of sand inside an hour glass; there they continue in isolation, or are compounded into complexes . . . . (1956:18)

This general conception of the human mind became commonplace among eighteenth-century philosophers. For Locke and for Berkeley, notes Berlin,

> what is characteristic is the assumption common to both (and to Hume and many other contemporary empiricists, particularly in France) that the mind is a container within which ideas like counters circulate and form patterns as they would in a complicated slot machine; three-dimensional Newtonian space has its counterpart in the inner 'space' of the mind over which the inner eye – the faculty of reflection – presides. (1956:19)

When Adam Smith came to write the foundational text for modern economics, *The Wealth of Nations* (1776), he had the example not only of Newton's material atomism, but also of Locke's extension of it, by analogy, to an altogether different area of inquiry. If atomism could form the basis of a theory of ideas, then why not apply it as well to a theory of human beings? The full title of Smith's essay on astronomy, 'The Principles Which Lead and Direct Philosophical Enquiries; Illustrated by the History of Astronomy', reflects both the direction in which he looked for inspiration and the then still existing unity of knowledge. Science and philosophy had not yet parted company, so, for Smith, Newton's physics is 'Newton's Philosophy' and his system, including his law of gravity, a 'philosophical hypothesis' (1986:34-5). 'Philosophy', explains Smith, 'is the science of connecting principles of nature' (1986:31).

Today, in the physical sciences, where their former linkage with philosophy is a usually forgotten fact and where metaphysics are employed mainly as means to ends, as heuristic devices for conceptualising the data, atomism is merely one of several narratives applied to the pursuit of empirical knowledge. This narrative pluralism holds true even within physics itself. For example, in describing the temperature of an individual atom as dependent on its relations with a set of atoms, thermodynamics takes as its metaphysic of explanation the reverse of the atomism of classical mechanics. Traditional chemistry employs still another method. Proceeding on the basis of low-level generalisations, it actively entertains the possibility that, when individual elements are brought into certain relations, their properties may change. As in the case of atoms of hydrogen and oxygen, such changes can be extremely radical. In the natural sciences these and other metaphysics of explanation coexist within an ethos of cooperative pluralism. The high-energy physicist does not perceive the thermodynamics expert as a dangerous heretic who should be deprived of his or her post. Instead there exists broad agreement that understanding nature does not come easily, and that, therefore, any mode of explanation which delivers observable results merits use and respect. It is indisputable that, if, following the success of Newton's mechanics, atomism had been made the required methodology of the natural sciences, then much of today's science and technology would not exist.

But something like this did happen in the social sciences, especially in economics. Instead of regarding different conceptual frameworks as tools to be applied according to their suitability to particular classes of phenomena, social scientists tend to treat them as rival systems of belief requiring, like religions, exclusive allegiance. The atomistic approach to social or economic phenomena which claims for itself sole access to truth is called methodological individualism, and the opposing view that such phenomena must be explained in terms of the relationship to social wholes is called methodological holism. These rival metanarratives tend to be held with great fervour, giving rise to sectarianism, each side zealously defending its enclaves of domination. Methodological individualism dominates economics. Its 'mainstream', which is nine-tenths of the whole, takes it as an article of faith that economic agents must be defined as individuals whose tastes and desires are formed and maintained independently of the desires of others, of institutions and of the market process, in other words, that human beings must be regarded as analogous to Newton's impermeable atoms. But this conception of the human being as socially impermeable, as exclusively *intra*subjective, is not the only mechanistic and Newtonian inspired element of *homo economicus*.

Economics also defines the human being as a pleasure machine. Again Locke appears to be the conception's ultimate source. He conceived of human perception as a process analogous to Newton's analysis of collision between material bodies. Material objects, Locke argues, stimulate our sense organs, producing in a 'natural and regular' way effects, called 'sensations', in our consciousness (1993:324). To this idea Locke coupled another, this one analogous to classical mechanics' principle of inertia or Newton's first law of motion. Newton says that a body remains at rest (or, if already in motion, remains in uniform motion) unless acted on by an external force. Locke says:

> The infinite wise Author of our being, . . . to excite us to these actions of thinking and motion that we are capable of, has been pleased to join to several thoughts and several sensations a *perception of delight*. If this were wholly separated from all our outward sensations and inward thoughts, we should have no reason to prefer one thought or action to another, negligence to attention, or motion to rest. And so we should neither stir our bodies, nor employ our minds. . . . *Pain* has the same efficacy and use to set us on work that pleasure has . . . (1993:66).

In other words, Locke assumes that like material bodies, the human personality will not be brought into 'motion' unless disturbed by extraneous forces, in this case, sensations bringing pleasure or pain. Just as classical physics attributes to every body in the universe a measure of mass, Locke's metaphysics of the human personality attributes to every sensation a measure of pleasure or pain belonging to a single scale applicable equally to every experience and every moment of a person's life (1993:135). It is this inbuilt system of reward and punishment which overcomes the presumed inertia of the human personality. Locke insists repeatedly that without the impetus of sensory pleasure and pain, no one would do anything.

Locke's next pair of concepts proved especially significant for the definition of *homo economicus*. He defines happiness on the basis of his mechanistic concept of pleasure: '*Happiness*, then, in its full extent, is the utmost pleasure we are capable of, and *misery* the utmost pain' (1993:136). He also deploys his sensationalist theory of desire to move into the realms of ethics and social justice:

> Things then are good or evil only in reference to pleasure or pain. That we call good which *is apt to cause or increase pleasure, or diminish pain in us, or else to procure or preserve us the possession of any other good or absence of any evil.* And, on the contrary, we name that *evil* which *is apt to produce or increase any pain, or diminish any pleasure in us, or else to procure us any evil, or deprive us of any good.* (1993:119)

A century later, these ideas became the basis of Utilitarianism. In his *An Introduction to the Principles of Morals and Legislation* (1789), Jeremy Bentham substitutes 'utility' for Locke's 'good': 'By utility is meant that property in any object, whereby it tends to produce benefit, advantage, pleasure, good or happiness . . . or . . . to prevent the happening of mischief, pain, evil or unhappiness to the party whose interest is considered' (1982:12). From the 1870s onward, this Lockean view, filtered through Bentham, of the human being as a simple pleasure machine was tightly incorporated into economic theory. Economists adopted it, on the one hand, as the universal principle of human action, and, on another, as the basis for a doctrine of social justice, a doctrine which usually comes down on the side of the status quo.[1]

The maverick American economist, Thorstein Veblen, a methodological holist, captures the 'spirit' of economics' *homo economicus* as follows:

> the human material with which the inquiry is concerned is conceived in hedonistic terms; that is to say, in terms of a passive and substantially inert and immutably given human nature. . . . The hedonistic conception of man is that of a lightning calculator of pleasure and pains, who oscillates like a homogeneous globule of desire of happiness under the impulse of stimuli that shift him about the area, but leave him intact. He has neither antecedent nor consequent. He is an isolated definitive human datum . . . (1898:373)

The development of the concept of *homo economicus* was part of a larger project to fashion an economic model in the image of Newtonian mechanics, one in which economic agents could be treated as if they were particles obeying mechanical laws, and all of whose behaviour could, in principle, be described simultaneously by a solvable system of equations. This narrative required the treatment of human desires as fundamental data, which, like the masses of physical bodies in classical mechanics, are not affected by the relations being modelled. It was to this end, and

1 For a given situation, social welfare judgements will depend on whether it is assumed that between individuals desires are independent or interdependent.

not to the understanding of economic phenomena, that *homo economicus*, including the hedonistic calculus, was invented. The dream of a determinate model of the economic universe was realised in the 1870s by William Stanley Jevons and, especially, by Léon Walras, both of whom were physicists by training. Called the model of general equilibrium, this elaborate mechanistic metaphor, proudly devoid of empirical content, remains the grand narrative of economic theory for students and economists worldwide.

Homo Economicus 2

In one sense the foregoing critique of *homo economicus* is less than fair. From a vantage point inside a consumer society, the notion that consumers are autonomous subjectivities and that, therefore, economic phenomena is exclusively *intrasubjective* appears patently absurd. But this was not always the case. When modern economics was in its formative stages, economic activity was primarily about satisfying material needs. Until this century, most people in the West lived at or near subsistence level. Intersubjectivity does not enter into the determination of the biological requirements of sustaining a human life and of providing it with basic physical comfort. So at the time of economics' founding and through much of the nineteenth century, basing *homo economicus* on atomistic individualism and sensationalist psychology, although limiting the scope of its inquiry, left it with a wide field to cover. In other words, there was an era when *intrasubjective economics* could claim as its domain the greater part of economic phenomena.

But it is a hundred years since Caroline Foley and Thorstein Veblen described the growing importance of non-intrasubjective factors in the determination of consumer demand and product design (Foley, 1893; Veblen, 1899). Since then this transformation has gathered momentum until today one is hard pressed to identify any product whose demand is not seriously mediated by the consumer's permeability to social influences. Intersubjective economics' brief is to inquire systematically into this realm of economic phenomena, as 'mainstream' economics has inquired into the realm of the intrasubjective. For this it needs a set of preconceptions, especially an idea of a new *homo economicus*, which is not flagrantly incompatible with the empirical phenomena it intends to investigate. In the space that remains I will summarise the Intersubjectivists' views about the nature of human beings and the elementary relations which pertain between them.

An implicit but key component of the Intersubjectivists' notion of human being is the principle of intentionality, based on the work of the late nineteenth-century Austrian psychologist and philosopher, Franz Brentano. This principle offers a way of thinking about mind and human experience which differs radically from those of both British empiricism and French Cartesian philosophy. Whereas the older traditions think of consciousness as a kind of *receptacle* for perceptions and images, the principle of intentionality holds that consciousness is a *relation* which humans have to objects, both real and imagined. The term 'intentional' merely refers to the idea that consciousness always intends an object, in other words, that consciousness is always consciousness *of* something. Several eminent twentieth-century thinkers, including Husserl, Beauvoir, Merleau-Ponty and Sartre, have explored the radical implications which the relational view of consciousness holds for the nature and structure of human desire and for the nature of self. But it is the explorations along these lines carried out by the polymath René Girard which have contributed directly to the establishment of the intersubjective approach to economics.

If consciousness is a binary relation reaching from the individual to the world of objects, then consciousness continuously requires objects for its existence, and so must continuously *project* itself toward the world. It is important to note that this conception of the human being reverses the view of radical empiricism upon which traditional economics bases its deductions. Rather than looking upon men and women as inherently passive and dependent on outside stimuli for overcoming inertia, the relational view of consciousness posits human subjects as inherently and unstoppably active, as structurally compelled to an endless projection of their existence beyond the present. Every moment and every act of consciousness begins as the need for an object, or, in other words, as a *lack* of being. Various thinkers in the relationalist tradition have identified this lack, this continuous need of consciousness for an object, as the ultimate basis of human desire.

The relational view of consciousness also voids the traditional view of self as a fixed entity residing *in* consciousness and knowable by introspection. If consciousness is not a container, but instead a relation which the human body has to the world, then a person's self (or selves) can only be, like anything else, an intermittent *object* of consciousness. Rather than an internal and fixed entity, like the soul of Christian theology, self is an image of one's being which undergoes continuous self-amendment throughout life. This school of thought views self as an ongoing project of self-construction and self-reconstruction, *a project which other people continuously influence*. This social and dynamic conception of the human individual which underlies the new economics is the antithesis of the atomistic conception which underpins traditional economic reasoning. Under the new vision there is no conceptual space for a fixed set of consumer preferences or for a set which is independent of other people's preferences. Individual subjectivities, rather than being perceived as static, autonomous and asocial, are perceived as dynamic and interdependent, that is to say, *intersubjective*.

Girard's elaboration (in *Deceit, Desire, and the Novel* and *Violence and the Sacred*) of the structure of intersubjective desire (he calls it 'triangular' or 'mimetic desire') provides an analytical framework now used in various fields, including literary criticism, anthropology and economics (1965; 1977). Like most non-economists, Girard regards it as self-evident that an individual's desires are influenced by what he or she perceives to be the desires of other people. In lieu of intrasubjective economics' model of 'desire according to Oneself', Girard offers a model of 'desire according to Another' (1965:4). Whereas *intrasubjective desire* (Girard calls it 'linear desire') can be represented by a straight line running from the subject to the desired object A, intersubjective desire presumes a *mediator* who is perceived by the subject as desiring object A. The mediator is someone, either real or imagined and either an individual or a group, whom the subject holds in some degree of respect. When desire is mimetic it is the mediator's desire for an object which makes that object 'desirable in the eyes of the subject. The mediation begets a second desire exactly the same as the mediator's' (1965:7). Girard introduces the concept of 'distance', social or intellectual or economic, between the 'universe' of the subject and that of the mediator. This enables him to identify 'two fundamental categories' of the mediation of desire: external mediation when there is no 'contact between the two spheres of *possibilities* of which the mediator and the subject occupy the respective centers', and internal mediation when these two spheres 'penetrate each other more or less profoundly' (1965:9).

This conceptual framework fits well the standard marketing procedures and consumer patterns of affluent economies. Girard explains this correspondence as follows:

> When modern theorists envisage man as a being who knows what he wants, or who at least possesses an 'unconscious' that knows for him, they may simply have failed to perceive the domain in which human uncertainty is most extreme. Once his basic needs are satisfied (indeed, sometimes even before), man is subject to intense desires, though he may not know precisely for what. The reason is that he desires *being*, something he himself lacks and which some other person seems to possess. The subject thus looks to that other person to inform him of what he should desire in order to acquire that being.

> If the model, who is apparently already endowed with superior being, desires some object, that object must surely be capable of conferring an even greater plenitude of being. It is not through words, therefore, but by the example of his own desire that the model conveys to the subject the supreme desirability of the object. (1977:145-6)

Girard's analysis of human desire suggests two fundamental economic categories. His bifurcation of desire between that based on the desires of others and that which is not, implies that every commodity's demand has its origin in one or the other or some combination of the two subclasses of desire. In other words, consumer demand divides between *intrasubjective demand and intersubjective demand.* As the human material lot rises above the level of biological subsistence, it is argued that intersubjective demand becomes an increasingly important component of the demand for an increasing number of commodities. It is precisely this intersubjective dimension of the market economy – the interdependence of individual demands – which is metaphysically excluded from economics' traditional research programme and which Intersubjective Economics has been founded to investigate.

For the past decade at the Centre de Recherche en Épistémologie Appliquée of the Ecole Polytechnique, Jean-Pierre Dupuy, André Orléan and others have developed economic and social description on the basis of the new intersubjective *homo economicus*. Mathematics, especially the calculus of classical mechanics, suitable to reasoning grounded on the assumption that humans are purely intrasubjective beings, fit poorly the new conceptional base, which requires much broader powers of description. At the level of fundamental research, this means the identification of the form of logical relations holding between intersubjective agents with changing preferences. Beginning with the conception of the individual agent as 'a being radically incomplete, in a state of lack', Dupuy, whose major works include *Introduction aux sciences sociales: Logique des phénomènes collectifs*, has enjoyed success at decoding intersubjective relations (Dupuy 1988:85; Dupuy 1992a). He is especially concerned to identify and describe self-referential structures (1989; 1991). An example is his elementary model of what he calls the 'mimetic universe' and what another intersubjectivist calls the 'intersubjective process' (Levy 1994:13).

> Two subjects, **A** and **B**, reciprocally imitate themselves. The object of their mutual imitation is by hypothesis indeterminate. But suppose that a noise, a false rumour reaches **A** to the effect that **B** desires . . . object **O**. From now on **A** knows what he should desire . . .: he makes the first move, indicating in this way to **B** the object **O**, and when **B** manifests in his turn his interest in **O**, **A** obtains proof that his initial hypothesis was correct. His representation, although perhaps implausible *a priori*, is *self-realized*. This emergence of an objective fact, of an exteriority by the closure on itself of a system of actors who all imitate each other, has a vigour which grows as the number of actors increases. The most absurd rumours can focus a crowd unanimously on the most unexpected object, each member finding the proof of the object's value in the look or the action of all the others. The process takes place in two phases: the first is a game of mirrors, . . . in which each watches the others for signs of a coveted knowing and which sooner or later ends by precipitating everyone in the same direction; the second is the stabilization of the object which has emerged, by forgetting the arbitrariness inherent in the conditions of its genesis. . . .
>
> This phenomenological description of the world of imitation can be clarified and confirmed by mathematical modelling. A very active branch of formal economics today explores the role of what it calls the intersubjective influences in economic activity. (my translation) (1992b:267-8)

John Maynard Keynes's theory of speculation, as shown by André Orléan, is an example of an explanation of a mimetic or intersubjective universe (Keynes 1973; Orléan 1988, 1989a, 1989b, 1990, 1992). Keynes distinguishes between investment, buying a security solely for yield, and speculation, buying it for appreciation in value. Speculation is a strategy of choosing to buy the same standard items which other people will subsequently choose to buy, or, as Keynes puts it, of trying 'to guess better than the crowd how the crowd will behave' (1973:157). By identifying speculation, like fashion, as a situation where buyers' choices are interdependent,

Keynes shows that neither the traditional idea of *homo economicus* nor its associated intrasubjec ive mode of explanation apply. Looking for an alternative mode, he sketches within the market context a concept of convention. Price stability in a speculative market results when buyers and sellers reach a convention regarding the value of the security in question. 'The essence of this convention', says Keynes, 'lies in assuming that the existing state of affairs will continue indefinitely' (1973:152). But behind this stability-creating assumption is knowledge that stability based on convention will not continue indefinitely. 'A conventional valuation', explains Keynes, 'which is established as the outcome of the mass psychology of a large number of ignorant individuals is liable to change violently as the result of a sudden fluctuation of opinion' (1973:154).

'Thanks to Keynes', writes Dupuy in a recent issue of *SubStance*, 'we understand the working of a conventional order that *contains* the principle of its own decomposition' (1994:97). But it is really thanks to Dupuy, not Keynes, that we begin to appreciate that the pattern identified by the British economist in financial markets is also a defining pattern of many fields of human activity. By identifying an otherwise disparate set of human *processes which violate themselves within themselves*, and which thereby possess an autonomy of change, Dupuy identifies a large field of human phenomena open to explanation neither by atomistic nor by holistic methodologies. He considers literature, law, religious ritual and philosophy as examples of orders which *contain*, in both senses of the word, the principle of their own decomposition. Dupuy explains this logical and ontological autonomy as due to the existence of a rule which 'violates itself within itself' (1994:89). Examples of the 'paradox of self-refutation' include literature's signified which 'is in fact the signifier of its supposed signifier' (Dupuy 1994:89), law's principle of self-amendment, the financial market's process of 'cross-imitation', philosophy's 'autonomy' through its dependence on writing, and, at the most general level, human desire which creates the desirable and human projects which set up their own ends.

Dupuy measures his position against that of Derridian deconstruction, which he sees as a philosophical convention offering only a halfway house to what this essay identifies as postmodernism. In showing that philosophical texts and other human processes contain the seeds of their destruction, deconstruction tells only half the story. Human orders contain their 'possible reversal, negation, violation, destruction' not only in the sense of '"to have within oneself", but also "to keep in check"', to establish autonomous orders for better or for worse (Dupuy 1994:93). To be fully postmodern is to recognise this paradoxical nature of human reality. In this sense, Dupuy sees himself as opening the gate to a second phase of postmodernism.

A century ago, it was highly improbable that economics' metaphysics of an exclusively intrasubjective human being would prove so durable. Yet, like the other orders noted above, economics' conception of the human being as analogous to Newton's conception of materiality has always been a convention facing an indefinite future. That this uncertainty currently is greater than in the recent past seems due partly to the perceived injustice of blocking systematic inquiry about the larger and growing part of economic phenomena, partly to the spreading of 'postmodernist' sensibilities, and partly to the human's eternal propensity to investigate the forbidden.

Edward FULLBROOK

The John Rylands University Library
Self-service loan receipt

Items may be recalled if
required by other readers

24/04/2009 20:37:39

Mr Lewey Bonathan-Metcalf

Complex adaptive systems : an introductior
ELKWO   Due: 22/05/2009

Postmodernism
D92KH   Due: 22/05/2009

Being and becoming : a critique of post-mc
DEK6T   Due: 22/05/2009

Just postmodernism
EH82W   Due: 22/05/2009

End of list

Works Cited

Bentham, Jeremy. (1789). *An Introduction to the Principles of Morals and Legislation*. London: Methuen, 1982.

Berlin, Isaiah. *The Age of Enlightenment*. New York: Mentor, 1956.

De Beauvoir, Simone. *The Ethics of Ambiguity*. (1948). Trans. Bernard Frechtman. New York: Citadel Press, 1970.

Dupuy, Jean-Pierre. 'The Self-Deconstruction of Convention'. *SubStance* 74 (1994): 86-98.

—–. *Introduction aux Sciences Sociales: Logique des phénomènes collectifs*. Paris: Ellipses, 1992a.

—–. *Le sacrifice et l'envie: Le libéralisme aux prises avec la justice sociale*. Paris: Calmann-Lévy, 1992b.

—–. *La panique*. Paris: Les empêcheurs de penser en round, 1991.

—–. 'Convention et Common knowledge'. *Revue économique* 2 (mars 1989): 361-400.

—–. 'L'individu libéral, cet inconnu: Adam Smith à Friedrich Hayek'. *Individu et justice sociale*. Eds. C. Audard, J. P. Dupuy and R. Sève. Paris: Le Seuil, 1988. 73-125.

Foley, Caroline A. 'Fashion'. *The Economic Journal* 3 (Sept. 1893): 458-74.

Fullbrook, Edward. (a) 'The Metaphysics of Consumer Desire and the French Intersubjectivists'. *International Advances in Economic Research* 2.3 (August 1996): 287-294.

——. (b) 'Consumer Metaphysics: The Neoclassicalists Versus the Inter-subjectivists'. *Archives of Economic History* 7.1 (Jan. 1996): 53-74.

Girard, René. (1961). *Violence and the Sacred.* (1972). Trans. Patrick Gregory. Baltimore: Johns Hopkins Press, 1977.

——. *Deceit, Desire, and the Novel: Self and Other in Literary Theory*. Trans. Yvonne Freccero. Baltimore: Johns Hopkins Press, 1965.

Keynes, John Maynard. (1936). *The General Theory of Employment, Interest and Money*. Cambridge: Macmillan, 1973.

Levy, Thierry. 'Measurement Economics, Value Theory and the Social Function of Money'. *Atlantic Economic Society Best Paper Proceedings* 4.2 (July 1994): 11-18.

Locke, John. (1690). *An Essay Concerning Human Understanding*. London: Everyman, 1993.

Orléan, André. 'Contagion des opinions et founctionnement des marchés financiers'. *Revue économique* 4 (julliet 1992): 685-98.

——. 'Le role des influences interpersonnelles dans la formation des cours boursiers'. *Revue économique* 5 (sept. 1990).

——. (a) 'Pour une approche cognitive des conventions économiques'. *Revue économique* 2 (mars 1989): 241-72.

——. (b) 'La crise du paradigme walrasian: reflexions sur quelques resultats theoriques recents'. *Cahier du CREA* 13 (sept. 1989): 148-66.

——. 'L'auto-reference dans la theorie keynesienne de la speculation'. *Cahier du CREA* 11 (avril 1988): 120-144.

Seldon, Arthur, and F. G. Pennance. *Everyman's Dictionary of Economics*. London: Dent, 1976.

Smith, Adam. 'The Principles Which Lead and Direct Philosophical Enquiries; Illustrated by the History of Astronomy'. *The Essential Adam Smith*. Ed. Robert L. Heilbroner. New York: Norton, 1986. 22-37.

Veblen, Thorstein. *The Theory of the Leisure Class.* (1899). New York: Dover, 1994.

——. 'Why is Economics not an Evolutionary Science?' *Quarterly Journal of Economics* 12 (1898): 373-97.

Mastering Timespace:

Virtual Reality and Postcolonial Time Travel

In an article that begins with Walter Benjamin's description of progress as being like a 'storm' – chaotic and disruptive – Anne McClintock takes to task the discipline known as 'post-colonialism' for tacitly colluding with the 'Enlightenment trope of linear progress', an idea unfortunately demonstrated for her by a New York art exhibition in which colonialism is concretised in a transitional space called The Passage:

> In colonial discourse . . . space is time, and history is shaped around two, necessary movements: the 'progress' forward of humanity from slouching deprivation to erect, enlightened reason. The other movement presents the reverse: regression backwards from (white, male) adulthood to a primordial, black 'degeneracy' usually incarnated in women.
>
> (McClintock 1994:253)

The prefix 'post', she says, 'reduces cultures of peoples beyond colonialism to prepositional time'. A consequence of the epistemological orientation of postcolonial studies ensures that 'the world's multitudinous cultures are marked not positively by what distinguishes them but by a subordinate, retrospective relation to linear, European time' (255). McClintock goes on to detail the failure of the First-World (US and Soviet) myth of industrial progress and technocratic development to deliver its promises to/in the Third World.

The critique is taken into another dimension – the third timespace – by Smadar Lavie and Ted Swedenburg:

> We stake out a terrain old in experience and memory but new in theory, a third timespace . . . . This is a terrain where opposition is not only responsive, but creative. It is a guerrilla warfare of the interstices, where minorities rupture categories of race, gender, sexuality, class, nation, and empire in the center as well as on the margins. The third timespace goes beyond the old model of culture, but not as another fixity – it designates phenomena too heterogeneous, mobile, and discontinuous for that, on the one hand, while remaining anchored in the politics of history/location on the other. (1996:165-6)

As cultural anthropologists, Lavie and Swedenburg mapped this 'terrain' in response to what they perceive as a persistent homology, on the one hand, 'between a timeless Out There culture and its indigenous space' and, on the other, another, oppositional, homology of 'the nation-state Here and linear time that progresses toward enlightenment' (1996:156). The persistence of these homologies, in spite of their equally persistent refusal by 'racialized non-White subjects' at 'the heart of the Eurocenter', is due to the location of power still being the 'Eurocentered mode of production': 'Even though racialized and gendered subjects might act out a multiplicity of fractal identities . . ., dominant forces still police the boundaries of binary opposition' (160). The counter-discourse to such dominance requires a rupture of the discourse of patriarchal Eurocentric identity through the persistence of diasporic and borderzone 'creolizations' – the seizure and hybridisation of the interstices of identity politics.

Another critic of postcolonialism, Bharati Mukherjee, has consistently inscribed the discourses of the 'New World' with a penetrating interrogation of the operation of 'worlding' and its consequent manifestation in victims, ghettos and cultural 'mosaics'. Benjamin's storm of progress blows through Mukherjee's violent and ironic disruptions of cultural identity, pushing all before it and piling up the debris behind (McClintock 1994:253); time and geography are the minefields of cultural confrontation in which individuals perish or survive depending on their ability to negotiate the danger. History, politics, literature, are all interrogated by this imperative, and are found wanting. The 'Enlightenment trope of linear progress' is thus apparently ruptured, wresting the future away from the binary politics of colonisation, from the linear history of Western civilisation, from the crude geography of centre and margin. In her most recent novel, *The Holder of the World*, Mukherjee continues to explore the persistence of rupture within the borderzone discourses of First- and Third-World confrontation.

McClintock, Lavie and Swedenburg, and Mukherjee, have in common that they recognise a future dominated, not by the imperial state, as in colonialist models, nor by nationalisms, as in some postcolonial models, but by a technocracy located in a paradoxically diffuse, geographically indifferent centre known by the trope 'the West' – controlled by those with the power to interpret the future on their own terms. Each recognises, too, the impossibility of 'a single theoretical term' (McClintock 1994:266) which could counter the 'globalisation of culture' (Grossberg 1996:169). McClintock calls for 'a proliferation of historically nuanced theories and strategies . . . which may enable us to engage more effectively in the politics of affiliation, and the currently catastrophic dispensations of power' (1994:266). Lavie and Swedenburg put their faith in the disorderly conduct of the third timespace, which distorts the reflective surface of hegemony and merges text and praxis in political activism (1996:171). What Mukherjee achieves in her work is the insistent articulation of the working within history of this third timespace – a space of hybrid and creolised lives existing invisibly in the interstices of Western time. In *The Holder of the World*, she enacts a strategy of 'mastering' timespace, whereby these lives are made virtually visible.

As feminist and postcolonial theorists alike have pointed out, however, the anticipated freedoms of the 'fracture and [dissolution of] old and supposedly exhausted unities' (Waugh 1992:121) for those who have but recently been admitted to full membership of the 'enlightened' confraternity, are double edged. It is true that postmodernism and postcolonialism share a concern 'with the state of what we could call ex-centricity' (Hutcheon 1991:172), but they do so, so to speak, from opposite sides of the concentric fence. The new orthodoxies of postmodernism problematise discourses of marginality which are rooted in political struggle against the repressive forces of the dominant. A compulsion towards hegemony infects the academic context of cultural theory. Postmodernism's 'complicitous critique' of dominant culture gives rise to an ambiguous and destabilising series of substitutions for the centre which simultaneously repeat and subvert its claims:

> Thus there arise complex layerings in which traces of old paradigms are embedded within new, resistances to mastery are enfolded with impulses toward mastery, totalizing moves are made in the service of local knowledge. The convoluted ambiquity [sic] that arises from these layerings . . . is deeply characteristic of what I shall call cultural postmodernism.
>
> (Hayles 1990:265)

The 'guerrilla warfare' engaged in by the marginal at each of these 'layerings' is therefore at risk from the impulse towards absorption of the systems in which the struggle is taking place.

The language of postmodernist and recent postcolonial critique is imbued with the new metaphors of the technocratic age: a paradoxical language of information technology and cosmology in which 'the end of history', 'historically empty space', 'timespace', 'virtual reality', 'fractal identities', jostle to articulate the inadequacy of the old representations to describe a new cognitive experience.

For the postmodernist and postcolonial writer and critic, concerned with the interface between simulation and reality, and with deconstructing borders between self and other, them and us, here and there, then and now, the potential of this marriage between the critique of Western metaphysics and the discourse of information technology is irresistible. Twentieth-century science offers an epistemological structure in which the ambivalences, blurred identities and political impasses described above might be contained and articulated. N. Katherine Hayles captures the cultural relevance of scientific discourse – in particular, the recent and evocative subject of chaos theory – in what she calls the 'denaturing' of the metanarrative. This is a recognition that scientific paradigms are not facts but constructions: they are the assembled articulations of theorisable or realisable phenomena into a pattern or structure which speaks to society about its own condition (Lyotard 1979). As new developments disrupt the existing paradigm or structure, from the disorder is created multiple new structures, each containing traces of the authority of the old. The chemical deconstruction of DNA, for example, paradoxically demonstrated the constructedness of the molecule and the potential for the 'artificial' reconstruction and reconfiguration of the gene. This discovery led to a whole new field of study and an attendant technology coming into being to develop and market this immensely powerful knowledge (Hayles 1990:265-6). Yet these new technologies serve in an instrumental sense the horizons and goals of scientific discovery; as these change, what is perceived is a series of substitutions for the ultimate goal, the truth about the nature of the universe. The starburst of late-twentieth-century technologies does not alter in any way the location of this centre both within and outside of the multiplicity of narrative structures under the umbrella of scientific discourse.

Extended to the understanding of culture, the postmodern absorption with, and of, the disordered organism is prevalent in an equivalent 'denaturing' of the human experience. As the human experience is increasingly conceived of in relation to the structures of meaning within which that experience is encoded, and as by deconstructing those experiences a system might be set up by which they could be simulated and/or re-constructed and re-encoded within a complex web of technology, it is possible to give assent to Hayles's suggestion that 'the postmodern anticipates and implies the posthuman' (1990:266).

At the far end of the spectrum of research, unencumbered by the imperatives of applied science, American cosmologist Frank Tipler suggests that the human being is 'a particular type of machine' and that the human soul is 'nothing but a program being run on a computer called the brain' (Tipler 1995:xi). It is therefore possible to reduce each individual soul to a computational set of digits and insert it into a data base with potential for recovery in 'a cyberspace in a computer's memory':

> Since the universal computer capacity increases without bound as the Omega Point is approached, it follows that, if only a bare bones description of our current world is stored permanently, then there will inevitably come a time when there will be sufficient computer capacity to simulate our present-day world by simple brute force: by creating an exact simulation – an emulation – of *all* logically possible variants of our world.
> (Tipler 1995:220)

Tipler does not, however, celebrate the chaotic potential of this view. He is motivated by a sense of the 'eternal progress' of human existence, brought about by the increasing heterogeneity of social interaction. Thus a postmodernist *desideratum* – the possibility of realising chaotic and ultimately infinite recombinative meanings, inclusive of human knowledge without recourse to metaphysics – is recuperated in the service of an Enlightenment principle of progress. It is also interesting that progress is defined by Tipler in terms of material as well as epistemological gains:

> From the human standpoint progress means an increase with time of per capita wealth, an increase in the average life span, an improvement in the health of the typical person, more generally an increase in the standard of living. Furthermore, progress means an increase of knowledge. 'Eternal' progress means that progress will continue literally without limit. Knowledge will grow without bound, per capita wealth will increase to infinity.
>
> (Tipler 1994:104)

The power to control this technology, and ultimately the resurrection of the dead, is with the Omega Point or God. A cybernetic future generation (seeing as Tipler's heterogeneity does not end with the human organism, but extends to the robotic) will rescue the data from the dying solar system. Resurrection is located within the desire of this future generation to experience, playfully, the possibilities of historical moments. Once re-activated within the machine, the individual consciousness can choose to refuse cooperation, can relive historical moments in order to experience them differently or can choose to continue in a different context. It will be possible to interact with new generations (in whatever form) and to experience an infinite number of new contexts:

> Once an emulation of a person and his/her world has been formed in a computer of sufficient capacity, the emulation can be allowed to develop further – to think and feel things that the long-dead original person never felt or thought. . . .
>
> The Omega Point could resurrect the original person at whatever stage in his/her development and against whatever background environment (simulated or fantasy) He/She wished and interact with His/Her emulated creatures. The Omega Point is God: author/game player.
>
> (Tipler 1994:228)

The fact that disorder or chaos is no longer the apocalypse it once was is the result of an ability to perceive and accommodate a sense of the 'deep structure' towards which chaos tends. Chaos theory has removed from the equation of reality the fearful factor of randomness (uncertainty) and has replaced it with an entropic variable – a strange attractor – whose unpredictability is paradoxically predictable and whose effects can be reproduced within a simulation of the whole system. Strange attractors occur in a mathematical dimension called 'phase space' which describes the exact moment in time and space where a system is vulnerable to the effects of change. The fractal geometry which arises from the repeated iterations of equations help us to understand the uncertainty of change through the patterning of chaotic behaviour, allowing us to gain a picture of the system on a macro and micro level. The Cassandrean predictions of ecologists or demographers are based on their ability to make comprehensible images of uncertainty. Newtonian physics' description of the world as a stable progressive and predictable organism, refuted by quantum mechanics, is being rethought through mathematics and technology.

Thus the apocalyptic tone of Hayles's pronouncement disguises the impact of the de- and re-construction of human experience that has been part and parcel of media technology since the advent of radio and television. Lives that were once lived according to local norms and conventions became subject to first national, then global (Western) 'panopticism'. The 'feedback loop' of deconstruction and reconstruction, as a theorist of postmodernism might see it, creates a system/human interface which has already reduced human life to the sum of its calculable and reproducible events (Baudrillard 1983). The science of decoding and encoding electrical impulses has given rise to other technologies that not only allow us to observe the behaviours, ideologies and ideas of strangers but also to reconstruct and interact with those behaviours and ideas within a context of our choice. The simulation of context adds a predictive function to the feedback loop: it is no longer only possible to emit data (behaviours, ideologies, ideas) in response to what happened in the past, but acting upon historical data, it is possible to simulate a context in response to what is likely to happen in the future. If as Fredric Jameson suggests, we have lost the ability to retain our own past (Jameson, cited in Woolley 1992:207), then perhaps we have gained the ability to reconfigure history within a virtual timespace, not necessarily to alter the future, but to make visible a past, present and future that might have been obscured by the 'Enlightenment trope of linear progress'. The significant question for the politics of globalisation is one of domination: what benefits will mastering timespace bring and to whom?

This, on a variety of levels, is the question addressed by Bharati Mukherjee in *The Holder of the World*. Rather in the vein of Frank Tipler, Mukherjee approaches the racial and cultural heterogeneity of societies and the role of information technology as symptoms of progress towards an infinity of material and spiritual gain through knowledge. The novel constructs a space of imaginative possibility in which Tipler's cosmology is reduced in scale to the operation of a single resurrection in the twentieth century of an historical moment in the seventeenth century which results in the advancement of both knowledge and material wealth for those involved. This project is presented by the narrator, Beigh Masters, as 'a hunger for connectedness, a belief that with sufficient passion and intelligence we can deconstruct the barriers of time and geography' (Mukherjee 1993:11). This is not just a philosophical issue; it is presented to the reader as a 'real' goal made possible by late-twentieth-century information technology. The two 'fictional' protagonists are attempting to arrogate powers to themselves that Tipler assigns to the CyberGod: the power to reconstruct from 'information overload' a timespace for 'time-tourists', who can interact with the resurrected, recontextualised inhabitants of a virtual dimension. Venn Iyer, the computer scientist who controls the technology, calls this a 'reality withdrawal' from 'history's big savings bank' (Mukherjee 1993:6). My question is whether this postulated 'time tourism' is any less exploitative than the kind of First-World tourism that is experienced by Third-World countries in 'reality' or is any less constitutive of the hyperreal than Disneyland, especially when the context for the latter is the timespace of American literature itself.

The structure of the novel is clearly founded on the issues of chaos theory and data processing technology. Driven by the conviction that 'there are no accidents' in life, or what we might call no random events, the novel's narrator articulates the 'tangled lines' of her own life and that of the object of her obsessive quest from a multitude of interconnected sources: histories, genealogies, artefacts and textualities. The object of this quest is the multiple identities and catastrophic effects of Hannah Easton, experienced between Salem, Massachusetts, the home of witches and the new America, and the Indian Subcontinent, where she appears in history as the Salem Bibi. Obvious convergences of time and place in Puritan Salem – the location of Masters's white, Anglo-Saxon, Protestant authenticity – are interwoven to create the illusion of an unbroken linear history – the history of America and of American literature. But it is clear that the historical congruence that links Masters to her subject is a 'tissue' of fantastic complexity and extraordinary historical, cultural and literary events ranging over half the world. Apparently random in their detail, these events, when examined, have an underlying order or pattern which is iterated on large and small scales in the narrative. The tiny flap of butterfly wings occasioned by the attraction between two people on one continent or in one reality dimension has momentous implications for the creation and destruction of nations and the future of civilisations. The novel's plot is built around this series of iterated patterns in which the 'normal' course of events are pulled out of alignment by an exterior alien force. In each case the 'strange attractor' (as it is referred to in chaos theory) at work is composed of the same elements: the mutual and antithetical attraction of West for East, of Coloniser for Colonised, of woman and man. Mukherjee appears to concur literally with Desmond Cory's description of the nature and action of a strange attractor: 'Maybe for a while things can go round and round in a nice smooth orbit . . . . But then some unknown factor interferes and attracts the particles – pulls them out of the pattern. And it all goes haywire. We call that factor a strange attractor. It's *strange* in the sense of *alien*, something that can't be included in the original equation' (cited in Hawkins 1995:126). Mukherjee iterates the unpredictable patterns of a strange attractor in precisely this sense in order to create an image of what Hawkins calls 'deterministic chaos' (Hawkins 1995:28).

The pattern is iterated on several levels. One is that of the narrator and her (subcontinental) Indian computer scientist lover. Their timespace is North America in the nineteen nineties, the geographical location is central to both the historical and technological effects of the story. Running parallel to this timespace is another, which begins as a collection of historical data on a single character and ends in a computerised virtual world with the late seventeenth-century India as a context. These two dimensions are constructed within yet another timespace – perhaps the third timespace – in which American literary history is diverted by the presence of yet another strange attractor – the hybridised fiction of Bharati Mukherjee. At each of these levels of operation, the appearance of the (literal) alien at moments of potential change effects a swerve in the linear direction of the character's or canon's momentum.

The first of these iterations is the framing one of the relationship between Beigh Masters and Venn Iyer. Beigh Masters is an asset retriever. She works for wealthy collectors of cultural artefacts, seeking out objects and art which will enhance her client's wealth and social standing. Her job requires the skills of an archivist, an historian and an art dealer; she is a retriever of information, an assembler of data which is then realised in a single object and a large paycheque. Masters' client, the one who funds her search for the Salem Bibi, is Bugs Kilken, the son of a Dachau survivor, a B-movie producer whose existence attests to the apparent workings of chance. Bugs is motivated by a desire to balance an irresistible attraction to the popular and vulgar on which his wealth is created with conscious appropriation of a more authentic culture: 'American colonial'. He has an uneasy relationship with Masters' blue-blooded culture – a relationship which recognises the necessity of authenticity. In acquiring Masters' services, it can be said that Bugs is buying her heritage in more ways than one. Later

Masters is quietly triumphant in cheating him out of it.

Venn Iyer is located as the intellectual centre of virtual technology, but he is also located in the institutional centre of technocracy, MIT, which has bought up the world's knowledge producers for half a century and 'will prosper on the patent' (278). He is an Indian from the Subcontinent; he grew up in the United States and, like the rest of his family, is successful: 'there was never a question of anything different' (31). Venn is a familiar Mukherjee character – an 'alien' who is at home with the ethos of America and indifferent to late-nineteenth-century Western handwringing over motives and morals. He is, Masters says, 'scornful of our habits of self-effacement and reasonableness, of our naive or desperate clinging to an imagined continuity' (31). Venn 'animates information'; his vision of 'time-tourism' is partly ironic, partly prophetic. His true vision is of a self-generative parallel and virtual universe in the interstices of 'real' time and space, set in motion by an overload of data input by this dimension. Masters' project is merely a diversion; he is drawn away from the pursuit of his goal by love and the promise of material incentives:

> Venn says, I know what you want me to do: time-travel. Not just to October 29, 1989, but back three hundred years. He and Jay Basu and all the other strategists at MIT are looking for an information formula, an Einsteinian theory that will organise facts, the billions of facts that swarm around us like microbes, like pond scum, into some sort of pattern. He wants facts to grow like a crystal garden, he wants to create a supersaturated medium, a data plasma, in which just a sprinkling of data cues on top will precipitate a forest down below.
>
> Yes, I say, that'll do.
>
> What's in it for me? he asks.
>
> How about the most perfect diamond in the world?
>
> (Mukherjee 1993:259)

The attraction of Iyer for Masters – one alien, erratic, the other apparently linear, ordained – creates the conditions for resurrection of Hannah Easton as the

Salem Bibi in seventeenth-century India and through her the retrieval of the diamond. Venn is aptly named, since it is in the overlap between two multilayered spheres, history and technology, New World and Old World, First World and Third World, asset buying and asset selling, that the timespace can be located. The condition of time-travel which Masters procures is within this unstructured, as yet unexperienced space, outside of time and geography: 'Neither we, nor time, will have traveled an inch, or a millisecond' (Mukherjee 1993:139). The space in which Hannah is resurrected in order to reveal to Masters the resting place of the diamond, is a narrative constructed from iterated narratives – historical and literary, Western and Eastern, seventeenth and twentieth century – interconnected in a web of hybridity.

The diamond and its setting – the Holder of the World – for which the book is named is, of course, a multifaceted metaphor. It is a commodity of enormous value, an incentive to Bugs Kilken and Venn Iyer, the symbol of success and power. It represents the passing of the world from the hands of a former empire built on patriarchal rules of honour and war into the hands of a future empire built on control of science and technology. It is also the world of the novel, a different kind of reality, and which shares with it the status of aesthetic object; its future in the hybridised world of American literature and its past in the hybridised history of colonial India: the crystalline prism of art.

The narrative of Masters and Iyer is iterated in Hannah's alien presence in seventeenth-century India. She becomes an inadvertent agent of British colonialism, disrupting the course of the relationship between the various elite factions in the country, by entering, unregulated and unaccountable, the lives of two princes: a Raja and a Mogul. She sets off a chain of events which are the cause of the destruction of the Raja and his people, and pregnant with the Raja's child she returns to America with her black child to become the inspiration for Nathaniel Hawthorne's *The Scarlet Letter*.

Thus, within the virtual world created first by the narrator's accumulated data and her 'literary prose' and then by Venn's intervention, the fractals of this equation are repeated both by and within Hannah's story. Each item of data, from the young girl's sampler with its light blue, computer screen background and fantasy exotic figures (44) to a series of miniature paintings featuring the Salem Bibi, from the multitude of documents of early American and colonial history to the story of Sita in the epic poem, *Ramayana*, demonstrates the pattern of attraction and irrevocable change. Hannah Easton's widowed mother, Rachel, is drawn to her native-American lover and disappears from her daughter's history, existing only as a repressed memory and the knowledge of medicine which both learned from the 'Indians'. Her story is repeated in written accounts by the story of Mary Rowlandson, who was 'restored' to her people but who refused to feel ashamed or defiled by her experiences and remained defiantly alive. Both Rachel's and Mary's stories are incorporated into Hannah's understanding of Sita's predicament as the attraction for women of what lies beyond the structures and strictures of patriarchal society. Each of these sources – historical, fictional, epic – becomes part of the data which will eventually reconstruct Hannah as the Salem Bibi, and, paradoxically, permit a reading of the story of Sita as more than an emblem of virtuous wife-hood:

> Where is Sita's version of her captivity in Lanka? I want to hear Sita tell me of her resistance to or accommodation with the multiheaded, multilimbed carnivorous captor. . . . I may not have Sita's words, but I have the Salem Bibi's; I know from her own captivity narrative what Sita would have written. (Mukherjee 1995:177)

Each trajectory of attraction and disorder, therefore, occasions an equal and opposite resistance to the safe, the normal, the acceptable, by which its deviation is judged. Moreover, by reading the actions of entropy within the system, and by understanding the fractal patterning of relationships, it is possible to resurrect other, unofficial lives which resist the systemic obscurantism of the dominant narrative. This is how virtual worlds are simulated and how they operate. Each fractal pattern reiterates the others and so can be built into a complex account of timespace which can reproduce itself on the principles of inevitable disorder and unpredictability. Thus, in Masters' virtual reality Hester becomes Bhagmati who once again becomes Hester – the pattern being suicide. An issue of this patterning is precisely the sense of connectedness – an irrelevance of time and place – for which Beigh Masters hungers at the beginning of the book.

Although both Beigh and Venn are preoccupied in their own ways with the desire to master time and space, the American woman, with her double-punning name, achieves the goal first on the knowledge of her lover. Beigh Masters' position in relation to the system – her ability to muster and master the resources of the dominant and to use them in order to generate the data which makes visible the disruption obscured by linear narrative – is therefore ambiguous and paradoxical. By mastering Venn (through the great wealth of her inheritance), she is mastering the creative disruption of his presence in her culture.

As in her previous work, in this novel Mukherjee repudiates the depiction of First- and Third-World in terms of victimiser and victim. None of the characters who are resurrected in either the seventeenth- or twentieth-century contexts appear in any sense other than masters of their own destiny. Even the servant, Bhagmati, escapes coercion. But the location of the quest in the putative centre of world economics, the intimate (and acknowledged) relationship between knowledge and wealth, and the conception of progress as being in some way equally bound up with both, makes this text once again problematic for the postcolonial critic. If the hybrid voices in the interstices of the discourse can only be recovered and interpreted by the technocratic and commodifying cultures of a new dominant, what happens to the disruptive force of such voices? If commodification results in nothing more than 'time-tourism' where marginal identities are subject only to the kind of reductive interaction that money can buy, in what timespace is this chaotic progress to be found? One can hardly imagine a virtual reality, based on this prospect which does not simply reproduce and perpetuate the injustices of this reality. Unless, of course, like Disneyland, it manages to absorb them into the hyperreal.

Of course, Mukherjee does not leave us with this scenario. By postulating a relationship between Hannah Easton and the white Pearl of Nathaniel Hawthorne's American classic *The Scarlet Letter*, Mukherjee offers her own work as the disruptive strange attractor in American letters. The hybridised voice, for Mukherjee, has entered the centre and is challenging the canon for the right to authenticity. Mukherjee's America is a paradigm shift from Hawthorne's. The location of the diamond might be in India, and in the body of the hybridised Bhagmati/Hester, but the mastery over that knowledge is with the time traveller from the West, wherever that is located.

Geraldine STONEHAM
De Montfort University, Bedford

Works Cited

Baudrillard, Jean. 'Simulacra and Simulations'. *Selected Writings*. Ed. Mark Poster. Cambridge: Polity, 1988. 166-84.

Eco, Umberto. *Travels in Hyperreality*. London: Picador, 1987.

Grossberg, Lawrence. 'The Space of Culture, The Power of Space'. *The Post-Colonial Question: Common Skies, Divided Horizons*. Eds. Iain Chambers and Lidia Curti. London: Routledge, 1996. 169-88.

Hawkins, Harriet. *Strange Attractors: Literature, Culture and Chaos Theory*. Hemel Hempstead: Prentice Hall/Harvester Wheatsheaf, 1995.

Hayles, N. Katherine. *Chaos Bound: Orderly Disorder in Contemporary Literature and Science*. New York: Cornell University Press, 1990.

Hutcheon, Linda. 'Circling the Downspout of Empire'. *Past the Last Post: Theorizing Post-Colonialism and Post-Modernism*. Eds. Ian Adam and Helen Tiffin. Hemel Hempstead: Harvester Wheatsheaf, 1991. 167-89.

Lavie, Smadar and Ted Swedenburg. 'Between and Among the Boundaries of Culture: Bridging Text and Lived Experience in the Third Timespace'. *Cultural Studies* 10.1 (1996): 154-79.

Lyotard, Jean-François. *The Postmodern Condition*. Manchester: Manchester University Press, 1985.

McClintock, Anne. 'The Angel of Progress: Pitfalls of the Term "Postcolonialism"'. *Colonial Discourse/Postcolonial Theory*. Eds. Francis Barker, Peter Hulme and Margaret Iversen. Manchester: Manchester University Press, 1994. 253-66.

Mukherjee, Bharati. *The Holder of the World*. London: Chatto and Windus, 1993.

Tipler, Frank J. *The Physics of Immortality: Modern Cosmology, God and the Resurrection of the Dead*. London: Macmillan, 1995.

Waugh, Patricia. *Practising Postmodernism/Reading Modernism*. London: Edward Arnold, 1992.

Woolley, Benjamin. *Virtual Worlds*. Oxford: Blackwell, 1992.

Living In-Between:

Interstitial Spaces of Possibility in Timothy Mo's *Sour Sweet*

Exploring the relationship between postmodernism and postcolonialism in the context of literary criticism is almost like being party to a particularly messy divorce. These erstwhile theoretical bedfellows have, in the last ten years, drifted further and further apart. Much of what each might offer the other has been lost beneath a growing volume of accusation, hostility and mutual suspicion. Once, it seems, postcolonial theory appeared entirely compatible with a postmodernist sensibility. Both attacked the tyranny of certainty, the relationship between language and power, and those metanarratives of legitimation that had acted as the philosophical props for such things as one's identity, the pursuit of reason, and colonial rule. As Michael Keith and Malcolm Cross neatly summarise when discussing the politics of identity, 'the questions which have dominated postmodernist cultural theory for the past decade are precisely those that writers in the anti-imperialist and post-colonial traditions have been addressing for the past century (and longer)' (Keith and Cross 1993:22). Yet it has become increasingly difficult to reconcile each aesthetic practice. Increasingly, postcolonial critics accuse postmodernists of dispensing with certain vital concepts – especially historical reference – in their proposal that all is now 'hyperreal' or 'simulacra'. As Simon During has pointed out, postcolonialism often functions 'by accepting and using those practices and concepts (representation, history, evaluation) which postmodernism most strenuously denies' (During 1985:369). These have been lost in the fun-house of postmodernism, threatened by its promiscuous, cheerful subjectivism. Reference and representation have denounced their previous intimacy, and the postmodernists endlessly celebrate the end of the affair. Furthermore, in a neat reversal of this logic, postmodernists decry those critical practices that still use 'outdated' empiricist notions of history and reality. Chances of a reunion between postmodernism and postcolonialism seem slim.

My summary of this supposed annulment necessarily leans towards caricature, and polarises into enemy camps a complex constellation of critical positions on the issue. But the substance and legitimacy of this separation is the preoccupation of this essay. Although there are strong reasons for keeping postmodernism and postcolonialism at some distance from each other, there are also appropriate circumstances when their confluence can be critically enabling. Postcolonial critics who declare a boycott on *all* things postmodernist are in danger of making precisely the kind of ahistorical generalisation that they would otherwise condemn as axiomatic of colonial discourse. If in the past literary criticism has swung too far in one direction, celebrating the happy matrimony of postmodernism and postcolonialism, it now seems to have swung too far in the other.

Postmodernism is fast becoming a dirty word in postcolonial criticism. Things were not always this way. In the 1980s Linda Hutcheon did much to bring postmodernist aesthetics into line with a postcolonial opposition to the dominant discourses of Western modernity. In a series of provocative, if repetitive, books (Hutcheon 1988, 1990) Hutcheon argued that the dominant modes of postmodernist writing – parody, irony, metafictional self-consciousness – were well suited to the attempts of postcolonial writers like Salman Rushdie to make 'the different, the off-centre, a vehicle for aesthetic and even political conscience raising – perhaps the first and necessary step to radical change' (Hutcheon 1988:70). But by the early 1990s she had become more pessimistic in the confluence of postmodernism and postcolonialism, arguing that 'the postcolonial, like the feminist, is a dismantling but also constructive political enterprise insofar as it implies a theory of agency and social change that the postmodern deconstructive impulse lacks' (Hutcheon 1991:183). In her recent article (Hutcheon 1994) concerning the ill-fated exhibition 'Into the Heart of Africa' that occurred between November 1989 and August 1990 at the Royal Ontario Museum, Canada, she turns her attention to the incompatibility of postmodernist aesthetics and postcolonial concerns, and the disastrous results their confluence can create. The criticism of others has reinforced this notion of incompatibility.[1] For example, Judie Newman's recent study of intertextuality in postcolonial fiction is at great pains to rescue intertextuality from its accustomed refuge within postmodernist aesthetics, as if labelling it 'postmodern' threatens its critical efficacy. For her, the resemblances between postmodernism and postcolonialism are 'illusory' (Newman 1995:ix). Postmodernism is practised in the main by critics 'almost entirely male, white and metropolitan. [It] is thus often a means of packaging and commodifying an acceptable form of dissent' (Newman 1995:ix). According to Newman, postcolonial writers are especially aware of the determining relationship between narrative and lived reality, how the stories that get told come to shape the lives we lead. Their intertextual experiments are an attempt to interrupt dominant imperialist ideologies that have previously defined them, assuming that power for themselves. Thus, 'postcolonial writers are

1 See in particular the arguments raised by Helen Tiffin and Stephen Slemon in *Past The Last Post: Theorising Post-Colonialism and Post-Modernism* (Adam and Tiffin 1991).

therefore often at their politically sharpest, when they are also at their most literary' (Newman 1995:4). But woe betide anyone who dares call this metafictional self-consciousness a postmodernist attribute, as Hutcheon did a decade previous.

A welcome voice in the debate comes from Elleke Boehmer. She concedes that postmodern and postcolonial critical theory cross 'in their concern with marginality, ambiguity, disintegrating binaries, and all things parodied, piebald, dual, mimicked, borrowed and second hand' (Boehmer 1995:244). But, as she warns, historical specificity must not be sacrificed too readily. 'Criticism must address itself to the particularity of different textual situations' (Boehmer 1995:248). Readers need to bear witness to cultural specificity in their reading practices, an omission made too frequently by postmodernists. However, I want to suggest that this point, ostensibly a warning against engaging too readily with a postmodernist sensibility, can be mobilised to sanction a productive reunion between postmodernism and postcolonialism. Obviously, not all postcolonial textual situations can be understood with recourse to postmodernist aesthetics. But some certainly can, and bearing witness to their situatedness requires a rendezvous between postmodernism and postcolonialism. In particular, there are a significant number of recent novels written in English, within Britain, whose textual situatedness can be explored by bringing together postmodernist and postcolonialist critical practices for a tense reunion. Such fiction has been produced by a group of writers that Steven Connor describes as 'outsiders who were once previously held spatially and culturally at a distance [and] have returned or have doubled-back to the distant imperial centres to which they had previously been connected, as it were, only by their separation' (Connor 1996:85). Connor cites Timothy Mo, Salman Rushdie and Kazuo Ishiguro as typical (Connor 1996:86). Such writers, I think, clearly engage with postmodern concerns yet are preoccupied with political issues and theoretical concepts akin to postcolonial critical practices.[2] A brief reading of Timothy Mo's second novel *Sour Sweet* (1982) will demonstrate, I hope, the productivity of working with the discourses of postmodernism and postcolonialism when reading this fiction, not least because the textual situation under study sanctions this approach.

One of the problems of working with both postmodernism and postcolonialism stems from the awkward task of defining these multifarious and wide-ranging concepts, more umbrella terms than accurate signifiers. As Hans Bertens warns: 'postmodernism is an exasperating term, and so are postmodern, postmodernist, postmodernity, and whatever else one might come across in the way of derivation' (Bertens 1995:3). Ann McClintock is similarly exasperated by the term 'post-colonial', especially as it is too often used as a singular category that 'may license too readily a panoptic tendency to view the globe within generic abstractions voided of political nuance' (McClintock 1993:293). As Stephen Slemon rightly argues, the term describes 'a remarkably heterogeneous set of subject positions, professional fields, and critical enterprises' (Slemon 1994:16). We are reminded once again of the importance of situatedness when tackling texts in this area. In what follows, then, I am using a specific theorising of postcolonialism and postmodernism derived from the work of Homi Bhabha. This is not to say that Bhabha's understanding of these terms is more accurate or theoretically sound than the work of others, or that his work is not free from problems. But it is to say that his approach aligns itself with the textual situation of novels such as *Sour Sweet*, and can enable a productive reading of this fascinating novel.

2 In making this claim I am not asserting an unproblematic identity for each novelist as postmodern, postcolonial, or both. For a detailed discussion of their relationship with each, see the introduction to my study of J. G. Farrell, Timothy Mo, Kazuo Ishiguro and Salman Rushdie (McLeod 1995:1-24).

Bhabha locates his model of postcolonialism squarely within the terms of the postmodern critique of the grand narratives of the West. He finds a contiguity between the lack of faith in Western modernity as rehearsed by Lyotard and a similar re-appraisal voiced by writers who have emerged from once oppressed cultural groups – indeed, the suggestion is that the former cannot be separated from the latter. This is an important manoeuvre, and I want to spend a moment exploring it. It is necessary to grasp a revealing correspondence between Bhabha's location of postcolonialism and his theorising of colonial discourse that needs examining. Much of Bhabha's work examines the apparently binary power relations between colonial self and other in colonial discourse. Yet he refuses such binary logic by locating an ambivalence that disrupts its authority. Bhabha returns constantly to 'the image of the post-Enlightenment man tethered to, *not* confronted by, his dark reflection, the shadow of the colonised man, that splits his presence, distorts his outline, breaches his boundaries, repeats his action at a distance, disturbs and divides the very time of his being' (Bhabha 1994:44). Bhabha's attention to the tethering of coloniser to colonised is especially interesting. In his essay 'Of Mimicry and Man', he focuses upon the colonial subject educated in the language and culture of the colonising West. This 'mimic man' unsettles the binary opposition of colonial self and colonised other. He occupies an ambivalent position between difference and resemblance. In one respect his identity is fixed as fundamentally different from the colonising subject. But his knowledge of the colonisers' language and culture disavows that difference. Bhabha describes the mimic man as partial presence, a '*subject of difference that is almost the same, but not quite*' (Bhabha 1994:86). As Robert Young summarises, when confronted with the colonised subject 'the coloniser sees a grotesquely displaced image of himself . . . the surveilling eye is suddenly confronted with a returning gaze of otherness and finds that its mastery, its sameness, is undone' (Young 1990:147). The ambivalent disruption of colonial discourse occurs interstitially – between coloniser and colonised, derision and desire, difference and resemblance. Resulting from Bhabha's work on identity is 'a strategy of ambivalence in the structure of identification that occurs precisely in the elliptical *in-between*, where the shadow of the other falls upon the self' (Bhabha 1994:60).

Although Bhabha refutes the binary logic of colonial discourse, there remains in place the circuit of power relations that keeps the coloniser and colonised tethered. My point is that Bhabha configures the postcolonial in very similar terms, as a kind of tethering to the dominant power. The postcolonial texts that feature in his criticism (specifically work by Toni Morrison and Salman Rushdie) are always located in an ambivalent circuit that binds them to the disruption of the master narratives of Western epistemology. Within this circuit an ambivalent, interstitial space is discovered that is assumed to be productive. Bhabha certainly shares Lyotard's affirmative sense of the end of grand narratives. Sensing perhaps the potential vacuity of postmodernist aesthetics, he aims to 'rename the postmodern from the position of the postcolonial' (Bhabha 1994:175). The end of grand narratives licenses the production of new histories by those previously silenced (Bhabha 1994:4-5). Bhabha argues that the West 'must confront its postcolonial history, told by its influx of postwar migrants and refugees, as an indigenous or native narrative *internal to its narrative identity*' (Bhabha 1994:6). But these new dissident histories remain ultimately tethered to the West because their purpose seems primarily the redefinition of Western knowledge. This begs the question whether these newly authorised voices are ever completely free from the hegemony of the traditional colonial centres. They seem to function like the mimic man, splitting the authority of the West by rewriting its history as an ambivalent shadow of its former self. And just as the tethering of coloniser and colonised subjects produced a mode of subversion that emerged from a space in-between, so too does the unequal encounter between two cultures facilitate an interstitial space of possibility that Bhabha names the postcolonial:

> The postcolonial perspective – as it is being developed by cultural historians and literary theorists – departs from the traditions of the sociology of underdevelopment or 'dependency' theory. As a mode of analysis, it attempts to revise those nationalist or 'nativist' pedagogies that set up the relation of Third World and First World in a binary structure of opposition. The postcolonial perspective resists the attempt at holistic forms of social explanation. It forces the recognition of the more complex cultural and political boundaries that exist on the cusp of these often opposed political spheres. (Bhabha 1994:173)

A space of possibility is opened interstitially and claimed as the location of the postcolonial. In this model, the postcolonial does not exist outside of the circuit marked by the polarities of coloniser and colonised. It emerges at an ambivalent border-space in-between a structure of opposition.

This is a particular kind of postcolonial perspective, one that bears witness to the tethering of the colonised to the colonising cultures while recognising within this relationship the room for subversion. Bhabha must be criticised for assuming the particular postcolonial perspective he builds as universal in his book *The Location of Culture*. He threatens to homogenise a vast and varied terrain of cultural practices. The assumption that all postcolonial literature is always writing back to the centre continues the privileging of the West common to colonial discourse, and is remarkably ahistorical in its lack of attention to the situatedness of postcolonial texts. But Bhabha's model can be returned to history if we notice how it speaks to a *certain* body of texts. His version of the 'postcolonial perspective' is indicative of a specific terrain that circumscribes the work of writers such as Timothy Mo, to whom I now turn in order to demonstrate the productivity of working Bhabha's model. In *Sour Sweet*, I suggest, we can discover Bhabha's interstitial spaces of possibility struggling to become concrete.

Mo is often described as 'Anglo-Chinese' (Facknitz 1991:648). He was born in Hong Kong to an English mother and Cantonese father. At the age of ten he moved to England, in 1960, where he later attended Oxford University and read history. The fact of Mo's birth in Hong Kong convinces many that his work is primarily preoccupied with postcolonial concerns, especially as he left a colonised location to be educated at, and later work in, the old centre of the British Empire. For Mark A. R. Facknitz, Mo is 'a quintessential writer of two Empires, the Celestial and the British, the one defeated, the second now gone beyond decadence to dust' (Facknitz 1991:649). As a migrant writer with his own tethering to the old imperial centre, Mo occupies that peculiar position place both within and without, belonging and not-belonging. His novel, *Sour Sweet*, at one level explores the productivity of this position in terms similar to Bhabha's. It enables us to assess the productivity of Bhabha's interstitial space of possibility by depicting a migrant Chinese family attempting to live at that peculiar border-space both between and beyond, here specifically the compulsion of British racism and Chinese obligation. Yet Mo's conclusions about the productivity of this space differ somewhat from Bhabha's; indeed, if Bhabha's work assists in reading the textual situatedness of *Sour Sweet*, then Mo's novel certainly enables a critical evaluation of Bhabha's model.

Set in the early years of the 1960s, *Sour Sweet* depicts the fortunes of two groups of Chinese who have migrated to London. One group is the family of the Chens, consisting of Chen, his wife Lily, their son Man Kee, and Lily's sister Mui. The other is the Triads, a Chinese secret society whose affairs include the trafficking of drugs in London. Chen is employed as a waiter in a restaurant in Chinatown. When his father runs into debt in Hong Kong, Chen borrows money from the Triads. Later he is approached by one of them, Roman Fok, and told he must assist in their illicit trade in narcotics. In an attempt to escape from this task, Chen buys a house he believes is remote from the Triads' influence in London. Here he opens a Chinese take-away with Lily and Mui. Lily remains oblivious to his involvement with the Triads. Eventually Chen is located and ordered to be killed. A bewildered Lily is left alone at the take-away, mystified by Chen's disappearance.

As migrant Chinese, the Chens face two forces of compulsion. The first concerns the attitudes of the British to the influx of migrants in the 1960s. The novel opens with the narrator describing Chen's sense of himself as an 'interloper' (Mo 1982:1) in the eyes of the British. He 'could sense [this] in between his shoulder-blades as he walked past emptying public houses on his day off; in the shrinking of his scalp as he heard bottles rolling in the gutter; in a descending silence at a dark bus-stop and its subsequent lifting; in an unspoken complicity between himself and others like him, not necessarily his own' (1). The second comes from the Triads, who control both the legitimate and illicit businesses in Chinatown. The violent world of the Triads is, of course, a caricature of Chinese culture. But the Triads function as an agency of control derived from the Chens' inherited culture, one that they attempt to live beyond. In short, *Sour Sweet* depicts a family attempting to clear a space where they might live at a remove from both British and Chinese coercive attitudes.

As the novel opens, there is already a sense of their existence between two cultures. The Chens have lived in Britain for four years, 'which was long enough to have lost their place in the society from which they had emigrated but not long to feel comfortable in the new' (1). This interstitial position is later suggested by some richly described physical locations. Two are worthy of comment. The first is a passageway that Chen uses as a short cut between the restaurant where he works in Chinatown, and Leicester Square:

> Chen's restaurant was in Soho, just off Gerrard street and its complex of travel agencies, supermarkets, fortune tellers, quack acupuncturists and Chinese cinema clubs, in a quiet lane whose only establishments were restaurants. At the end of the row was a passage with a double bend, so that what seemed to *strangers* like a blind alley was in reality a concealed entrance, constructed on the same principle as a lobster trap. A sharp right turn after passing an iron bollard took the knowledgeable or *intrepid* into a gloomy canyon formed by the blind backs of two forty-feet high Georgian terraces. Rubbish filled the alley. At night the rats scrabbled in the piles of rotting vegetable leaves and soggy cardboard boxes. There was a muffled silence in the enclosure. At the other end another series of baffles led, *quite suddenly*, into the brightness and sound of Leicester Square. This was Chen's habitual short-cut to the Underground station.
>
> (26-7 – emphasis added)

This quotation is interesting for several reasons. The detail accumulated in the description seems recorded for those who are unfamiliar with Chinatown and also, quite obviously, English-speakers. The passageway is a short-cut for Chen but appears a dead end for 'strangers'. To whom does this space belong? Native Londoners, it seems, are unfamiliar with this particular route. Those that hazard beyond the sharp right turn are either 'knowledgeable' – like Chen or the narrator – or 'intrepid', the latter term conveying a sense of an explorer wandering into an unknown and faintly threatening space. The use of the phrase 'quite suddenly' in describing the emergence into Leicester Square suggests an element of surprise for the stranger, a surprise not shared by the Chen to whom the emergence into the square would be quite familiar. Spatially, the passage is in-between Chinatown and conventional London. It is not the sole property of either place. This passageway suggests the space the Chens search for in the novel, one that is between the English and the Chinese. It is a space both enabling and dangerous, one that provides a helpful passage, but is for the intrepid only.

In similar terms, the acquisition of the Chens' take-away can be understood as an attempt to secure a space that is interstitial, and both enabling and dangerous. Chen wants to open a business as far away from the reach of the Triads as possible. The house he eventually buys exists at a place that is also at a remove from the British. The narrator's description of the house and its surroundings suggest that a new space is being opened by the Chens that had not existed previously in quite the same form. Consider the narration of the Chens' journey to their new home, as they walk through an unfamiliar and deserted part of London:

> It became apparent that the main road formed *an unofficial kind of boundary*. The side they were now on was older, more dilapidated than the north side, a change which took place with startling swiftness. They had been walking for three minutes and already the houses were visibly decayed. They passed a derelict terrace, the doors and windows covered with corrugated tin sheets; through rusted holes in the crinkled metal they could see grass growing in the roofless rooms. There was still a sofa in one of the ruined houses and its springs had burst out of the rotten cloth like a robot's innards. This was more like it, Chen thought with satisfaction; they would start here. It was ideal. (84 – emphasis added)

The location of their house is on this site, beyond a boundary. It rests upon the remains of a previous community. The site bears the traces of an earlier habitat, but it now lies vacant. If this derelict space signifies the decline of a community that was once the home of the British, for the Chens it is a place of new possibility. Its existence beyond the boundary of the main road is perhaps symbolic; it suggests that Chen has discovered a boundary that marks the limits of the influence exerted by both the Triads and the English. It is interesting that the Chens also consider a property *within* the boundary of the main road, one that is being repaired by some workmen. The workmen unsettle Chen as they remind him of the 'peppery' (83) English he avoids when walking past pubs at night. He recalls that sense of hostility towards his difference that is mentioned in the novel's opening. But beyond the boundary of the main road there seems no interest in rebuilding or maintaining the houses that lie derelict. The British do not seem to cross the boundary regularly. The 'demolition site' (85) offers the Chens the possibility of establishing a space within Britain that is not the sole property of the English and Chinese. The only other occupant Chen meets on the site is Mr Constantinides, the proprietor of a garage, who is presumably a Greek migrant. The house Chen eventually chooses in this location is similarly suggestive:

> Their shop, their home, could not pretend to have been anything other than an ordinary house up till then. Originally it had been the eastern wing of a terrace of three houses. The centre and western wing had been hit by a bomb in the war and subsequently demolished but a freak effect of the blast had left Chen's house unscathed. Two big braces, such as they had seen on the big demolition site, supported the western wall. The previous occupant, and Chen had no idea who he or she had been, had left over five years ago. No one had wanted the property. Being so near a garage hadn't helped either. (89-90)

Like the site as a whole, the house is vacant and unwanted. The fact that its west wing has been demolished while its eastern wing remains is particularly apposite. It tempts us to consider the demolition site as the beginnings of another 'east wing', a place that will support those newly arrived from the East. These forgotten ruins existing just beyond a boundary promise a site of possibility for the Chens, a place they can fashion for themselves beyond outside interference.

It is, however, a fragile space that requires constant protection. The Chens continue to be encroached upon by those forces across the boundary that Chen in particular wishes to escape. Once the Chens have settled in their home, decorated it and opened the take-away, they are still threatened by forces of coercion. In particular, Lily and Mui in different ways work hard to defend their space from threats beyond the border. At one point, Man Kee suffers an attack at his school. This prompts Lily to teach her son some basic boxing techniques she learned from her father as a child. She is unwilling to approach the school authorities to complain, as 'that way you drew attention to yourself, made trouble for the powers that be, and then they got at you indirectly' (231). Mui is critical of the tradition of fighting that Lily teaches her son, condemning it as a 'fierce and mindless' (233) response to Man Kee's attack. Lily is motivated by a continuing fear of encroachment, and her resilience and determination make it difficult to condemn her response to the aggression of others. Mui also protects their space. She devises the means to keep the business financially independent. She provides the link between the take-away and Mr. Constantinides' garage, carrying food to the many truck drivers who buy from the take-away by placing an order at the garage. Her connections with the truck drivers enable the Chens to buy a cheap supply of Coca-Cola which they sell at a large profit. It is also her 'brainwave' (141) to sell chips that proves highly successful. Like Lily, Mui also uses some of the things she learnt as a child to cope with the contingencies of the present. For example, when Mui buys a van from Mr Constantinides, she defends her decision to a sceptical Lily by recounting a lesson she learnt from her father:

> 'Which of Mr. Constantinides' cars was best? I will tell you: the little one with the window so dirty you couldn't even look inside. It had a stout heart. Do you remember the story Father used to tell us about the blind

> sage and how he could tell which of the Duke of Chou's race-horses was the fastest?'
>
> Lily smiled pityingly at Mui.
>
> But Mui was right. The motor ran sweetly when an obliging mechanic tuned it for them. When Lily kicked the tyres (secretly hoping to bring down the van down in a heap of folding, groaning metal) the tyres were hard and springy. (147-8)

Importantly, the sisters do not defend their space with recourse to a blind faith in the validity of inherited learning. The tension between Lily and Mui throughout the novel forces each to appropriate critically the knowledge they learned in childhood in China, conscious of its potential shortcomings. Mui objects to Lily teaching Man Kee to fight; Lily scoffs at Mui's reasons for choosing the van. This critical revisiting of the past, I suggest, is one component of their attempt to open a space beyond conventional holistic boundaries. As Bhabha argues, to move to a space beyond the limits of received culture is not an act of complete repudiation: 'the "beyond" is neither a new horizon, nor a leaving behind of the past . . . there is a sense of disorientation, a disturbance of direction, in the "beyond": an exploratory, restless movement caught so well in the French rendition of the words *au-delà* – here and there, on all sides, *fort/da*, hither and thither, back and forth' (Bhabha 1994:1). Lily's and Mui's defence of their space is an example of that continual movement back and forth between the past and the present for the purposes of survival. They cannot access the past nostalgically, without an awareness of its potential limitations. This is one purpose of their several disagreements throughout the novel. They appropriate the past critically to confront present contingencies. As such, they protect their fragile space through productive negotiation. This strategy begs comparison with Bhabha's notion of the 'past-present'. This involves the 'renew[al] of the past, refiguring it as a contingent "in-between" space, that innovates and interrupts the performance of the present. The "past-present" becomes part of the necessity, not the nostalgia, of living' (Bhabha 1994:7). The sisters select from their past in an attempt to forge a new life in the present in-between Chinese and English cultures: necessity constantly thwarts an uncritical nostalgic return.

But the Chens never break free completely from the influence of the British and the Triads. Lily is unsettled by the visits of the tax-man and the social worker, and these visits remind both the reader and the Chens that the Chens' space is still not fully their own to do with as they please. Lily's relations with the English, especially her customers, remain antagonistic. The influence of the Triads also reaches across the boundary. They locate Chen's whereabouts through the remittances Lily sends to Hong Kong, as these reveal his postal district in London. The murder of Chen exposes the fragility of the Chens' space. Coercive forces still have the power to move back and forth across the symbolic boundary of the main road, confronting the Chens with a series of continuing challenges. The Chens' space is not particularly stable nor as remote from coercion as Chen and Lily might wish, and this is a cause of concern in the text. The boundary that separates their home from the influence of the British and the Triads is permeable, not absolute. The Chens ultimately remain tethered to the forces they wish to live beyond. In contrast to Bhabha's optimistic theorising, in the novel tethering is never fully transformed into a secure foundation of possibility.

Sour Sweet suggests in concrete terms the productivity of a postcolonial space of possibility where coercive forces no longer function. But there remains a fracture between the promise of this space and its establishment. The novel closes with the departure of Mui from the Chens' take-away, when Mui leaves to get married. She invites Lily to join her, but Lily declines. The vocabulary used by the narrator in describing the sisters' separation is interesting in the current context:

> this was the end of the old life, the life of the loving, closely knit family Mui and Lily knew they had been. . . . There had been parturition, the single cell had contracted, swelled, and through the wall had escaped matter from its very nucleus. Now there were two cells, sharing the same territory, happily co-existing but quite autonomous.
>
> And, later, Lily discovered there was nothing much to regret about this, not too much to be wistful about; or only in so far as it gave her something in common with Mui. (277)

There is a powerful dissonance in this passage that raises questions about the space the Chens make for themselves in the novel. Mui's leaving marks an end to a way of life that emphasised resilience and resourcefulness. The 'loving, closely knit' family may have been a place of tension, as evidenced by the friction between Lily and Mui. But there is a sense that something is also lost in its dissolution. The narrator informs us in the first paragraph that the new units of the family will happily co-exist. But in the next, doubts are raised immediately about Lily's happiness. The fact that she takes time to learn that there was nothing 'much' to regret about Mui's departure suggests a melancholy on Lily's part. Lily's disquiet implies that something is being lost as her family splits. A dissonance is created through the conjuring of two moods, one happy, the other more muted and pensive. This dissonance is supplemented by the metaphor of parturition the narrator uses to describe what has happened to the Chens. On the one hand, parturition suggests fertility, growth and development. It implies that the Chens have survived happily, and have coped positively with the challenge of their migrancy. But parturition is also an organic process of change and refinement, devoid of stability or fixity. Such stability might be vital to a strategy of survival. The mobility of the family unit perhaps disqualifies the possibility of a loving, closely knit family. This constant mobility and emphasis upon change is a source of trauma as well as a strategy for survival. For Bhabha mobility is inherently positive. *Sour Sweet* questions that assumption. The splitting of the family perhaps disqualifies resources that could prove useful to Lily and Mui, in particular a protective sense of community that can compensate for the disorientation of living in a new place.

This novel, then, can be read *against* Bhabha's location of the postcolonial perspective. If we approach his work through *Sour Sweet*, I believe we discover a pessimism that constitutes a critique of the productivity of a space at the cultural boundaries of the English and the Chinese. For Bhabha, boundaries are exciting and valuable as they 'initiate new signs of identity, and innovate sites of collaboration, and contestation, in the act of defining the idea of society itself' (Bhabha 1994:1-2). *Sour Sweet* can be read as approaching this space with caution, perhaps pointing up the difficulties involved in preserving a space between and beyond cultures, one that is not already the property of any one cultural group. We are left to ponder the extent to which the Chens have negotiated successfully strategies sufficient for survival as well as their success in fulfilling the promise that the demolition site suggested. I believe *Sour Sweet* qualifies an enthusiasm for Bhabha's space at the cusp of the postmodern and the postcolonial by exposing its fragility and exploring the trauma of protecting it from coercive forces that still have agency. In *Sour Sweet*, such a space seems fragile. The constant negotiations and splittings of the family enable strategies of survival that involve a critical appropriation of past knowledge, but also produce a dissonant, muted tone of melancholy as the novel closes.

In conclusion, I am suggesting that the failed relationships of the Chen family act to subdue an enthusiasm for Bhabha's confidence in the productive confluence of postmodernism and postcolonialism. But this does not disqualify the appropriateness of forging their reunion between them in order to bear witness to the textual situation of Mo's novel. Bhabha's work enables a productive reading of *Sour Sweet*, even if its exuberance and optimism for interstitial sites of possibility are held up to question as a consequence. These sites are at once physical, as in the passageway or the location of the take-away, and aesthetic, as expressed by Lily and Mui's negotiation between past pedagogy and present contingency. They figure the possibility of survival while recognising the fragility and loss this involves, troubling the confidence that Bhabha places in the boundary as an interstitial space of possibility. In this instance, then, the confluence of postmodernism and postcolonialism assists us in considering Mo's representation of a specific historical situation. Hopefully, a heightened attention to situatedness might return some of the historical specificity all too often missing in the discourses of both postmodernism and postcolonialism, but also stop those working with the latter dismissing out of hand the potential productivity of appropriating the former when necessary. Such separation can create its own silences.

John McLEOD
University of Leeds

Works Cited

Adam, Ian and Helen Tiffin, eds. *Past the Last Post: Theorising Post-Colonialism and Post-Modernism*. New York: Harvester Wheatsheaf, 1991.

Bertens, Hans. *The Idea of the Postmodern: A History*. London: Routledge, 1995.

Bhabha, Homi K. *The Location of Culture*. London: Routledge, 1994.

Boehmer, Elleke. *Colonial and Postcolonial Literature: Migrant Metaphors*. Oxford: Opus, 1995.

Connor, Steven. *The English Novel in History 1950-1995*. London: Routledge, 1996.

During, Simon. 'Postmodernism or Postcolonialism?'. *Landfall* 39 (1985): 368-380.

Facknitz, Mark A. R. 'Timothy Mo'. *Contemporary Novelists* (fifth edition). Ed. Leslie Henderson. London: St. Martin's Press, 1991. 648-9.

Hutcheon, Linda. 'The Post Always Rings Twice: the Postmodern and the Postcolonial'. *Textual Practice* 8.2 (1994).

---. 'Circling the Downspout of Empire'. *Past the Last Post: Theorising Post-Colonialism and Post-Modernism*. Eds. Ian Adam and Helen Tiffin. New York: Harvester Wheatsheaf, 1991. 167-90.

---. *The Politics of Postmodernism*. London: Routledge, 1990.

---. *A Poetics of Postmodernism*. London: Routledge, 1988.

Keith, Michael and Malcolm Cross, eds. *Racism, the City and the State*. London: Routledge, 1993.

McClintock, Anne. 'The Angel of Progress: Pitfalls of the Term "Post-colonialism"'. *Colonial Discourse and Post-Colonial Theory*. Eds. Patrick Williams and Laura Chrisman. New York: Harvester Wheatsheaf, 1993. 291-304.

McLeod, John. *Rewriting History: Postmodern and Postcolonial Negotiations in the Fiction of J. G. Farrell, Timothy Mo, Kazuo Ishiguro and Salman Rushdie*. University of Leeds: Unpublished PhD Dissertation, 1995.

Mo, Timothy. *Sour Sweet*. London: Abacus, 1982.

Newman, Judie. *The Ballistic Bard: Postcolonial Fictions*. London: Edward Arnold, 1995.

Slemon, Stephen. 'The Scramble for Post-colonialism'. *De-Scribing Empire: Postcolonialism and Textuality*. Eds. Chris Tiffin and Alan Lawson. London: Routledge, 1994. 15-32.

Young, Robert. *White Mythologies: Writing History and the West*. London: Routledge, 1990.

The Racial Dominant:

Postmodernism and American Ethnic Women's Fiction

It is a curious and ironic state of affairs that the work of key ethnic women writers like Maxine Hong Kingston's *The Woman Warrior* and *Trickmaster Monkey*, Sandra Cisneros's *The House on Mango Street*, Louise Erdrich's quartet beginning with *Love Medicine*, Denise Chavez's *The Last of the Menu Girls*, Toni Morrison's *Beloved* and *Jazz* especially of all her writing, Amy Tan's *The Joy Luck Club*, Ana Castillo's *The Mixquiahuala Letters* and Paula Gunn Allen's *The Woman Who Owned the Shadows* (the list could go on) represents a degree of narrative experimentation that ought to place these writers squarely within the category of postmodernists. Instead, however, this body of fiction presents us with the paradoxical case of texts that in terms of their form exhibit significant similarities with the postmodern mainstream yet in terms of ideology this fiction represents a powerful dissent from the masculine bias of postmodernism in favour of the marginal female ethnic voice. These writers deliberately distance themselves from the discourse of postmodernism and a postmodernist model of fiction that is perceived to have failed in crucial ways to engage with America's most pressing social and cultural problems. In this essay I want firstly to explore those narrative features that are most like postmodernist characteristics (ontological uncertainty, discontinuous narrative forms, complex stylistics, fractured subjectivities, and the like) and then to ask how it is that the stylistic innovation of ethnic women's writing offers a critique of postmodernist fictional experimentation.

Shifting the Dominant: From Epistemology to Ontology to Race and Gender

Perhaps the single most influential account of postmodernist fiction is that set out by Brian McHale in *Postmodernist Fiction* (1987). The simplicity and elegance of his definition of postmodernism create a seductive appeal, irresistible to students and scholars alike. The idea that postmodernism can be distinguished from its modernist forebear with relative ease according to a narrative equivalent of Roman Jakobson's linguistic 'dominant' allows us to categorise texts, some of which are notorious for a stubborn refusal to keep within established generic bounds. McHale's clear definition of a postmodernist text is concerned with ontological questions such as 'What is a world?; What kinds of world are there, how are they constituted, and how do they differ?; What happens when different kinds of world are placed in confrontation, or when boundaries between worlds are violated?' (McHale 1987:10) in contradistinction to a modernist text that asks primarily epistemological questions like 'What is there to be known?; Who knows it?; How do they know it, and with what degree of certainty?; How is knowledge transmitted from one knower to another, and with what degree of reliability?; How does the object of knowledge change as it passes from knower to knower?; What are the limits of the knowable?' (McHale 1987:9). Such a shift from epistemological to ontological questioning, from the modernist dominant to the postmodernist, is apparent in the writing of prominent American ethnic women. The example I would like to consider in some detail is Maxine Hong Kingston's *The Woman Warrior*. I will then turn to a discussion of Louise Erdrich's *Love Medicine*, Sandra Cisneros's *The House on Mango Street*, and Amy Tan's *The Joy Luck Club*, to consider the significance of this ontological questioning in the twin perspectives of race and gender.

The Woman Warrior is a feminist *Künstlerroman* and is therefore a hybrid form, comprised of autobiography, biography, myths and legends, fiction and historical reconstruction. In each of the five sections of the narrative there is explored a character – or more ambiguously Maxine in a public mask (daughter, student, warrior, writer) – who offers a specific model of femininity. However, the effect of this multiplicity of roles is to render the whole concept of identity mysterious. Narrative form seeks to articulate the forces that have shaped Maxine's identity but these forces are overwhelmingly disjunctions: between China and America, the past and the present, mythic and mundane worlds, the world of the real versus that which exists only in recollection. Maxine tries to find a voice with which to express her relationship with her mother, especially, and so reach an understanding of how women can relate to each other within the terms of a brutally misogynistic Chinese culture and a hostile and conflicting American culture. Consequently, the narrative voice is both complicated and confusing – varying from subjective reconstruction (the No-Name Aunt), imaginative construction (Moon Orchid), or historical verisimilitude (the biographical account of her mother in the section entitled 'Shaman'). This fragmentation of the narrative form – emphasised by the shifts from first to third person narration – attempts to represent the pervasive condition of doubleness with which Maxine lives. And with which all Chinese-Americans live, as Maxine reveals when she asks:

> 'Chinese-Americans, when you try to understand what things in you are Chinese, how do you separate what is peculiar to childhood, to poverty, insanities, one family, your mother who marked your growing with stories, from what is Chinese? What is Chinese tradition and what is the movies?'
> (Kingston 1975:13)

All of these different worlds – of fantasy, insanity, memory, tradition, mythology – some of which are of ambiguous ontology – collide in *The Woman Warrior* in alarming ways.

The issue of fractured or cross-cultural identity and how to express the peculiar demands made by the condition of cultural hybridity is absolutely central to Kingston's project in *The Woman Warrior*. Maxine tries to understand the conflicting demands made of her by both her worlds: those of her Chinese ancestry and her American childhood. She is critical of China and the culture that belittles her for reason of her gender. She hears degrading proverbs: 'Girls are maggots in the rice' and 'It is more profitable to raise geese than daughters' (41). Language itself embodies the assumption of feminine inferiority – '"There is a Chinese word for the female I – which is 'slave'. Break the women with their own tongues!"' (49). She learns that 'Girl' and 'bad' are assumed to be synonymous: '"I'm not a bad girl, I would scream. . . . I might as well have said, 'I'm not a girl"' (48). Looking upon the world of Chinatown from an American perspective she hears Chinese voices and thinks 'You can see the disgust on American faces looking at women like that. It isn't just the loudness. It is the way Chinese sounds, chingchong ugly, to American ears, not beautiful like Japanese sayonara words with the consonants and vowels as regular as Italian' (154). Maxine finds that the effort to analyse and to understand is very difficult but the only alternative is that represented by Moon Orchid, who finds the two different ethnic lifestyles impossible to deal with and so she loses her sanity.

Maxine herself is torn between the two cultures: she is aware of her difficulties in understanding Chinese culture (166), but she is also aware that she doesn't belong entirely to American culture. Only as a woman warrior can she imagine bringing the two together: 'Nobody in history has conquered and united both North America and Asia' (50). The difficulty of conquering her hyphenated state is emphasised by the narrative's preoccupation with silence and the difficulty of self-articulation. The ability of a woman to express herself is related to the recurring motif of mutilation. Physical mutilation is experienced by Ma Fu Lan, the woman warrior, who bears the villagers' wrongs carved into her back or Maxine's own experience of her mother who cuts her daughter's frenum (either to silence her and repress the 'ready tongue [that] is an evil tongue' [148] or else to free her daughter's tongue so she may learn many languages). The No-Name Aunt gives 'silent birth' (18), Maxine bullies a classmate who refuses to talk but herself suffers a period of hysterical muteness, Moon Orchid is unable to talk about her confusions and goes mad: Maxine reflects, 'I thought talking and not talking made the difference between sanity and insanity. Insane people were the one's who couldn't explain themselves' (166). Kingston is haunted by a fear of being thought insane and fears that her parents will betroth her to the retarded boy who visits the laundry (174ff). But in the final chapter she compiles a list of grievances to tell her mother and so make her mutilated tongue work in the cause of her own liberation (179-80).

The colliding worlds of *The Woman Warrior* are basically the worlds inhabited by the immigrant and the descendants of immigrants: Anglo-America, Chinese-America and the China that has been left behind, though not in memory, language and belief. These worlds and the secondary conflicts generated by their problematic relations (conflicts between memory, myth, imagination and present reality) are articulated not only by the disjunctive narrative style of *The Woman*

Warrior but also through Kingston's skilful use of imagery and narrative motifs. The book is subtitled 'Memoirs of a Girlhood Among Ghosts' and ghosts provide a multifaceted imagistic thread even as this image introduces a further complication in the ontological relations among the worlds Kingston describes. Ghosts threaten Chinese traditions by drawing people away from traditional Chinese culture: these include Taxi Ghosts, Police Ghosts, Grocery Ghosts, or the ghosts that terrify Moon Orchid as she is consumed by her paranoid hysteria, the Panhandler Ghosts and Mugger Ghosts and Mexican Ghosts. Ghosts are not necessarily of non-Chinese cultures; the No-Name Aunt threatens the Chinese community that has driven her to commit suicide by drowning herself in the village well thus promising to wait there 'silently by the water to pull down a substitute' (22). The challenge to traditional culture represented by the story of the No-Name Aunt haunts Maxine and eventually motivates the entire narrative of which she becomes a crucial part.

Storytelling or 'talk-story' is then crucial to *The Woman Warrior*: stories can sustain superstitions and embody warnings, they can also offer the chance to imagine previously unrealised possibilities (the No-Name Aunt's story does all of these). The act of saying can be a form of vengeance and in this sense the entire text is a discontinuous talk-story, telling the story of how Maxine develops as an artist and a woman. *The Woman Warrior* then can be seen as a feminist *Künstlerroman* but the artist's skill that Maxine develops is the skill of holding in balance, without making easy equations, the competing and conflicting worlds that define her identity and her experience. And so she warns us: 'Be careful what you say. It comes true. It comes true. I had to leave home in order to see the world logically, logic the new way of seeing. . . . Shine floodlights into dark corners: no ghosts' (182). The perception of diverse worlds that refuse to become the same and the need to sustain the integrity of these worlds that define her condition give rise, at the end, to Maxine's new view of herself as a translator, a mediator, between cultures and between worlds.

In what follows I intend to highlight the shift away from ontological questioning to the analysis of the construction of racial subjectivities in Louise Erdrich's *Love Medicine*, Sandra Cisneros's *The House on Mango Street*, and Amy Tan's *The Joy Luck Club*.

In her review of *The Beet Queen*, Leslie Marmon Silko criticises Louise Erdrich for a style of linguistic virtuosity which, while it is 'dazzling' and 'a poet's prose' betrays a self-referentiality that belongs rather to the academic discourses of postmodernism than to the representation of the conditions of life for Native American people (Silko 1986). Silko argues that the shared communal ethic that infuses the oral tradition of tribal culture is anathema to a postmodernist style designed to convey powerfully the alienated condition of a Western writer seeking to portray a fragmented and devastated contemporary world. But the perception of the world as ontologically fragmented is not necessarily divorced from political commitment and indeed in texts like *Love Medicine* Erdrich reveals the enormous part played by racism in fragmenting the very world inhabited by the native people she portrays. Erdrich's experimental style, with its postmodernist borrowings, enables her to represent the fragmented subjectivity of characters who are alienated precisely for historical and political reasons of race. In an address to the English Institute, Silko describes the centrality of storytelling in Laguna culture: 'Whatever literature we received at school (which was damned little), at home the storytelling, the special regard for telling and bringing together through the telling, was going on constantly' (Silko 1981:67-8). And it is this concern to bring together the fragments of contemporary Chippewa life through language and through storytelling that

Erdrich identifies as the motive behind her formal experiments with narrative point of view and novelistic structure.

In the quartet of novels that begins with *Love Medicine* Erdrich comes to terms with the alienated reality that is the condition of life for her tribal characters. She does this by creating worlds of distinct ontology that go beyond differences of perception, interpretation or individual subjectivity to embody Reservation versus off-Reservation worlds; the world of tribal culture in conflict with the dominant Anglo culture (which is the hybrid world of the half-breed); the world of the historical past versus the mythical world of inherited tribal culture versus the contemporary world; the insanely alienated world of fractured cultural and personal identities: these are the worlds of Erdrich's rich fictional diversity.

Louise Erdrich and Michael Dorris, in an interview with Hertha Wong, agree that one of the most perceptive comments about their work by a reviewer is Kathleen Mullen Sands' claim that in *Love Medicine* the 'storytelling technique is the secular anecdotal process of community gossip' (Wong 1987:204). There is no single privileged narrative voice; there is no single authority to order the characters' lives. The reader seems to hear bits of gossip rather than a full, correct, story. For Erdrich, this technique reflects memories of a childhood lived in a small community: 'You were who you were in relation to the community' (Wong 1987:205). So in *Love Medicine* there is no central consciousness, but all the characters share the experience of being haunted by June's death. Questions of responsibility and guilt are shared by all in the community, and the narrative takes account of both personal and historical/political factors. The central concern, then, is with June's problematical and failed return home.

Erdrich's storytelling technique gives voice to a plurality of characters, telling parts of the larger story from different points of view. If one voice dominates, it is the voice of the community. The story asks how the community deals with the upheavals that occur within it: like June's death, the threat to Lulu's land, the influence of whites and white urban culture, poverty. Erdrich's tone is humorous but hardbitten, stoical; her multi-voiced method allows her to sustain a balance between pessimism and optimism at the end. The world of the tribal community is given vivid representation by Erdrich's conscious decision to locate the action in a community where non-tribal society (for example, Washington DC, where Nector visits on tribal business) is not very present nor is it relevant to the lives of the characters. The entire world is encompassed by the community and the primary interest of the narratives is focused upon how the community deals with itself and its members. But even within the boundaries of the Reservation and the tribal community still other worlds intersect and intervene: the world of memory, of myth and of Anglo-American racism.

Imagery is used by Erdrich to introduce these conflicting worlds into the narrative and to maintain narrative unity which would otherwise be threatened by the diversity of narrative voices. In *Love Medicine* the main recurring image is that of water – the experience of transformation or of crossing over between worlds is signified by walking over snow or water. The image of the river signifies a boundary which is related to the concept of transcendence; moving to a higher world. In Chippewa mythology, after death the soul goes west until it reaches a stream in the land of spirits, a land which is full of lakes and streams. In the interview with Hertha Wong, Erdrich describes in this connection one of the stories in Ojibway (Chippewa) mythology: 'there are different myths, but one of them is the bear coming through different worlds, breaking through from one world into the next, from the next world into the next world' (210-11). This is what June does, crossing the snow-covered landscape to her death: 'The snow fell deeper that Easter than it had in forty years, but June walked over it like water and came home' (Erdrich 1984:6). At the end of the narrative, June's son Lipsha completes her ritual return. He stops his car half-way across the 'boundary river' and as he gazes into the river he thinks of June:

> I'd heard that this river was the last of an ancient ocean, miles deep, that once had covered the Dakotas and solved all our problems. It was easy to still imagine us beneath them vast unreasonable waves, but the truth is we live on dry ground. I got inside. The morning was clear. A good road led on. So there was nothing to do but cross the water, and bring her home.
> (Erdrich 1984:272)

The transformation undergone by Lipsha is represented by his ability to assume agency in his own life and to leave behind the debilitating knowledge of his mother's abandonment of him. In Erdrich's fiction the characters' lives are balanced against the qualities of nature: shifting human history in contrast with enduring nature; human experience set against the elements like light and dark, dust and snow; but it is especially water that offers an imagistic commentary on the experiences of the characters. Water is extremely important in Chippewa tradition: water is needed for the very existence of the nation; it is needed for transportation, fishing, drinking; the benevolence of the Great Spirit is measured according to the concern to provide water for the people. Traditionally, Chippewa people have strong religious and historical affinities with water but as we discover through the conflict between the traditional tribal world and the world of modern America, nature and religion are no longer compelling for characters, both on and off the reservation.

This clash between worlds is perhaps most dramatically imaged in Erdrich's work by the figure of the half-breed. In nineteenth-century American literature, the mixed-blood Indian was the invisible aspect of racial integration that took the form of 'whitening' the Indians. But in contemporary writing, according to the poet Wendy Rose, the mixed-blood is 'a condition of history, . . . a political fact' (Coltelli 1990:123). The half-breed is significant in relation to the theme of the loss of culture and of land since the mixed-blood Indian is already partially dispossessed by blood. The effect of mixed blood is often poisonous, tainting one's self-image and relations with others and the tribe. The young Marie Lazarre, under the destructive influence of French Jesuitical Catholicism, attempts to deny her own Indian part: 'I don't have that much Indian blood' she claims (40). Among the most precious of all that is lost by the half-breed is the loss of native language. The loss of tribal language means losing the bond between what you express and who you are. The denial of native language is disempowering because in so doing one denies the ability to name things. Erdrich gives as an example of this the character Lulu Lamartine in *Love Medicine*: 'This is a woman that has been silenced because she's not allowed to speak in her native language. . . . Like so many people of various cultures who were denied language and the subsequent ability to name things, she [Lulu] is disempowered' (Pearlman 1990:146). Erdrich describes native language as the language of survival (Pearlman 1990:146), and of resistance to cultural annihilation (Wong 1987:200). And so the loss of language is the loss of connection with the protective, enabling forces of the tribal world.

It is as a result of the impact of colonisation that the tribal world has been challenged so aggressively: the historical influence of the French upon the Chippewa is apparent in the Catholicism that engages destructively with tribal beliefs and practices. Sister Leopolda – Pauline in *Tracks* – and her illegitimate daughter Marie in *Love Medicine* both succumb to an hysterical rejection of their tribal identities in response to their Catholicism. The perverse and crazy relationship between Pauline and Marie offers an example of the impact of the external political world upon the fabric of tribal society. As Sister Leopolda,

Pauline tries to murder her illegitimate daughter Marie, interpreting as signs of satanic possession Marie's Indian part: 'She always said the Dark One wanted me most of all, and I believed this. I stood out. Evil was a common thing I trusted. Before sleep sometimes he came and whispered conversation in the old language of the bush. I listened. He told me things he never told anyone but Indians. I was privy to both worlds of his knowledge' (Erdrich 1984:43). Leopolda sucks Marie into her hysterical worldview by the threat, 'You have two choices. One, you can marry a no-good Indian, bear his brats, die like a dog. Or two, you can give yourself to God' (45). So Marie embarks upon an insane race with the woman whom she knows not as her mother, to see who will make it first to heaven. Family relationships are at the heart of tribal kinship structures. Families have become dysfunctional; families are displaced, broken as a consequence of poverty, alcoholism, promiscuity and illegitimacy, violence, and self-hatred of the kind that is directed towards children and spouses. The violence done historically to tribal unity is represented through broken families: Lulu's eight boys each of whom has a different father, the orphans taken in by Marie. Violence is now domestic and the only hunting is done by the police. But the family unit reveals how enmeshed have been and still are the personal and the political, the present and the past, in Indian life.

The historical past itself constitutes a separate world, of ambiguous ontology because it relies so precariously upon human memory for its existence. Erdrich's fiction emphasises both the unreliability of memory at any given moment but also the powerful structuring ability of memory. Erdrich's plurality of narrative points of view produces a 'multilayered racial memory' (Pearlman 1990:147). The ambiguity of this recollected racial world and the conflictual nature of its relations with the other worlds experienced by the characters underlines the challenge of self-definition they confront within the context of

Native American history and those pressures applied by institutions such as the tribe, the Church, the police, the Bureau of Indian Affairs. Memory, language, storytelling traditions – they all contribute to the personal and historical recollections that structure the characters' distinctive identities. The past merges with the present in the context of continuing traditions, like Lipsha's medicine in the title story. Lipsha tries to reconcile his estranged grandparents as a gesture of gratitude for raising him. But the old tribal ways have become so corrupted by Europe, as the tribal medicine has been corrupted by Catholicism, that Lipsha no longer knows how to ask the tribal gods for assistance. He relies instead upon his own instinct, firstly in choosing geese hearts as the medium for his love medicine, secondly in assuming that since he has failed to hunt any real geese frozen turkey hearts bought from store will do ('I told myself love medicine was simple. I told myself the old superstitions were just that – strange beliefs. . . . I took an evil shortcut. I looked at birds that was dead and froze' [Erdrich 1984:203]), and finally in blessing with holy water the turkey hearts himself when no-one at the convent is willing to perform such a pagan blessing for him. It is hardly surprising then that this medicine fails: rather than reconcile his grandparents the medicine separates them completely by choking Nector to death.

Characters like Lipsha seek in fumbling ways modern identities through this interplay of past and present social realities. But this raises the question of home and the possibilities for belonging within the context of dispossession. In the interview with Mickey Pearlman, Erdrich describes how 'there is a certain freedom in and peace that comes from home, the feeling of having a homeland' (144). In *Love Medicine*, June is heading home through an empty landscape; for her, home is what Erdrich describes as a mix of family and place. But the freedom of a completely open space is not a place in which to live – it leads to alienation, madness, and, for June, death. On the Reservation, characters experience a conflict between the desire to leave and a longing for home. June lives alternately in the tribal world of the Reservation and in the off-Reservation world of Anglo-America. The conflict she experiences between these two worlds, in neither of which she finds a sense of belonging, is resolved only in death. Within the narrative itself the conflict is never resolved. These distinct worlds and the ambiguous ontological relations among them are never resolved into unity or harmony.

The difficulty of self-definition is compounded in a hybrid or 'hyphenated' culture like that of Native-Americans, Chinese-Americans, Mexican-Americans. Sandra Cisneros and other Chicana writers use a *dis*continuous narrative technique in order to represent authentically the fragmented nature of the Chicana's world. This is the world of the marginal subject, disempowered and disenfranchised, where transient individuals appear and disappear, where glimpses of life are captured but there is no grand narrative to give them meaning. There is no sense of belonging, no sense of living within a fully integrated and unified community. Cisnero's narratives, like the lives they describe, are fragmented into scenes and isolated images; within the narrative, selves are fragmented as are the female characters Cisnero creates. This fragmentation can be both debilitating or alienating but it can also be liberating. In *The House on Mango Street*, the woman 'Mamacita' who speaks no English and is paralysed with homesickness for Mexico fails, as a result, as both wife and mother; she is reduced to a pathetic figure sitting alone at her window. But Alicia, who must rise before dawn to do her dead mother's work before going to school, resists the pressure of normalisation (expressed by her father) and spends her nights studying so that through education she might escape the destiny set down for the women of Mango Street.

Esperanza, the narrator, encounters a number of women who are able to find some relief, if not escape, from the subjectivity imposed upon them by a patriarchal culture: Minerva and Aunt Lupe take refuge in poetry and it is they who encourage Esperanza to seek freedom through her artistic intelligence. The fragmented narrative of *The House on Mango Street* embodies this quest for freedom, for a voice: 'When you leave you must remember to come back for the others. A circle, understand? You will always be Esperanza. You will always be Mango Street. You can't erase what you know. You can't forget who you are' (Cisneros 1989:105). Only by discovering precisely who she is, by learning from all the women that surround her, can Esperanza find the voice that is her poet's voice. Maria Elena de Valdes describes precisely how Cisneros's narrative technique relates to the twin themes of gender and racial identity:

> The open-ended reflections are the narrator's search for an answer to the enigma: how can she be free of Mango Street and the house that is not hers and yet belong as she must to that house and that street. The open-ended entries come together only slowly as the tapestry takes shape, for each of the closed figures are also threads of the larger background figure which is the narrator herself. (de Valdes 1993:293)

Cisneros uses poetic forms of expression, a highly metaphoric and allusive style which is subversive of rational patriarchal structures of thought. But the resolution of such radical narrative disjunction must remain tenuous and fragile. The threads which are the individual stories come together at the very end when the historical present gives way to the narrative present and the adult Esperanza takes over the narrative from her adolescent self. The conclusion is one of highly qualified optimism. Esperanza escapes to find a voice with which to speak of and for Mango Street but the grim reality of life for the Mexican-American women who remain dominates to the very end.

The vignettes that make up *The House on Mango Street* are connected in such a loose and associative fashion that critics still debate whether the book is better read as a short story collection rather than a single narrative. Amy Tan's work also threatens to fragment in much the same way. In *The Joy Luck Club* a framework is supplied by the story of June's enactment of her mother's return to China and reunion with her daughters. The novel is divided into four sections, with the life histories of the four mothers providing the context for their daughters' narratives. So there is a danger that the narrative will fragment into distinct short stories. However, this is overcome by the use of threads of imagery that lend coherence to the entire narrative. Each of the four sections of the narrative focuses on a particular personal crisis. First-person narrators are employed to tell their own stories. This means that cross-cultural confusions are represented impressionistically as personal experience rather than objectively as sociological fact. The limitations and partialities of the narrators become apparent when those characters are reported as actors in another's narrative. For example, Jing-mei reports her mother's theory of five personal elements and uses An-mei as an example (Tan 1989:31): she says that An-mei has no spine but it is An-mei who later tells her daughter Rose that she has no spine and that she lacks wood in order to explain her lack of self-assertion (191). Also, we learn from other characters' stories further explanations of why each is as they are. Each chapter concerns a crucial incident in the life of that character. Consequently, the novel does not present a comprehensive historical account of Chinese-American relations in the twentieth century but is focused thematically upon the issue of generational change and the possibility of communication across the distinct cultural worlds. This gap between the generations is exaggerated by the cultural distance separating Chinese-born mothers from their American-born children.

Tan uses imagery for several narrative purposes: to lend coherence and unity to an otherwise discontinuous narrative structure; to emphasise the difference and conflict between the worlds of China and America; and finally to suggest points of continuity or shared experience that bring together the generations. It is generally mundane imagery, or imagery of the mundane, that stresses the everyday objects of cultural ritual and so emphasises the differences between Chinese and American culture, mothers and daughters. It is the exotic imagery that represents intangible qualities and points of continuity that emphasise the fundamental commonalities between mothers and daughters.

A pervasive example of mundane imagery is food. As a symbol of luck food operates as the central part of the ritual of Joy Luck: 'The hostess had to serve special *dyansyin* foods to bring good fortune of all kinds – dumplings shaped like silver money ingots, long rice noodles for long life, boiled peanuts for conceiving sons, and of course, many good-luck oranges for a plentiful, sweet life' (23). The supernatural power with which food is imbued – the power to bring good-luck or evil – lends Lena to interpret her mother's stories in such a way that she develops an eating disorder and later anorexia: for Lena, food is both a symbol of future (the supernaturally charged grains of rice that act as omens of her future) and a symbol of her present malaise in form of the ice cream upon which she binges and of which she purges herself in an act of almost ritual purification. Food is an extremely important point of cross-cultural incomprehension and appears in this connection on the very first page of *The Joy Luck Club*. At the very beginning June explains her inability to remember Chinese concepts because she doesn't understand them in the first place, by telling of her confusion between two terms: 'She said the two soups were almost the same, *chabudwo*. Or maybe she said *butong*, not the same thing at all' (19). Among the threads of exotic imagery used by Tan in *The Joy Luck Club* is the motif of the wind: the invisible yet undeniable power of the wind's elemental force represents to her Lindo's dawning self-possession; as she dresses for the arranged wedding she abhors, Lindo becomes aware of the billowing: 'And then I realized it was the first time I could see the power of the wind. I couldn't see the wind itself, but I could see it carried the water that filled the rivers and shaped the countryside. . . . I had genuine thoughts inside that no one could see, that no one could ever take away from me. I was like the wind' (89). Much later Lindo advises her daughter Waverly about 'the art of invisible strength' (Tan 1989:89), that she must listen to the wind if she would win at anything, including chess games, and as a result Waverly becomes a champion. Waverly's knowledge of chess secrets are like the instructions given to Jing-mei about playing Mah Jong: the Joy Luck aunties seat her at her mother's corner of the table, the East, 'the direction from which the sun rises, where the wind comes from' (33).

The commonalities discovered by Tan's fictional mothers and daughters focus upon the importance of the maternal bond, a relationship that sets the foundation for personal and cultural identity and which transcends incidental differences of time and space. In an interview with Katherine Henderson, Amy Tan describes:

> the [metaphorical] umbilical cord . . . [that] gets stretched over time; whether it's the mother or daughter who severs it or tries to pull it tighter, part of that is individual and part is cultural. In a Chinese family the mother pulls very tightly on the bond to a point where [the daughter] asks, 'Why can't I know about such and such?' and the [mother answers], 'Because I haven't put it in your mind yet'. The notion that your mother puts every thing in your mind – the blank slate theory – is part of Chinese culture.
> (Henderson 1990:16)

This kind of thinking informs the relationship between Waverly and Lindo Jong and the power struggle between them. To challenge maternal authority is to transgress an invisible boundary and to enter a world of isolation and alienation. The challenge to maternal authority is characteristically met with silence, as in both *The Joy Luck Club* and *The Kitchen God's Wife* where the daughter Pearl describes how 'my mother looked at me with a blank face and absolute silence. And after that, she did stop complaining to me. In fact, she stopped talking to me for about two months' (Tan 1991:13). The relative importance to personal esteem and sense of self of individuality versus cultural characteristics is explored by Tan through the stories of two generations of women, with very different experiences of China, of America, and of each other. One of the most important shared experiences they discover is the common suffering of women under patriarchy. Patriarchal oppression is represented in terms of the powerful influence exerted by masculine power upon feminine relationships, for example, the relationship between An-mei and her concubine mother – a relationship modelled upon that between Tan's mother and grandmother. Katherine Henderson reports Tan as saying '[that] her mother has for most of her life felt oppressed by unhappiness; she feels that "everything is cumulative; that if the sequence begins wrong everything is wrong; only in the past few years has she felt that she can be happy"' (Henderson 1990:20). A disruptive relationship between a woman and her mother will then poison all aspects of that woman's life. In *The Joy Luck Club*, Lena and Rose neglect the examples offered by their mothers' experiences and are so concerned about racism and fairness that they do not see how they are being exploited by husbands. These women have been conditioned to blame themselves and other women for any unhappiness they experience (156). But in the course of the narrative they discover that their mothers have experienced in their lives the combined effects of racism and sexism. It is the assumption that only racism operates in the US that traps Lena and Rose in oppressive relationships. The feminine world is not significantly different in America: Mrs Jordan treats Rose as a Chinese mother-in-law would – interested only in her son's welfare. Gender roles within marriage are only quantitatively different. The obedience demanded of a Chinese wife is not so very different to the conformity demanded of women in America.

The question of how to communicate across distinct generational and cultural worlds raises in Tan's work, as much as in Erdrich's, Kingston's and Cisneros's, the importance of language and of cultural conventions: the adhesive of social unity and belonging. This is the primary issue of *The Joy Luck Club*, especially after Jing-mei scandalises the Joy Luck aunties by confessing her ignorance of what her mother was, her inability to tell her newly-discovered sisters in Chin who their mother was: 'What can I tell them about my mother? I don't know anything. She was my mother' (Tan 1989:40). The fear that their own daughters may be just as ignorant of them motivates these women to tell their stories. But they come up against the difficulty of cultural incomprehension on both the large and the small scales, as when Jing-mei mistakes social conventions of the Joy Luck aunties; she believes they ask her to stay as a gesture of politeness, they want her to stay so they can broach the issue of her recently discovered sisters. Even more than the lack of shared conventions, manners and assumptions is the lack of a shared language. After speaking with her mother about her marriage break-up, Rose recognises the extent to which some Chinese words or concepts cannot be translated: 'maybe they can't be easily translated because they refer to a sensation only Chinese people have' (Tan 1989:188). Waverly only knows Chinese baby-talk and Lindo wonders, 'How can she talk to people in China with these words? Pee-pee, choo-choo train, eat, close light sleep' (Tan 1989:253-4).

Historical change operates to fragment families, as is seen in the fate of Suyuan's daughters and her inability to trace them. Tan underlines the importance of knowing where you come from and who your family is, so that you can understand who you are. This narrative framework also offers Amy Tan the opportunity for a happy ending – happy for Jing-mei because her family is complete; for her sisters because they discover their mother through their sister; for Suyuan because her wish is granted and her daughters are finally found. But this happy ending is qualified because Suyuan does not live to participate in the reunion – the experience of loss is therefore firmly inscribed in the ending. Amy Tan is able to answer the question addressed to Chinese-Americans by Maxine Hong Kingston – 'How do you know what is Chinese tradition and what is the movies?' (Kingston 1975:13) – with greater confidence than Kingston herself. But in both narratives, techniques of fragmentation, discontinuity, the decentred subject and ontological uncertainty are used to dramatise the possibilities for transcendence of these conditions, for continuing to live despite the real conditions of alienation that continually threaten the lives of ethnic women in America.

Conclusion: Race, Gender and the Critique of Postmodernism

Maxine Hong Kingston has described something of her own writing in relation to the canon of American literary postmodernism. In an interview with Paula Rabinowitz in 1987, Rabinowitz questioned what was Kingston's perception of her relationship with what Rabinowitz called the 'white, male, postmodernist establishment of writers, who have outlined the boundaries of what is considered contemporary writing' (Rabinowitz 1987:184). Kingston replied by describing her sense of connection with the work of other ethnic women, specifically Toni Morrison and Leslie Marmon Silko, and then she went on to elaborate:

> I do feel an affinity not only because I love them as people but because we seem to write alike. There is so much human emotion and richness and story and imagery and colors and things to eat. Nobody is alienated from life; everybody is warm. When I compare our work with some of the mainstream work, it seems as if many of them are *only* playing with words. The 'language' people's world seems grey and black and white. . . . We do not live in new subdivisions without ceremony and memory; and if those other writers have to draw from that non-magical imagination, then of course, their writing will be grey and black and white.
>
> (Rabinowitz 1987:184).

But the work of the 'language people' is not merely colourless, by contrast with the women's fiction discussed above. What Kingston does not mention is the misogyny often found in classic postmodernist texts of the sixties – texts like Robert Coover's *Pricksongs and Descants*, John Barth's *The End of the Road*, Thomas Pynchon's *V*, and many of the novels by Jerzy Kosinski. A compelling reason for ethnic women writers, and their commentators, to dissociate their writing from the postmodernist mainstream is the rather vicious attitude towards women found there. Coover's story 'The Babysitter', for example, juxtaposes male fantasies (both adolescent and middle-aged, of fathers and sons) of sexually assaulting the babysitter with the absurd and demeaning image of the mother, Dolly, writhing on the bathroom floor as she tries to get into her girdle. The overweight and overbearing mother is a figure of contempt as her fellow party-goers make her the subject of a game called 'Get Dolly Tucker In Her Girdle Again' and she herself is overcome with anxiety that all the future holds for her is the prospect of her children forcing her into a nursing home. The host's son and his friend imagine raping the babysitter whilst Dolly's husband Harry fantasises interrupting the boys and then seducing the babysitter himself. The narrator, the consciousness that reports these fantasised vignettes, describes lasciviously the prospect of the babysitter taking a bath while the children sleep. The context for these imagined snapshots is a violent movie of cops and robbers playing on the television. The description of physical violence, violent pursuit and ugly murder sets the tone for the imagined scenes of sexual violence that comprise the main part of the story. Violent and cruel sexual behaviour is, in important respects, the very stuff of Jerzy Kosinski's fiction. In novels like *Cockpit* and *Blind Date* scenes of rape and violent sexual congress stud the narrative: the woman smothered near to death during sex; a woman simultaneously raped vaginally, anally and orally by filthy derelict men brought in off the street; a teenager repeatedly raped in an act that gives the novel *Blind Date* its title. In Kosinski's writing women are the passive subjects of an extreme sexual cruelty that frequently they are seen to deserve: the woman who is smothered is punished for her sexual pride – she claims sexual aids or devices can satisfy her desire as well as a man; the woman raped by three bums is punished for an act of betrayal. Feminine sexual passivity is therefore complemented by feminine duplicity, in Kosinski's view. John Barth's *The End of the Road*, ends with Rennie's botched abortion and death, and Thomas Pynchon's eponymous feminine figure 'V', who comes to reify the inhumanity, materialism and cruelty of the twentieth century, do not present us with such uncompromisingly ugly images of women yet they do represent women as entirely subject to male interests (sexual or otherwise) and as seen from an intensely masculine perspective.

Many of the canonical writers of postmodernist fiction share a concern with the impersonal, abstract systems of repression to which we are subject in post-industrial society but this interest betrays a patriarchal bias in that the repression highlighted by these writers is not linked to the kinds of oppression ethnic women deal with every day of their lives: poverty, illiteracy, lack of birth control, lack of education, disenfranchisement, and so on. It is the vast impersonal world of 'Them' and 'Their' politics that is of concern to Pynchon, DeLillo, Gaddis and the like. In the poem 'Notes from a Chicana Coed' Bernice Zamora writes of exactly this situation:

> To cry that *gabacho*
> is our oppressor is to shout
> in abstraction, *carnal*.
> He no more oppresses us
> than you do now as you tell me
> 'It's the gringo who oppresses you, Babe'.
> You cry, 'The gringo is our oppressor!'
> to the tune of $20,000 to $30,000
> a year, brother, and I wake up
> alone each morning and ask,
> 'Can I feed my children today?'
> (Zamora 1990:131)

Zamora addresses the compulsion felt by ethnic women writers to write of the oppression suffered as a consequence of Anglo-American racism and the simultaneous imperative to write of oppression as it is experienced in a diversity of repressive cultural practices and as this oppression impacts upon the conditions of everyday life: 'Can I feed my children today?' This urgency, this concern with grassroots oppression, lends the fictional experimentation of ethnic women writers its significance and its power, its 'color', in Maxine Hong Kingston's terms. Not an empty playing with words and messing around with the formal possibilities of literary expression, the vitality of ethnic women's writing arises from the necessary break with a misogynistic and patriarchal postmodernist mainstream in which they cannot, thankfully, find a part.

Deborah MADSEN
University of Leicester

Works Cited

Barth, John. (1958). *The End of the Road.* London: Granada, 1962.

Cisneros, Sandra. (1989). *The House on Mango Street.* London: Bloomsbury, 1992.

Coltelli, Laura. *Winged Words: American Indian Women Writers Speak.* Lincoln: University of Nebraska Press, 1990. 'Wendy Rose'. 121-33.

Coover, Robert. *Pricksongs and Descants.* New York: New American Library, 1969.

De Valdes, Maria Elena. 'The Critical Reception of Sandra Cisneros's *The House on Mango Street*'. *Gender, Self and Society: Proceedings of IV International Conference on Hispanic Cultures of the United States.* Ed. Renate von Bardeleben. Frankfurt: Peter Lang, 1993. 287-300.

Erdrich, Louise. (1984). *Love Medicine.* London: Abacus, 1990.

Henderson, Katherine Usher. 'An Interview with Amy Tan'. *Inter/View: Talks with America's Writing Women.* Eds. Mickey Pearlman and Katherine Usher Henderson. Lexington: University Press of Kentucky, 1990. 15-22.

Kingston, Maxine Hong. (1975). *The Woman Warrior: Memoir of a Girlhood Among Ghosts.* London: Picador, 1981.

Kosinski, Jerzy. (1977). *Blind Date*. London: Corgi, 1978.

---. *Cockpit*. London: Hutchinson, 1975.

McHale, Brian. *Postmodernist Fiction*. New York: Methuen, 1987.

Pearlman, Mickey. 'An Interview with Louise Erdrich'. *Inter/View: Talks with America's Writing Women*. Eds. Mickey Pearlman and Katherine Usher Henderson. Lexington: University Press of Kentucky, 1990. 143-48.

Pynchon, Thomas. (1961). *V*. London: Picador, 1975.

Rabinowitz, Paula. 'Eccentric Memories: An Interview with Maxine Hong Kingston'. *Michigan Quarterly Review* 26.1 (1987): 177-87.

Silko, Leslie Marmon. 'Here's an Odd Artifact for the Fairy-Tale Shelf'. *Studies in American Literature* 10 (1986): 177-84.

---. 'Language and Literature from a Laguna Pueblo Perspective'. *English Literature: Opening Up the Canon*. Eds. Leslie A Fiedler and Houston A. Baker, Jr. Selected Papers from the English Institute. Baltimore: Johns Hopkins University Press, 1981. 54-72.

Tan, Amy. *The Kitchen God's Wife*. London: Harper Collins, 1991.

---. *The Joy Luck Club*. London: Heinemann, 1989.

Wong, Hertha D. 'An Interview with Louise Erdrich and Michael Dorris'. *North Dakota Quarterly* 55.1 (1987): 196-218.

Zamora, Bernice. 'Notes from a Chicana Coed'. *Making Face, Making Soul: Haciendo Caras*. Ed. Glori Anzúldua. San Francisco: Aunt Lute, 1990. 131-2.

Lesbian Fiction and the Postmodern:

Genre, Narrativity, Sexual Politics[1]

Introduction

The intervention of lesbian representational practice in postmodern culture, which has taken place in the 1990s, is by no means a simple event but is marked by contradictions. As Judith Roof argues: 'The lesbian and the postmodern appear to be analogous, if not related phenomena' (Roof 1994:49). They have features in common and display, in certain respects, a similar trajectory. They are linked, Roof observes, by historical period, since the emergence of lesbian and gay groups in the mid-1950s coincided with the initial use of the term 'postmodern' by Arnold Toynbee (Roof 1994:48-52; Connor 1989:65). They also reveal – to a degree at least – intellectual and ideological affinities. Just as the postmodern, as defined by Jean-François Lyotard, is characterised by the loss of a totalising vision and the breakdown of the concept of the centre, so the emergence of lesbian and gay liberation movements challenges the notion of a norm of sexual behaviour by foregrounding a transgressive plurality of sexualities and lifestyles. Whereas the postmodern deconstructs the metanarratives of

---

1 For Cambridge Lesbian Line.

Western civilisation and the traditional notions of truth and knowledge which they serve to legitimatise, the lesbian problematises essentialist ideas of sexuality and gender. In achieving this, the lesbian, like the postmodern, employs intellectual and linguistic approaches involving deconstruction and denaturalisation. The definition of 'lesbian' proposed by the theorists Monique Wittig and Judith Butler as a sign or subject position which disrupts the conventional binaries of masculine/feminine, since the woman who adopts a lesbian identification rejects the role of sexual commodity and object of exchange assigned to woman in phallocentric culture, is pertinent to the postmodern, which likewise challenges binary gender categories.[2]

However, the lesbian and the postmodern, while sharing a common interest in deconstructing traditional metanarratives and institutions, display significant ideological differences. As is the case with the tensions existing between the feminist and the postmodern, these hinge on the issues of 'politics' and 'agency'. Unlike the postmodern, which, as Linda Hutcheon illustrates, tends to be 'politically ambivalent, doubly encoded as both complicity and critique' (Hutcheon 1989:168), the lesbian is committed to a political agenda which champions the rights of a particular category of women and seeks to achieve social and political change. Whereas the postmodern regards subjectivity as decentred and in a state of flux, the lesbian affirms a belief in the power of the individual to transform both herself and society. The difficulty of reconciling these disparate perspectives is recognised by Christine Di Stefano, who argues that:

2 Wittig, *The Straight Mind and Other Essays* (1992:9-20); Butler, *Gender Trouble: Feminism and the Subversion of Identity* (1990:5-34). For a discussion of the changing meanings of the term 'lesbian', see Bonnie Zimmerman, 'Lesbians Like This and That: Some Notes on Lesbian Criticism for the Nineties', in Sally Munt, ed., *New Lesbian Criticism: Literary and Cultural Readings* (1992-1-15).

> [the] postmodernist project . . . would make any semblance of a feminist politics impossible. To the extent that feminist politics is bound up with a specific constituency or subject, namely, women, the postmodernist prohibition against subject-centered inquiry and theory undermines the legitimacy of a broad-based organised movement dedicated to articulating and implementing the goals of such a constituency.
>
> (Di Stefano 1990:76)

As Di Stefano's comment indicates, the relationship between the lesbian and the postmodern is characterised by tension. Strategies of deconstruction and denaturalisation, associated with the postmodern, figure prominently in contemporary lesbian culture. In the field of fiction and theory, writers interrogate traditional attitudes by foregrounding the constructed aspect of institutions such as heterosexuality and the family which, in the past, were regarded as natural and unchanging. In problematising heterosexual values and codes of conduct, they utilise, as we shall see, approaches of a postmodern kind. These include: appropriating and reworking popular genres, such as the thriller; foregrounding the artifice and fictionality of the text; and breaking down the distinction between popular and high-style genres by creating an interplay between the two. However, they utilise these approaches and strategies with a specific aim in view – to explore issues relating to gender and sexuality. While recognising the role that culture and the unconscious play in the formation of the subject, they simultaneously seek to highlight, with differing degrees of emphasis, concepts of agency and self-determination.

The interaction between the lesbian and the postmodern in works of fiction takes a variety of forms, finding expression in numerous different ways. To illustrate its diversity, I have chosen to concentrate attention on two particular genres – historiographic metafiction and the thriller. Both have postmodern connotations and have proved popular with writers in the 1980s and '90s. The novels exemplifying them, in addition to indicating the range of styles employed in lesbian representation, illustrate the way that writers, in appropriating and reworking mainstream genres, employ postmodern strategies in relation to sexual politics. They transform the narrative forms and structures produced by hetero-patriarchy, along with the values informing them. As the novels of Ellen Galford and Jeanette Winterson illustrate, historiographic metafiction gives the writer the opportunity to critique phallocentric versions of history, question the values it embodies, and construct alternative images of the past focusing on marginalised groups. The thriller, as is apparent from the fiction of Sarah Schulman and Mary Wings, enables her to problematise the masculinist stereotypes associated with classic crime fiction. By centring the narrative on female characters and exploring the contradictory position of the lesbian in contemporary society, she can construct a more complex model of subjectivity and social relations than is generally associated with the genre. The thriller also offers the writer scope for parody and, by introducing elements from other genres such as Gothic, creating a generic interplay. The four writers, by portraying the protagonists they depict transgressing accepted social and sexual codes and challenging phallocentric images of femininity, interrogate the scripts conventionally assigned to women in Western fiction, creating alternative representations of femininity and relations between women.

Historiographic Metafiction

Galford's *Moll Cutpurse*, a relatively early example of lesbian historiographic metafiction published in 1984, takes the form of a re-evaluation of the adventures of Mary Frith, seventeenth-century trickster and crossdresser. The novel treats a number of themes and ideas pertinent to a postmodern approach to history. The most important are: an emphasis on the partisan and provisional nature of all accounts of the past; a focus on the problematic aspects of storytelling; reference to the difficulty the researcher and biographer encounter in establishing a clear line of demarcation between history and literature (Hutcheon 1988:106-23). Galford gives these themes political relevance, utilising them to affirm the value of a lesbian/feminist version of history, while at the same time acknowledging the problems involved in investigating constructs of femininity in earlier periods. Bridget, Moll's lover and one of several narrators whom Galford employs to tell her story, explains that her account is motivated by an urge to correct the 'lies and fables' circulated about Moll by her male contemporaries who unjustly vilify her by depicting her as a 'a monster . . . halfway between man and woman' (Galford 1984:11). Here Bridget, speaking on behalf of Galford, adopts the role of lesbian/feminist historian and biographer. She expresses the intent of intervening in male accounts of history and, by exposing the falsity of the image of woman as grotesque Other which they perpetrate, setting the record straight. Galford, however, does not fall into the trap of representing male accounts as unitary. Bridget has no quarrel with Thomas Dekker's portrayal of Moll in his play *The Roaring Girl* (1611) since he wrote it in the spirit of friendship and produced it while she was still alive. However, she strongly objects to the version of her life produced by the unnamed 'dull scribbler' (12) who, despite the fact that he never knew Moll, seeks to pass it off as her personal diary.

Bridget's self-appointed task of feminist historian/biographer is, Galford indicates, by no means easy. The proliferation of rival stories which Moll's larger than life personality generates and the difficulty of ascertaining their veracity is complicated by the fact that Bridget and her male contemporaries are not the only sources of information about her. Moll herself furnishes her own eccentric account – one which, since it is embellished with fictional elaborations, is far from reliable. As Bridget admits, Moll, in addition to having a huge ego and 'a voice like a bellowing ox' (11), enjoyed performing in front of an audience; she loved 'to be the centre of it all, and if there weren't enough tales with her name in them abroad in Paul's Churchyard and Cheapside, she'd grow restless and start up a few new rumours herself' (11). Here Galford mischievously problematises the simple distinction between the 'truth' of feminist versions of history and the 'falsity' of patriarchal accounts which she initially appeared to be setting up. Not only is Bridget's version of Moll's life recognised to be subjective and fallible, but also Moll's own autobiographical account, which we might naively expect to be the truth, is perceived to be untrustworthy. The partisan and subjective nature of all accounts of the past is acknowledged, as is the difficulty which the historian/biographer experiences in distinguishing fact from fiction.

Galford's treatment of lesbianism, the focal theme of her novel, is multifaceted. She succeeds in highlighting both its feminist dimension, reflected in the contribution it makes to improving women's circumstances and building a strong female community, and its transgressive aspect, illustrated by its capacity to disrupt and undermine the patriarchal *status quo*. She assigns the former to Bridget, who earns her living as an apothecary and specialises in female healing and counselling, and the latter to Moll, who occupies the roles of trickster and n'er-do-well. This division enables both the 'positive' and the 'negative' challenges which lesbianism directs at the forces of patriarchy to be acknowledged. Both, it is interesting to note, furnish Galford with the opportunity to foreground female agency and self-determination.

Emphasising Moll's strong-willed personality and contempt for convention, Galford gives a lively account of her experiences as a picaresque rogue, living on the margins of society and surviving by her wits. This role, as Galford depicts it, carries Bakhtinian associations of carnivalesque misrule and the grotesque body. In one episode, she dresses as a boy and joins a troupe of travelling players. Though appearing from a conformist point of view a monster and a freak, she emerges, from an anti-establishment perspective, as the epitome of carnivalesque mirth. She describes how, on one occasion, on finding herself confronted by a hostile audience angered by the delay of a theatrical performance, she entertains them with an irreverent display of cartwheels and flying:

> I flipped over into a handstand, stared out at the crowd from my upside-down vantage point, and began to tell what I thought of them: 'You pack of country idiots with dung for brains and toadstool faces – you deserve to live in a god-forsaken midden-hole like this place. . . . Your stupid faces and scabby flesh are living proof of the Seven Deadly Sins . . .
>
> (Galford 1984:28-9)

The inverted posture which Moll adopts, the stream of playful abuse issuing from her lips, and her insulting references to the audience's physical defects, recall Mikhail Bakhtin's description of carnivalesque behaviour and the way it challenges orthodox values. He describes how, in a typical carnivalesque stance, 'the essential topographical element of the bodily hierarchy [is] turned upside down; the lower stratum replaces the upper stratum' (Bakhtin 1984:309). In carnival raillery, moreover, 'the theme of mockery and abuse is almost entirely bodily and grotesque' since 'wherever men laugh and curse . . . their speech is filled with bodily images' (Bakhtin 1984:319). These comments are applicable to Moll and her antics.

A grotesque approach to the morphology of the lesbian body, illustrated by the description of Moll in the passage quoted above, alerts attention to the excess which lesbian sexuality signifies in phallocentric culture, since the lesbian rejects woman's conventional role of object of exchange and the Other of man. Galford balances this approach with other representations which are more attractive and wholesome. At the start of the novel, Moll, disgusted with the subordinate role which society expects her to play and regarding gender in an essentialist light, requests Bridget, in her professional capacity as herbalist, to sell her a potion which will transform her into a man. Bridget, who has fallen in love with her, eventually succeeds in convincing her that gender differences are cultural and persuades her to value the female body which, up to now, she has despised. She tells Moll that she is 'a lovely woman' and expresses admiration for her 'welcoming bosom and comfortable belly' (Galford 1984:42).

Two features cited by critics as typifying postmodern fiction are the problematising of the distinction between history and literature, and an emphasis on the production of the self through acts of narrative (Hutcheon 1988:87-123; Peter Brooks 1984:3-7). These are reflected in *Moll Cutpurse* in the pivotal role which storytelling plays in the text and in Galford's skilful utilisation of intertextuality. Both contribute to the novel's analysis of sexual politics. Allusions to the works of Dekker and Thomas Nashe, as well as creating a period flavour, alert attention to the male-dominated nature of the culture which Bridget and Moll, in living together, have to negotiate. Their partnership, while forming the centre of the text, is not the only focus of interest. Minor characters such as Mother Bunch, the owner of a London Alehouse, and Judith Shakespeare, a figure based on Woolf's creation in *A Room of One's Own* (1929), also recount their adventures. This interplay of voices, in addition to illustrating the contribution which women make to the production of history, foregrounds the theme of communal interaction, transforming the text into a polyphony of female voices and narratives.

Winterson's *The Passion* (1987), while sharing with *Moll Cutpurse* certain common features such as a focus on rival accounts of the past and the problematising of the distinction between 'history' and 'fiction', differs from it in many respects. Winterson's treatment of ideas and strategies associated with the postmodern is, on the whole, more radical and inventive than Galford's. She deconstructs gender binaries, introduces examples of fantasy and magic realism, and, as is signalled by her choice of title, centres her narrative on the psychoanalytic theme of the formation of subjectivity in terms of 'passion' and desire. An unusual feature of *The Passion*, when regarded in the context of lesbian fiction in general, is its utilisation, in certain sections, of a male narrator. This, as Lisa Moore argues, far from precluding a lesbian perspective on events, paradoxically contributes to it, since Henri, the French peasant employed as a cook in Napoleon's campaigns, is represented as respecting lesbian involvements and envying their emotional intensity (Moore 1995:112). Winterson utilises his portrayal to deconstruct conventions of sexual difference. Whereas Henri displays attributes of sensitivity and imagination generally regarded as feminine, Villanelle, the Venetian girl with whom he falls in love and who acts as the signifier of lesbian throughout the text, enjoys crossdressing and has qualities of initiative and daring conventionally seen as masculine.

Winterson's treatment of subjectivity in the novel is notably complex since, while ascribing to her characters a degree of agency, she simultaneously represents them, in typically postmodern manner, as subject to historical and psychological forces beyond their control. These include the social upheavals resulting from the Napoleonic Wars and, in terms of internal drives, the imperative of 'passion'. By 'passion' Winterson signifies the subject's obsessive involvement with the Other, the object of desire. Obsessions of this intense kind, she illustrates, override barriers of class and gender, and assume a variety of different manifestations. They can be romantic, as is Henri's love for Villanelle and Villanelle's for the Queen of Spades, the mystery woman whom she encounters while working at the Venice Casino. They can reflect hero worship and be oedipal in nature, as are Henri's feelings for Napoleon, whom he describes as 'a little father' (Winterson 1988:81). They can be motivated by a desire for power, as is the case with Napoleon's ambitions of territorial domination. They can be religious, as is the devotion of Henri's mother for the Virgin Mary.

Passions of such an obsessive nature, Winterson illustrates, are involuntary, irrational and, more often than not, self-destructive. Villanelle's involvement with the Queen of Spades results in her losing her heart literally as well as metaphorically, while Henri's love for Villanelle gives rise to his incarceration in the island edifice of San Servelo. Napoleon's passion for conquest, as well as resulting in an immense loss of human life, eventually brings about his own defeat and death. The intensity of the passion which the individual feels, as is illustrated in numerous episodes, bears little or no relation to the value of the object on which it centres but, like the Lacanian concept of desire, is a projection of the subject's inner needs.

However, despite its destructive effect, passion is nonetheless depicted as life-enhancing since it is capable of transforming the individual's powers of perception and bringing an element of magic to an otherwise drab world. As Henri observes, commenting on the magnetic attraction which Napoleon exerts on himself and his fellow countrymen, the romance which it involves is 'not a contract between equal partners but an explosion of dreams and desires that can find no outlet in every day life. Only a drama will do and while the fireworks last the sky is a different colour' (Winterson 1988:13).

The contradictions inherent in subjectivity and its formation are particularly apparent in the characterisation of Villanelle. Her portrayal represents, in fact, an intriguing combination of the 'lesbian' and 'postmodern', bringing together the polarities of agent and subject. From the moment of her first appearance, she appropriates the role of narrator from Henri – and proceeds to dominate both his life and the action of the novel. However, she, in turn, is dominated by her emotional involvement with the Queen of Spades. Acknowledging the way that this infatuation rules her life, reducing her assertive identity to a state of humble submission, she confesses: ‘Passion is not so much an emotion as a destiny. What choice have I in the face of this wind but to put up sail and rest my oars?’ (Winterson 1988:62).

Winterson’s treatment of sexuality in the novel has generated controversy among critics. Moore argues that Winterson’s representation of lesbianism lacks political resonance since, in her view, it depicts lesbian relations in hetero-patriarchy as in no way ‘problematic’ and fails to engage with the issue of homophobia. I, however, disagree with this reading. The reason for the abrupt termination of Villanelle’s relationship with the Queen of Spades is that the latter, in keeping with the conventions of the era, is married. A particularly moving incident, one which carries sexual-political implications and depicts the position of the lesbian in hetero-patriarchy as ‘problematic’ in the extreme, is the episode in which Villanelle, positioned in the marginal role of outsider and voyeur to which throughout history the lesbian has generally been relegated, gazes through the window of the Queen of Spades’ villa and watches her conversing with her husband in the social and financial security of the family home. He plants a kiss on his wife’s forehead, affirming his ownership of her and signalling the control which he exerts on her life. This episode illustrates the constraints which a phallocentric economy imposes on women, inhibiting relationships between them by curtailing their sexual and social freedom.

Winterson’s indirect allusion, in this episode, to the pressures exerted by codes of compulsory heterosexuality is underpinned by other explicit references.

The oppressive effect which heterosexual conventions and expectations have on women is illustrated on a number of occasions, linking a diverse assortment of female characters who, in other respects, have little in common. Henri recounts how his mother, prevented by her parents from following her religious vocation and entering a convent, is forced to accept the only other option then available to women – marriage. The prostitute whom he encounters in the military brothel is brutally coerced by one of the clients into performing fellatio, while Villanelle is treated as a chattel by her husband who gives her to a friend as the result of a wager. These episodes illustrate that Winterson, far from ignoring the political implications of female sexuality, as Moore suggests, employs postmodern strategies as a vehicle for their analysis.

As is the case in *Moll Cutpurse*, storytelling and the part it plays in the formation of the psyche is a key theme in *The Passion*. The stories the characters tell, though generally employing a familiar setting, often focus on preposterous, larger- than-life events. Villanelle recounts the curious origins of her webbed-feet and describes how she walked on the surface of the Venetian canal, while Henri relates anecdotes about the exceptional powers of vision enjoyed by his comrade Patrick. As in other works of historiographic metafiction, such as Angela Carter's *Nights at the Circus* (1984) and Salman Rushdie's *The Moor's Last Sigh* (1995), the focus on the fantastic is accumulative, and bizarre events increase in number as the narrative progresses. The distinction between history and fiction is blurred not only by the stories the characters tell, and the interplay between fact and fantasy which they reflect, but also by the paradoxical phrase acting as a refrain to them: 'I'm telling you stories. Trust me' (Winterson 1988:5). Repeated at intervals throughout the text, it emits contrary messages to the reader. Our uncertainty about the precise nature of the story increases its fascination by raising the crucial question: 'Is it fact or fiction? Truth or lies?'

Winterson's self-conscious preoccupation with narrative is accentuated by her introduction of intertextual allusions. Her treatment of the heart, a key motif in the novel, re-works the conceits of sixteenth-century poets such as Sir Philip Sidney and John Donne, utilising it to explore lesbian, instead of heterosexual, love relations. Villanelle tells the Queen of Spades, in a manner reminiscent of Donne, 'If you should leave, my heart will turn to water and flood away' (76). When subsequently she loses her heart, the conceit acquires literal significance in the episode in which Henri, at her instigation, breaks into the Queen of Spades' house to retrieve it. He finds it there, just as she had told him he would, concealed behind a rail of clothes. Incidents of magic realism, such as this, occur at moments of particularly intense emotion, illustrating the way that our passions and fantasies have the power to transform the mundane rational world by generating events which defy the laws of nature. Here as elsewhere in the novel, strategies associated with postmodernism are employed by Winterson to explore and represent the complexities of lesbian love.

The Thriller

The popularity which the thriller is currently enjoying with writers of lesbian fiction reflects a variety of different cultural and social factors. In addition to offering the reader the excitement of a crime-mystery and furnishing a vehicle for the representation of lesbian romance, the thriller is a highly flexible genre, capable of responding to and reproducing, with a degree of displacement, changes in the literary and ideological climate. Indicative of this sensitivity of response are the modifications which the lesbian thriller has undergone since its advent in the early 1980s. It has moved from being a form of fiction associated with realism, as exemplified by Catherine V. Forrest's *Amateur City* (1984) and Barbara Wilson's *Murder in the Collective* (1984), to one which, while maintaining the emphasis on female psychology and the focus on the problematic aspects of the lesbian's position in hetero-patriarchal society which characterise these early works, displays features of a postmodern kind. The most significant are an emphasis on the decentred nature of the self and society, a self-conscious utilisation of parody and pastiche, and the interweaving of elements from different genres. Changes have also occurred in the character constituting the hub of the narrative, the lesbian sleuth herself. While continuing to maintain a degree of agency and self-determination, she has shifted from being a figure who dominates the action and imposes order on a disordered world, to one revealing signs of a fractured self who often finds herself subject to forces beyond her control.[3] The latter feature links her to the protagonist of the Gothic novel – and it is no coincidence that examples of the lesbian thriller published in the late 1980s and '90s frequently introduce Gothic conventions and motifs.

Wings's *Divine Victim* (1992) and Schulman's *After Delores* (1988), while differing radically in style and subject-matter, exemplify the tendency of the lesbian thriller to move into postmodern territory, and illustrate a number of the features cited above. Both novels problematise the concept of a unitary self by introducing episodes focusing on role-play and masquerade. In addition, they intersperse the structures of crime-fiction with motifs and conventions appropriated from Gothic. In both the sleuth is by no means a free agent but, like the protagonist of novels treating the theme of spectral visitation, is haunted by figures and events from the past. This introduces a note of contradiction into her characterisation, creating a tension between the roles of agent/subject. While the

3 For discussion of the figure of the female investigator and the modifications which occur in her representation, see Sally Munt, *Murder by the Book? Feminism and the Crime Novel* (1994); and Paulina Palmer, *Contemporary Lesbian Writing: Dreams, Desire, Difference* (1993:70-7).

positioning of her in the role of investigator foregrounds her agency, the portrayal of her as the victim of disturbing memories and spectral occurrences reduces her to the position of subject, portraying her as ruled by psychological and cultural forces.

As is illustrated by her series of crime novels focusing on the adventures of the Boston investigator Emma Victor, which create a lesbian version of the Chandleresque thriller, Wings excels in the art of postmodern parody and pastiche. In *Divine Victim*, however, she lays aside the format of the hard-boiled crime novel and applies her skills of parody to an acclaimed example of Gothic romance: Daphne Du Maurier's *Rebecca* (1938). Though structured on the Gothic theme of 'the return of the repressed',[4] *Rebecca* introduces in the latter stages of the narrative, with the discovery of the Maxim De Winter's murder of his glamorous but morally decadent first wife, strategies of detection and suspense associated with the thriller. The ambiguous response to bourgeois femininity which, as Alison Light illustrates, Du Maurier's novel reflects, combined with the lesbian subtext hinted at in the references to Rebecca's illicit love affairs and in the feelings of passionate devotion which she inspires in her maid Mrs. Danvers, have understandably provoked discussion among feminist critics (Light 1984:7-25). They raise a number of intriguing questions. Is the second Mrs. De Winter, who accompanies Maxim to Manderley as his new wife and performs the role of narrator, sexually attracted to Rebecca or does she merely admire her and envy her beauty and sophistication? What precisely are the 'unspeakable' vices in which Rebecca engages on her surreptitious trips to London? And, as Wings herself asks in an the essay in which she discusses the writing of *Divine Victim* and refers to Du Maurier's own emotionally-fraught lesbian involvements, 'Was Rebecca an inner drama related to Du Maurier

4 See Rosemary Jackson, *Fantasy: The Literature of Subversion* (1981:63-70).

herself? Was killing Rebecca symbolically killing the lesbian impulse?' (Wings 1994:13). By teasing out and developing the lesbian subtext in Du Maurier's novel, Wings contributes to the debate which it has provoked. She also creates a fast-moving Gothic thriller which, set in present-day America, addresses lesbian and queer issues with wit and panache.

In commenting on the writing of *Divine Victim*, Wings enumerates the features of Du Maurier's novel which particularly caught her eye and discusses the way that, in creating 'a twentieth-century Gothic for queers', she transmuted and remodelled them (Wings 1994:13). She explains that, like Du Maurier, she chose to centre her novel on 'a nameless narrator who is additionally a world wanderer' (Wings 1994:31). Du Maurier's heroine, who earns a living by accompanying the rich Mrs Van Hopper on her travels and subsequently becomes Maxim's second wife, is transformed in *Divine Victim* into an untenured academic who travels the globe in search of employment. Like Du Maurier's heroine, her relationship with her present partner is haunted and destabilised by the memory of a female figure from the past. As Wings comments, 'Her new girl friend Marya, like Maxim, is boring. The sex isn't exciting the way it was with Ilona' (Wings 1994:31).

Another character in Du Maurier's novel who, Wings acknowledges, inspired her talent for parody, is Rebecca's devoted handmaid Mrs. Danvers. Danny is transformed in *Divine Victim* into Helen Danroy. Whereas Danny seeks to destroy the second Mrs. Winter because she resents her usurping Rebecca's place, Danroy attempts to kill the narrator in order to protect the reputation of her grandmother, Rebecca Cascia's lover. Developing the hint of lesbianism in Du Maurier's portrayal of Danny, Wings depicts Danroy as a rural dyke whose final appearance in the novel takes the form of a parodic image of lesbian S/M.

Wings's portrayal of Danroy/Danny is certainly imaginative but it is her re-creation of Du Maurier's femme fatale Rebecca which is her real *tour de force* of wit. As Wings observes in commenting on the writing of *Divine Victim*, the description of Rebecca's lingerie in Hitchcock's film of the novel as 'made by the nuns in the convent of St. Clare' inspired her not only to 'create roles for the underwear-producing nuns' but also to 'develop an entire subplot for them and give them a few steamy relationships of their own' (Wings 1994:31-2). The sacred associations of Rebecca (or rather, her underwear!) are developed in the figure of the renegade nun Rebecca Cascia, while the profane are elaborated in the character of Ilona Jorgensen, the narrator's former lover. Rebecca and Ilona both assume, in different ways, the role of 'divine victim'. Rebecca and her sister novices are expected, on taking their vows, 'to become something other, something holy, something divine', whereas Ilona is represented as divinely beautiful and, as emerges in the final pages, is the victim of a murder (Wings 1992:146).

Wings addresses *Divine Victim* to a youthful and intelligent lesbian readership whose members, as well as being familiar with the conventions of Gothic romance, are capable of recognising the allusions to lesbian and queer culture embodied in the numerous squibs of wit she lets fly. Lesbian S/M, the queer Sisters of Perpetual Indulgence who dress as nuns, and the tendency of urban lesbians to patronise and ridicule their country cousins, are some of the queer topics to which she playfully alludes. However, though written primarily for entertainment, the novel also touches on serious issues and, like Du Maurier's *Rebecca*, challenges female stereotypes. Whereas Du Maurier, as Light illustrates, problematises the respectable model of bourgeois femininity by juxtaposing it with the glamorously transgressive image of Rebecca, Wings, in her portrayal of the quarrelsome and promiscuous Ilona, subverts the politically-correct image of the lesbian associated with the 1970s Lesbian Feminist Movement.

Wings's *Divine Victim*, in ingeniously teasing out and developing the lesbian subtext of Du Maurier's *Rebecca*, illustrates the witty manner in which contemporary writers utilise strategies of postmodern parody to treat lesbian themes. Schulman's *After Delores*, in contrast, employs a postmodern focus on the fractured self and the fragmented nature of present-day society to explore the problematic situation of the woman who identifies as lesbian in Western urban culture. Schulman's narrator resembles Wings's in that she is unnamed and is haunted by a memory of a former lover. In other respects, however, her characterisation is wholly different. A member of the casual labour force which services New York City, she works as a waitress in a diner and, as she herself sullenly admits, is marginalised and underprivileged. Distressed by her lover Delores's infidelity, she suffers from bouts of anger and fits of depression. These compel her, as she bleakly puts it, to 'think about sad things' (Schulman 1988:9). As the narrative progresses, she drifts into alcoholism, and experiences increasing difficulty in decoding the fractured world of urban life. Her lack of agency, combined with her emotional outbursts and errors of judgement, are totally at odds with the attributes of perception and self-control which we expect from the figure of the sleuth. Not only is she, like the majority of lesbian investigators, an amateur but she embarks on the search for the murderer of Marianne Walker, the disco dancer whom she nicknames Punkette, by accident rather than design. Her decision to track down Punkette's killer and achieve justice, like her behaviour in general, is motivated by passion rather than reason.

These aspects of the narrator's portrayal, while limiting her abilities as a crime investigator, make her an obvious candidate for an encounter with the uncanny – and the opening lines of the novel portray her in the act of trying to avoid or, at any rate postpone, such an event. As she laconically remarks, as if recording an everyday occurrence, 'I walked out in the snow trying to get away from Delores's ghost. It was sitting back in the apartment waiting for me' (Schulman 1988:1).

The narrator's efforts to elude the uncanny are, however, unsuccessful since, like other Gothic heroines before her, she discovers that, in turning her back on the spectral presence, she is, ironically, moving towards it. On leaving her apartment to escape the ghost of the faithless Delores, she runs headlong into the realm of Gothic experience.[5] Schulman updates and urbanises this realm, making it applicable to the present-day lesbian, and transforming it to accommodate urban locations such as the disco hall, the park and the subway. It takes the form of a labyrinthian world of doubling, encounters between the self and Other, and sexual and theatrical role-play where the familiar is defamiliarised and things turn out to be the reverse of what they initially appear.

The first scene the narrator comes across in her lonely promenade through the wintry streets of New York is a gay fancy-dress party taking place in a local basement. In this visually surreal setting where, as she observes, 'The winter night that had been walls turned into men and women dancing together and by themselves' (1), she meets the larger-than-life character Priscilla Presley. Priscilla's sudden appearance in the surreal arena of the disco hall is, in fact, the first of a series of displacements and substitutions which proliferate throughout the novel, signalling to the reader that the narrator's encounters with the characters she meets, while existing on a realist plane and open to literal interpretation, simultaneously represent a journey of exploration into her own disturbed psyche, forcing her to confront her own personal fears and desires. Another character who plays a similar role in her life is Punkette, the disco

5 For reference to this realm, see William Patrick Day, *In the Circles of Fear and Desire: A Study of Gothic Fantasy* (1985:21-50).

dancer whose murder prompts her to assume the role of sleuth. Punkette is involved in an unhappy love affair and, in referring to her lover Charlotte and Charlotte's partner Beatriz, she introduces yet another set of displacements and substitutions which lead the narrator still deeper into the Gothic world.

Charlotte and Beatriz epitomise for the narrator a sophisticated realm of culture and artifice from which she feels excluded, and she is intrigued by the air of the uncanny which pervades them. They are involved in alternative theatre, and their passion for role-play, reflected in their personal life as well as in their performances on stage, exemplifies a duplicitous, though fascinating, world of illusion and deceit where the distinction between fact and fiction becomes blurred. The propensity for lying and pretence which they display, instead of alienating the narrator, serves, in fact, to bind her more firmly to them. It feeds her craving for emotional scenarios, ones spiced with an element of S/M. As she smugly comments, congratulating herself on the masochistic attachment which she forms with the couple, 'Their lies enabled them to keep a passionate relationship. I was one of them now. I was so evil. I was in love with them' (126).

The narrator's surreal experiences in New York City, with their proliferation of mirror-images and displacements, is accompanied by the introduction of Gothic imagery evoking horror and death. She continues to feel haunted by 'the phantom devil Delores' (80) and, in a fantasy which brings together images of physical violence, the grotesque body and woman as menstrual monster, dreams that she is wearing a white corset which fills with blood. When, in the dream, she sees Delores approaching, she attempts to hide the corset under a chair but fails to conceal it successfully. On waking, she purchases a picture postcard ironically representing the Statue of Liberty and mails it to Delores.

The narrator's increasing immersion in the Gothic world has the effect of severely diminishing her agency, making her vulnerable to forces (passions people, events) over which she has little or no control. Although she succeeds, more by luck than judgement, in avenging the murder of Punkette and achieving a form of justice, this does not give her sense of fulfilment. On the contrary, it leaves her feeling lonely and depressed. It fails to exorcise Delores's ghost or liberate her from her infatuation with her. As she wryly observes in the concluding lines of the novel, alerting attention to the circular trajectory of entrapment which she has traversed since she was first portrayed, on the opening page, leaving her apartment on a snowy winter's night to escape the presence of Delores's ghost, 'None of it meant anything to me. There was only one thing I really missed. I missed Delores' (158).

Paulina PALMER
University of Warwick

Works Cited

Bakhtin, Mikhail. *Rabelais and His World.* Trans. Helene Iswolsky. Bloomington: Indiana University Press, 1984.

Brooks, Peter. *Reading for the Plot: Design and Intention in Narrative*. New York: Random House, 1984.

Butler, Judith. *Gender Trouble: Feminism and the Subversion of Identity.* London: Routledge, 1990.

Connor, Steven. *Postmodernist Culture: An Introduction to Theories of the Contemporary*. Oxford: Blackwell, 1989.

Day, William Patrick. *In the Circles of Fear and Desire: A Study of Gothic Fantasy*. University of Chicago Press, 1985.

Di Stefano, Christine. 'Dilemmas of Difference: Feminism, Modernity, and Postmodernism'. *Feminism/Postmodernism*. Ed. Linda J. Nicholson. New York: Routledge, 1990. 63-82.

Du Maurier, Daphne. *Rebecca*. London: Gollancz, 1938.

Galford, Ellen. *Moll Cutpurse*. Edinburgh: Stramullion, 1984.

Hutcheon, Linda. *The Politics of Postmodernism*. London: Routledge, 1989.

---. *A Poetics of Postmodernism: History, Theory, Fiction*. London: Routledge, 1988.

Jackson, Rosemary. *Fantasy: The Literature of Subversion*. London: Methuen, 1981.

Light, Alison. '"Returning to Manderley" – Romance, Fiction, Female Sexuality and Class'. *Feminist Review* 16 (1984): 7-25.

Moore, Lisa. 'Teledildonics: Virtual Lesbians in the Fiction of Jeanette Winterson'. *Sexy Bodies: The Strange Carnalities of Feminism*. Eds. Elizabeth Grosz and Elspeth Probyn. London: Routledge, 1995. 104-27.

Munt, Sally. *Murder by the Book? Feminism and the Crime Novel*. London: Routledge, 1994.

Palmer, Paulina. *Contemporary Lesbian Writing: Dreams, Desire, Difference*. Buckingham: Open University Press, 1993.

Roof, Judith. 'Lesbians and Lyotard: Legitimation and the Politics of the Name'. *The Lesbian Postmodern*. Ed. Laura Doan. New York: Columbia University Press, 1994. 47-66.

Schulman, Sarah. *After Delores*. London: Sheba Feminist Publishers, 1988.

Wings, Mary. 'Rebecca Redux: Tears on a Lesbian Pillow'. *Daring to Dissent: Lesbian Culture from Margin to Mainstream*. Ed. Liz Gibbs. London: Cassell, 1994: 11-33.

---. *Divine Victim*. London: Women's Press, 1992.

Winterson, Jeanette. (1987). *The Passion*. Harmondsworth: Penguin, 1988.

Wittig, Monique. *The Straight Mind and Other Essays*. Hemel Hempstead: Harvester Wheatsheaf, 1992.

Zimmerman, Bonnie. 'Lesbians Like This and That: Some Notes on Lesbian Criticism for the Nineties'. *New Lesbian Criticism: Literary and Cultural Readings*. Ed. Sally Munt. Hemel Hempstead: Harvester Wheatsheaf, 1992. 1-15.

The Godfather:

Borges and the Ethics of the Labyrinth

Jorge Luis Borges died in 1986. At the end of 1995 his widow announced that fourteen biographies of the twentieth-century grand master of metaphysical fiction were under preparation (Woodall 1996:261). As the centennial of Borges's birth in 1899 approaches, the blind librarian of Buenos Aires looks like becoming the focus of an international carnival of writing of gargantuan proportions. In this, there is no element of reparation for neglect. It is not as if Borges has been left out of the literary limelight. From 1961, when he shared the first Prix Formentor with Samuel Beckett, until his death, Borges remained one of the most feted and interviewed authors on the planet. Or rather, his public persona, 'Borges', about whom he wrote with such wry charm in 'Borges and I' (which is one of the most perspicacious statements about the experience of that ubiquitous twentieth-century phenomenon, not fame but celebrity), ascended innumerable public platforms and gave incessant interviews in North and South America and in Europe in the guise of a gentlemanly old literary buffer – genial, bookish, harmless – ready to reveal practically nothing about himself, with the utmost graciousness. He gloried in inconsistency. Borges enjoyed his celebrity in the way that only the congenitally modest can. He was amused by it and it gave him more in material and experiential terms than he ever asked. Only the Nobel Prize, which he did crave, eluded Borges: Argentina's turn for the award did not arise during his lifetime, and Borges scarcely helped his case with anti-democratic pronouncements in old age, which loomed larger, because more recent, than his repeated denunciations of anti-semitism, Nazism, and dictatorship in the more personally dangerous decades of the 1930s, 1940s and 1950s. Borges never understood the politics of the Nobel Prize, but then, he seems never to have understood politics at all. He despised Hitler, he despised Perón (who lost him his job, kept him under surveillance, and briefly imprisoned his mother and sister): beyond that, he judged politicians by their manners. One might just as well enquire into the detailed politics of the Cheshire Cat.

If the political 'Borges' was simultaneously a mildly-anarchic, aristocratically-minded anachronism and his own worst enemy, the writerly 'Borges' could not be more definitively significant. The publishing consortium which initiated the Prix Formentor in 1961 proved itself absurdly prescient in their choice of Beckett and Borges as the most important contemporary authors on which to focus international attention via the prize. The two cosmopolitan writers belong together. Like Beckett, the young Borges had been soaked in high modernism; like Beckett, too, his work elides the boundaries between philosophy and literature. Like Beckett, the Irish writer, Borges the Argentinean writes in ways which transcend the merely national (both claim the whole of the Western tradition as their own), while retaining elements which proclaim their ex-centric national identities. However, unlike Beckett, whose legacy is everywhere and nowhere, and whose work tends to defy incorporation into others' texts, there is no writer who figures so prominently in the development of postmodern fiction as Borges. The writers who name Borges, whether enthusiastically or reluctantly, as a godfather for their own work provide the nucleus of the international stellar register of literary postmodernism: Angela Carter, Umberto Eco, John Barth, Italo Calvino, Robert Coover, Mario Vargas Llosa,

Gabriel Garcia Marquez, Carlos Fuentes. Critics and theorists, too, feed on Borges's legacy. Foucault invokes Borges in the preface of *The Order of Things*; Derrida calls up Borges in 'Plato's Pharmacy'. Gérard Genette took the title for one of his books from a Borges story, and ascribes part of his method to him (Aizenberg 1990:128-38, 109-21, 107-8). As early as 1971, Tony Tanner identified Borges, along with Nabokov, as the presiding genius of the new American fiction (not then generally called 'postmodernist') leading it onto 'lexical playfields' (Tanner 1971:33-49). Borges was fond of quoting Dr. Johnson's remark that 'no one wants to owe anything to his contemporaries'.[1] In the case of Borges, the accumulated contemporary literary and intellectual debt is not only enormous, but acknowledged to be so. Borges, simply, provides the postmodern intertext.

Borges is read as postmodern before postmodernism, regarded as *the* ur-postmodern author in his attention to paradox, intellection, surface as opposed to psychological depth. His erudition, and his scrupulous willingness to acknowledge sources from all eras of literary and philosophical history (as well as his delight in inventing spurious and sometimes fictional antecedents) slots in perfectly with postmodern debates regarding the instability and yet ubiquity of history, and with its pleasure in the disordered plundering of the costume-box of the past. His anti-realist aesthetics and relish for the fantastic also recommend him to the fabulists of the fantastic who occupy postmodernism's literary mainstream. His intellectual suppleness as a writer who lucidly plays with time and tigers attracts affection. With only Kafka as a rival, he remains the twentieth-century's pre-eminent composer of the philosophical parable. In critical and theoretical terms, recent accounts of Borges's impact on the shaping of postmodern fictional practice tend to concentrate on the metafictional dimensions of his work, on the aspects of Borges's writing

1 See, for example, 'Deutsches Requiem' (Borges 1970:174), and 'The Approach to Al-Mu'tasim' (Borges 1991:40).

which open sympathetically to narratives of poststructuralist theory and to concentration on the reflexivity and self-referentiality of language and texts (Molloy 1994; Bloom 1986; Aizenberg 1990). There is something very curious (and faintly amusing) in watching the reception of Borges's work being tailored according to these currently fashionable intellectual norms. No one understood this historically-driven process of the formation of what is noticed in reading better than Borges himself who wrote frequently about the book as not so much an object or 'series of verbal structures', not as 'an isolated being', but rather 'a relationship, and axis of innumerable possibilities' which calls up a 'dialogue' with readers which is 'infinite' because this dialogue takes place in time which always generates new ways of reading (Borges 1970:248, 129). The reading of texts is, for Borges, a perfect example of both persistence and change. The text does not change, but reading always does. And like Gertrude Stein (and Heraclitus), Borges insisted both on the inevitability of repetition and its impossibility. And, as his narrator/reader illustrates in 'Pierre Menard, Author of the *Quixote*', as he judges the twentieth-century replication of *Don Quixote* richer than the sixteenth-century original, Borges understood well how the obsessions of one era condition the terms of individuals' dialogues with the artifacts to which they attend.

The current readerly dialogue with his writing which features the postmodern 'Borges' relegates many other possible 'Borgeses' to the sidelines. In this essay, I want to look at one of these excluded facets of Borges's work and concentrate on its ethical tendencies.[2] This is scarcely an accidental or untimely project. One of the most troubling aspects of postmodernist thought is its inability to defend itself convincingly against charges of philosophical nihilism, or of the evaporation of agency and choice into linguistic effects, or, indeed, the similar disintegration of the

2 This is, for example, in direct contrast with Paul de Man, who argued in 1964 that Borges should be read not as a moralist, but as an aesthete. See 'A Modern Master' (reprinted in Bloom 1986:21-2).

concepts of justice and mercy, good and evil. Borges, the godfather of literary postmodernism, is very far from occupying this position. Abhorring the ethics of the line which leads to the power-mania of Nietzsche's Zarathustra and to Heidegger's version of existentialism, which he saw as 'immoral' in its flattering of human vanity by positing an illusory, heroic ego in secret (and self-aggrandising) dialogue with the void (Borges 1970:251), Borges locates himself in quite another ethical genealogy. As a man of the book, who noted that the chief event in his life was his father's library (Borges 1971:140), Borges's most significant ethics are those which deal with writing and its uses. His are the ethics of intellection, and of its writerly signs, so disturbingly at issue in the postmodernist debate. Borges's ethics are the ethics of the book.

Precisely how Borges should be read on this matter is indicated, to a certain extent, by the philosophical and literary lineage he constructs for himself. Famously, following T. S. Eliot, Borges noted 'that every writer *creates* his own precursors', modifying the earlier authors' reception in the light of the selected traces of their practice which reappear in their descendants' work, and thereby modifying the interpretation of the past (Borges 1970:236). Borges himself constantly invokes the names of his selected (and eclectically assorted) literary precursors: Kipling, Dante, Stevenson, Kafka, Shaw, Wells, Cervantes, James, Whitman, Poe, Sir Thomas Browne, Heine, Blake, Conrad, Browning, Hawthorne, De Quincey, Carroll, Emerson, Twain, Chesterton, Shakespeare. Borges translated Virginia Woolf, Melville, Faulkner, Henry James and Kafka. Among the philosophers, the recurrent names are those of the idealists: Plato, Berkeley, Leibniz, Bradley, along with Hume and Schopenhauer. His favourite, Swedenborg, must be ranked with the often anonymous mystics Borges found so interesting. Borges claims all mythographers, from the Greek to the Chinese, the Norse to those of Chile, as his own. More than any other text, he declares his affinity with the *1001 Nights*. He adored the

Encyclopedia Britannica. His is the lineage of the intersection of the intellect and the dream, of the storyteller whose tales beguile time and support life. This is, in itself, an ethical commitment of sorts. As one of Borges's shrewdest recent commentators, Sylvia Molloy, puts it, Borges enacts in his writing an ethics of the text, by which he maintains 'the honest conduct and conveyance of a text, seemingly deceitful yet aware of its deceptions, admitting to its inevitable traps, confessing to the creation of simulacra it does nothing to conceal'. In this sense, and it is an important one, Molloy argues that Borges provides 'a constant and honest disquisition on writing, his own writing, the writing of others' (Molloy 1994:4). This strikes me as importantly true, and especially valuable in the light of postmodernism's tendency to a certain dishonesty regarding its own textual games. But Borges's interest in terms of ethics goes beyond the characteristic textual honesty Molloy so rightly identifies. And he is perhaps at his most ethically compelling in his commentary on the Bible and its interpreters, its devotees and its renegades. Borrowing from the Talmud or the Kabbalah, or contemplating the possibilities of Christian heresies, are classic Borgesian strategies which he uses to explore the logical twists in human ideas of redemption and the good. A man of no religious affiliation, Borges nevertheless found the Jewish tradition of meditation on ethics the most profound and meaningful. And one strand of this elective filiation seems to me to be of particular importance for postmodernism as a facet of Borges's practice, one that stands in direct contradistinction to the neo-Heideggerian line.

Of the precursors who figured significantly in terms of ethics to Borges, Baruch Spinoza is perhaps the most important, and it is Spinoza as a tutelary figure for Borges that I want to examine here. Throughout his work, and especially in his late fiction, Borges frequently invokes Spinoza. For example, in the collection *Doctor Brodie's Report*, the young medical student in 'The Gospel According to Mark' who attempts to explain Christ's sacrifice to the utterly ignorant family of ranch hands he befriends and who crucify him in imperfect imitation of his teachings is given the name of 'Espinosa'. In 'The Unworthy Friend', in the same late collection of stories, a man, trying to expiate an act of betrayal, has among his projects the compilation of an anthology of Spinoza's writing. Spinoza is cited in 'Tlön, Uqbar, Orbis Tertius' as attributing to 'the inexhaustibly divine in man the qualities of extension and of thinking' (Borges 1991:24), and in the essay, 'The Wall and the Books' for his famous pronouncement that 'all things long to persist in their being' (Borges 1970:222). In 'Death and the Compass', Spinoza is used as the cipher by the murderer of Jews who decoys Borges's detective to his death. Borges wrote a poem on Spinoza. But his fullest commentary on this particular precursor comes in a lecture on Spinoza which Borges delivered at the Argentine-Israeli Institute for Cultural and Scientific Exchange in Buenos Aires in the 1960s. The Spinoza lecture was one of two: the other took *The Book of Job* as its subject. In his 'Autobiographical Essay' Borges remarked that his interest in Jewish culture 'as an integral element of our so-called Western civilization' (Borges 1971:183) went back to his early days as an adolescent in Geneva during the First World War. His life-long hatred of anti-semitism was augmented by his enthusiastic support for Israel. In an interview at Columbia in 1980 he declared his affinity most forcefully, saying 'I have done my best to be a Jew' (Barnstone 1982:75), pointing to the possible Jewishness of some of his ancestors, and defining Western culture, like Matthew Arnold, as, in essence, a mixture of Greek and Jewish thought.

By turning to Spinoza for the subject of his lecture, Borges speaks to this richly mixed ethical and intellectual inheritance. In his essay 'The Argentine Writer and Tradition', he declares that nationalist anxiety about the proper field of the Argentine writer constitutes a 'pseudo problem' (Borges 1970:211). Citing Thorstein Veblen on the 'pre-eminence of Jews in Western culture', pointing to the fine achievements of the Irish within English culture, and saying that the Argentine writer's is an analogous case, he forcefully argues that, not only is their tradition 'all of Western culture', to which they have a claim greater than writers more mired in stronger and therefore more limiting national cultures, and that this advantage is conferred because they are both within and slightly apart from the culture within which they work. He broadens his claim to include all of South America: 'we can handle all European themes, handle them without superstition, with an irreverence which can have, and already does have, fortunate consequences'. The culture on the margins, he notes, is likely to generate the innovation on which all cultural life depends (Borges 1970:218).

Just as Borges, who spent his childhood in Argentina and his youth in Europe, who grew up speaking both English and Spanish, and who claimed all of world literature as his own, was an embodiment of the multiplicity of cultural allegiances which he thought so important for excellence, so Spinoza was, famously, a man of the margins (Collinson 1987:61-4; Blackburn 1994:359-61; Russell 1961:552-62). The seventeenth-century philosopher was born in Amsterdam to a Jewish family who had fled from Lisbon to the relative tolerance of the Netherlands in the face of the Spanish Inquisition. Trained both in Jewish and in Islamic theology, Spinoza's enthusiastic acceptance of Descartes' philosophy moved him away from Judaism. Declared a heretic, he was excommunicated from the Jewish community and anathematised. Most of his subsequent friendships were with Protestants. The civil authorities were persuaded to banish him from Amsterdam, and there seem to have been attempts on his life. Later, living very simply in the Hague, following his trade of lens-polishing, Spinoza was attacked as a spy and almost killed by a mob after undertaking a minor peace mission to the French army. He died young, in his early forties, of a lung disease probably brought on by his craft. Spinoza is one of the great philosophers of tolerance and liberty. Accounts of the man stress his personal sweetness of temperament, his extraordinary virtue and simplicity. He was one of the last philosophers to write in Latin, the universal language of medieval Europe, yet couched his *Ethics* in a geometric form which borrowed from the modern universal language of mathematics. A stoic of sorts and a humanist Spinoza straddled many lines. He stands between the medieval and the modern; is informed by Jewish, Arab, and Christian cultures; looks back to the legacy of a metaphysics of the divine, while looking forward to the modern rationalist and scientific methods which were then in formation. His *Ethics* (Spinoza 1951) are an attempt to reconcile reason and nature within a notion of divinity which is all-inclusive, and which can only be apprehended within eternity. For Spinoza all substance was one and that substance was God. He emphasised logic and materiality equally. Like Borges, Spinoza was a man on the cusp.

Borges begins his lecture on Spinoza by citing Bertrand Russell's comment 'that of all the great philosophers the most lovable is Baruch Spinoza' (Alzenberg 1990:276), a sentiment with which he declares himself in full agreement. It is, I think, useful to reproduce Russell's opening remarks on Spinoza in the *History of Western Philosophy*, which drew such assent from Borges. Russell writes:

> Spinoza (1632-77) is the noblest and most lovable of the great philosophers. Intellectually, some others have surpassed him, but ethically he is supreme. As a natural consequence, he was considered, during his lifetime and for a century after his death, a man of appalling wickedness. He was born a Jew, but the Jews excommunicated him. Christians abhorred him equally; although his whole philosophy is dominated by the idea of God, the orthodox accused him of atheism. Leibniz, who owed much to him, concealed his debt, and carefully abstained from saying a word in his praise; he even went so far as to lie about the extent of his personal acquaintance with the heretic Jew.
>
> (Russell 1961:552)

Borges, with his metaphysics of time (as he writes succinctly in 'A New Refutation of Time', 'Time is the substance I am made of' [Borges 1970:269]), could not be expected to align himself with Spinoza's metaphysics of substance, and he announces his scepticism regarding Spinoza's ontological views and his system early in his lecture. But he also declares his admiration for the Dutch philosopher as well, praising his 'near saintliness' while noting the discordance of Spinoza's exemplary life with the monstrous inhumanity, indeed, the near divinity, of his philosophy and his philosophical system. Borges relished the curious circumstance that 'in Spinoza, love, sober, laconic, modest love is never far away', a fact that assorts oddly with, but nevertheless informs all 'the theorems, definitions, axioms, postulates, and corollaries of his *Ethics*' (Aizenberg 1990:277). Spinoza presents an example of an archetypally Borgesian figure: the warmly humane man seduced by and then caught up in the inexorability and inevitability of a mathematical process which may be (and probably is) his own invention.

After noting Spinoza's debt to Descartes and to the Kabbalah, Borges praises his work as lens-grinder, as well as the Jewish tradition that the writer should not earn his living from his writing, which is judged, not in terms of professional success in the present, but against the writing of all time. Borges stresses the love that Spinoza attracted, the 'bliss' in which he lived his life. He explains this in terms of the great pleasure in the pursuit of the life of the mind: 'for there is no greater joy', Borges notes, 'than the exercise of one's intelligence' (Aizenberg 1990:278). But Borges's curiosity persists with regard to Spinoza's strange choice of a geometrical method as the system best suited to the exposition of his ethical philosophy.

Noting Russell's explanation that 'mathematics is a vast tautology', which is intuited as universally true rather than dependent on experience for its proof, Borges links Spinoza's adoption of a mathematical method with his suspicion of the vulnerability of empirical observation. And because he believed in the logical nature of the universe, mathematics recommended itself to him as the vehicle for its exposition (there is also, adds Borges, the example of Descartes, and perhaps of the Kabbalah, with its obsession with the divine properties of number, to take into account as sources for this unlikely system). Further, Spinoza, like Descartes, wanted to ground his philosophy on the simplest of first principles, and, for him, this meant starting with definitions. He takes his initial first principle from the classic theological argument that God is an infinite substance and moves on to state that humans have knowledge of two of the 'infinite modes of the divinity: thought and extension', which Borges equates with space and time, both of which are parts of the mind of God, 'attributes of God, *parts* of God' (Aizenberg 1990:281). This is an ancient idea, he notes, found equally among the Greeks and the Hindus.

But it is at this point, argues Borges, that what is 'marvelous' and 'new' in Spinoza's philosophy comes into operation. This is the idea that, in addition to God being everything, God includes all of time and all of space, as well as existing in infinite numbers of ways which go beyond human imagination. Thus God includes consciousness and imagination, dreams and memories as well as events, in addition to material things. Locked within our own attributes of time and space, humans nevertheless, says Borges, 'are an infinitesimal part of the infinite divinity. This is, without a doubt, an invention or discovery of Baruch Spinoza' (Aizenberg 1990:282). The divine, to humans, is, and always will be, inconceivable, but even our limitations form part of an infinite divinity which we can never comprehend.

Nature and God, says Borges, are coextensive for Spinoza, although nature is simply one of God's attributes. He goes on to point out that Spinoza insists that humans must love God with an 'intellectual love', which consists of love for the order of the universe. Borges notes Spinoza's famous statement that humans must love God with no hope of being loved in return, a position which follows logically from the serene order of Spinoza's concept of divinity. Humans, as well, must cultivate serenity, tranquillity, and free themselves equally from hope and from fear, which erroneously orient humans toward futurity, while only eternity is real. Borges, the poet of time, finds this idea 'very strange' (Aizenberg 1990:283), but finds

Spinoza's resultant quiet and profound optimism extremely attractive. For Spinoza, rather than philosophy being a meditation on death, it is a calmly joyful meditation on life. For Spinoza, explains Borges, evil 'doesn't exist because it is a negative'. While everything is predestined, we can only act as if we are free, because our sense of being demands that we believe this, and everything wants to persist in its being. Borges ends his exposition of Spinoza's philosophy by calling attention to the inconclusiveness of his own remarks on the philosopher who he invokes as an incantatory precursor in his stories.

Much of Spinoza's metaphysics clearly leaves Borges bemused. But he finds the man utterly sympathetic and relishes his dedication to the intellectual life which overshadowed all Spinoza's other loyalties. In describing his own father, Borges noted that he 'was very intelligent, and, like all intelligent men, very kind' (Borges 1971:138). What he admires in the ethics of Spinoza is just this pairing of intelligence and kindness, its audacity, its tolerance, and its cultivation of serenity and joy. As Edna Aizenberg, who translated Borges's lecture on Spinoza into English, remarks, 'it is precisely the ingenuity of Spinoza's system, the "powerful imagination" at work behind the "deliberate aridity of the philosopher"', which constructs 'an imaginary being – an infinite substance called God' (Aizenberg 1990:265) which is so attractive to Borges. For Borges, says Aizenberg, Spinoza is one of the mythmakers, who himself becomes a 'substance' and an archetype to be called up throughout Borges's oeuvre, one which stands for the encroachment of the dizzying logic of the universe into Borges's stories, a logic beyond human understanding which defies all human notions of reason (Aizenberg 1990:265). For both Spinoza and Borges, the universe is, finally, inconceivable, and both utilise logic and mathematical games to lead beyond that which can be expressed logically.

But the shared penchant for unusual deployment of logic and of mathematical forms is only one facet of Borges's long felt affinity with Spinoza. More profound, I think, is the similar ethical orientation, which pulls together intellect and kindness, modesty and courage, stoicism and tolerance as the highest values in a finally impersonal universe in the view both of the Dutch philosopher and of the Argentine fabulist. And, while it is probably Schopenhauer for whom Borges has the deepest philosophical respect, it is with Spinoza that his most important ethical affinities lie, in his scepticism regarding the ego, in his consequent rejection of romanticism, and in his constant underlining of the limits of human understanding. In an interview with his English translator, Norman Thomas di Giovanni, at New York University in 1971, Borges was asked if God played a part in the mystic themes of his stories. His answer is telling:

> 'Well, if you, Sir, are thinking of a personal God, the answer is decidedly no. If you think of God as an ethical purpose, as an intellectual purpose, as what Matthew Arnold called "the something not ourselves that makes for righteousness", in that case I believe in God. Perhaps there is a moral purpose or intellectual purpose to the universe; however, I know nothing about that. I know I am attempting in my own tiny way to further that purpose by writing quite unimportant short stories'.
>
> (Newman 1972:402)

Asked about the basis of his ethics in 1980, Borges notes, with great simplicity: 'at every moment of our lives we have to choose. We have to act one way or another. As Dr. Johnson had it, we are moralists all the time . . .' (Barnstone 1982:103). For Borges, the only justice is private justice, the justice that accompanies our constant judgement of our every action. As he explained in another interview in 1976:

> 'At the very moment of our lives we know whether we're acting the right way or the wrong way. We might say that doomsday is going on all the time, that every moment of our lives we're acting wrongly or rightly. Doomsday is not something that comes at the end. It's going on all the time. And we know, through some instinct, when we have acted rightly or wrongly'.
>
> (Barnstone 1982:19)

For Borges, ethics is an instinct which we recognise but cannot comprehend. We are back to the humility before the absolute which lies at the heart of the complexity of Spinoza's extraordinary system, and which lies, as well, at the heart of the literary complexities which are now called Borgesian. As Angela Carter said at the end of her lecture on Borges in 1989, 'The library may be a maze, a trap with a Minotaur at the centre; the Aleph might turn out to be, at last, a false Aleph. But, alas, that's all we have – our systems. Our systems are what keep us human'. Borges's stories, she argues, are tales of 'how we know what we know and even of what we think we know' (Thomas di Giovanni 1995:46, 47). And in the honesty of his investigation of the systems which may be called human and of the need to pull together the sometimes alien virtues of kindness and intelligence one can discern in Borges's work the ethics of the labyrinth, an ethics which feeds directly into the production of postmodern fiction and which is its godfather's most profound legacy.

Kate FULLBROOK
University of the West of England

Works Cited

Aizenberg, Edna. *Borges and His Successors: The Borgesian Impact on Literature and the Arts*. London: University of Missouri Press, 1990.

Barnstone, Willis, ed. *Borges at Eighty*. Bloomington, Indiana: Indiana University Press, 1982.

Blackburn, Simon. *The Oxford Dictionary of Philosophy*. Oxford: Oxford University Press, 1994.

Bloom, Harold, ed. *Jorge Luis Borges*. New York: Chelsea House Publishers, 1986.

Borges, Jorge Luis. *Fictions*. Ed. Anthony Kerrigan. London: Calder, 1991

—. *Doctor Brodie's Report*. Trans. Norman Thomas di Giovanni. Harmondsworth, Middlesex: Penguin, 1976.

—. *The Aleph and Other Stories, 1933-1969*. Ed. and trans. Norman Thomas di Giovanni. New York: Bantam, 1971.

—. *Labyrinths: Selected Stories and Other Writings*. Eds. Donald A. Yates and James E. Irby. Harmondsworth, Middlesex: Penguin, 1970.

Collinson, Diané. *Fifty Major Philosophers*. London: Routledge, 1988.

Molloy, Sylvia. *Signs of Borges*. Trans. Oscar Montero. London: Duke University Press, 1994.

Newman, Charles and Mary Kinzie, eds. *Prose for Borges*. Evanston, Illinois: Northwestern University Press, 1972.

Russell, Bertrand. *History of Western Philosophy*. London: Allen & Unwin, 1961.

Spinoza, Benedict de. *The Chief Works of Benedict de Spinoza*. Vol. II. Trans. R. H. M. Elwes. New York: Dover Publications, 1951.

Tanner, Tony. *City of Words: American Fiction 1950-1970*. London: Jonathan Cape, 1971.

Thomas di Giovanni, Norman, ed. *The Borges Tradition*. London: Constable, 1995.

Woodall, James. *The Man in the Mirror of the Book: A Life of Jorge Luis Borges*. London: Hodder & Stoughton, 1996.

From Elitist Modernism to Populist Postmodernism?

> La letteratura deve essere nello stesso tempo elemento attuale di civiltà e opera d'arte, altrimenti alla letteratura d'arte viene preferita la letteratura d'appendice che, a suo modo, è un elemento attuale di cultura, di una cultura degradata quanto si vuole ma sentita vivamente.[1]
>
> A. Gramsci, *Quaderni del carcere*

The Two Aesthetics

According to Andreas Huyssen (1993), the Great Divide between 'high' and 'low' literature can be traced back to ancient literature. There, among aristocratic society, the seriousness of tragedy and epic was intended for 'high' social topics (politics, heroic deeds, courtly love) and the humour of comedy for the representation of bourgeois and peasant daily life; Auerbach *docet.* However, since the beginning of the modern age, which corresponded to the rise of the middle-classes, such class-biased criterion has fallen into disuse. Boileau's

1 'Literature must be, at the same time, an up-to-date document of civilisation and a work of art. Otherwise, "serialised" literature will be preferred to "literary" fiction, because it is a contemporary element of culture: a debased culture but deeply felt' (Antonio Gramsci, *Prison Notebooks*).

precepts and the rigorous classicist categories were no longer the models with which to distinguish 'high' literature from 'low'. The *Ancien régime*'s literary apparatus began to waver along with the socio-political one, firstly with the Romantics and then with Baudelaire, until it was replaced by the cult of the *nouveau*. Subsequently, the criterion of literary evaluation was no longer class-biased, but, so to speak, historicist: no more 'high' *versus* 'low' but 'old' *versus* 'new'. The rise of the bourgeoisie, with its utilitarian way of life, signed the beginning of an art that had to compete and survive in a market-oriented social system: a social system no longer based on the cult of the Past and Beauty, but on the cult of the present and business. It was an art of the new which, up to Edgar Allan Poe at least – possibly the first important writer totally exposed to the pervasive capitalist social web – had been able both to gratify the growing mass of readers, more and more alienated by the uniformity of everyday work, and to fulfil the needs of art *per sé*. The novel, in fact, as Stuart Hall and Paddy Whannel point out, emerged both in its popular and its high forms: 'Its themes are common both to the outstanding novelists – Defoe, Richardson and Fielding – and to the more popular novelists. . . . For nearly a century and a half the line between the popular and the serious in the novel is almost impossible to draw' (Hall and Whannel 1964:84). After Poe, indeed, things change. Either novelty is apparent and shocking only at the surface level, and therefore easily consumed by the mass of the reading public, or it is 'real' and deeply shocking, difficult to understand and thus less likely to be appropriated by the machinery of commerce. Poe, then, who might be considered the father both of Baudelaire and Conan Doyle, might also be seen as the last representative of that stage of modernity in which the newly-born mass culture and the progressive *intelligentsia* of the middle-classes set themselves the same task. Ever after, one is either an avantgardist or a mass novelist: either Baudelaire or Conan Doyle.

It is important to recall here the idea of the 'two conflicting modernities' of Calinescu, who says: 'at some point during the first half of the nineteenth century an irreversible split occurred between modernity as a stage in the history of civilisation – a product . . . of the sweeping economic and social changes brought about by capitalism – and modernity as an aesthetic concept' (Calinescu 1987:41). The same irreversible split occurred between literary modernity as mass culture, which obligingly yielded to the art-as-commodity, that is, to the first of Calinescu's modernity, and literary modernity as elite culture (Calinescu's aesthetic modernity), which furiously tried to resist commodification.

The first symptom of the rising contradiction between the *base* of the new society and its *superstructure* – the rising elite's first cry of danger – was Wordsworth's preface to *Lyrical Ballads* (1800). There the poet anxiously denounces that 'a multitude of causes, unknown to former times, are now acting with a combined force to blunt the discriminating powers of the mind . . . to reduce it to a state of almost savage torpor'. One of these causes is 'the increasing accumulation of men in cities, where the uniformity of their occupations produces a craving for extraordinary incident which the rapid communication of intelligence hourly gratifies', that is, the first forms of mass culture (1961:735). However, it is with Baudelaire and Sue that the Great Divide between 'high' art and mass art is evident. Since the mid-nineteenth century, when the 1848 revolution failed and the bourgeoisie showed its counter-revolutionary face, when capitalism wholly consolidated its system and cleared the way for the commodification of culture, a sort of silent division of artistic labour took place: on the one hand, those who tried to oppose aesthetic modernity both to tradition and to practical bourgeois modernity (Baudelaire's *maudit* cult of transitoriness, of the 'infinite new', of pointless *flânerie*), and on the other hand, those who upheld the commodification process by writing sensationalist stuff (Sue's fostering of social redemption fantasies through opiate *feuilletons*). Of course, these divisions are not quite so schematic. As Andreas Huyssen points out:

> the salient fact is that with the universalization of commodity production mass culture begins to cut across classes in heretofore unknown ways. Many of its forms attract cross-class audiences, others remain class-bound. Traditional popular culture enters into a fierce struggle with commodified culture producing a variety of hybrid forms.
>
> (Huyssen 1993:18)

Nevertheless, the core of the matter is that the mid-nineteenth century witnesses the rise of that aesthetic *coupure* which, during the twentieth century, will be variously called 'high' literature/'low' literature, elite literature/mass literature, *Kunstliteratur/Trivialliteratur*, literature/paraliterature, and which reaches an unthinkable depth with modernism. But more: 'modernism constituted itself through a conscious strategy of exclusion, an anxiety of contamination by its other: an increasingly consuming and engulfing mass culture' (Huyssen 1993:vii). Consequently, 'paraliterature occupies the space outside the literary enclosure, as a forbidden, taboo, and perhaps degraded product – held at bay, and yet rich in themes and obsessions which are repressed in high culture' (Marc Angenot, cited in Parrinder 1980:46). Finally, their mutual exclusiveness could be the sign of their secret interdependence: on the one hand, mass culture as 'the family ghost rambling in the cellar' (Huyssen 1993:16), on the other hand, modernism as 'the strawman desperately needed by the system to provide an aura of popular legitimisation for the blessing of the culture industry' (Huyssen 1993:17).

The Negative Aesthetics of Modernism *versus* the Positive Aesthetics of Postmodernism

As early as the last decades of the nineteenth century, a radical change occurred in the reading public. As George Bernard Shaw explained: 'the Education Act of 1871 was producing readers who had never before bought books, nor could have read them if they had' (cited in Carey 1990:34). In other words, Shaw witnessed the increasing standardisation of culture in modernity at a time when a huge literate public came into being, bringing about deep changes in literary production and consumption. As Shaw himself realised, adventure stories like Stevenson's *Treasure Island* were liked better than his 'excessively literary' works. But Shaw, unlike most of his contemporary colleagues, as John Carey stresses, 'made the conscious decision to write for the millions [... and] by the end of the 1880s he had made himself, as Max Beerbohm acknowledged, "the most brilliant and remarkable journalist in London"' (Carey 1990:34). Therefore, a gulf was opening up between writers and readers of the popular *Strand Magazine* and *Daily Mail*, and writers and readers of T. S. Eliot's cultural periodical *Criterion*, which used to have a print-run of 800. Even the father of modern science fiction, H. G. Wells, who was not, after all, a Conan Doyle, was included by Henry James in 'a bundle with a company of young men of questionable quality' (cited in Zabel 1979:480). Wells' reply was sharp, claiming that 'the only living human motives left in the novels of Henry James are a certain avidity and an entirely superficial curiosity' (Zabel 1979:479). 'There is of course a real and very fundamental difference in our innate and developed attitude towards life and literature. To you literature like painting is an end, to me literature like architecture is a means, it has a use' (482).

But it is Woolf's famous claims in 'Modern Fiction' (1919, 1925) which are the clear emblem of modernist elitist poetics and of a proud distancing from Wells-like art:

> Our quarrel, then, is not with the classics, [... but] with Mr Wells, Mr Bennett, and Mr Galsworthy [... who] have excited so many hopes and disappointed them so persistently that our gratitude largely takes the form of thanking them for having shown us what they might have done but have not done; what we certainly could not do, but as certainly, perhaps, do not wish to do. . . . If we tried to formulate our meaning in one word we should say that these three writers are materialists. It is because they are concerned not with the spirit but with the body that they have disappointed, and left us with the feeling that *the sooner English fiction turns its back upon them, as politely as may be, and marches, if only into the desert, the better for its soul. . . . He* [Wells] *is materialist from sheer goodness of heart, taking upon his shoulder the work that ought to have been discharged by Government officials* . . . (Woolf 1984:147-8, emphasis added)

Actually, by that time 'high' English fiction had already turned its back upon Wells-like fiction and was set to enter the modernist 'waste land' of the 1920s.

Modernism, to resist the market place, that is to say, to avoid the reduction to commodity status, actually 'marched into the desert': warping its forms and bracketing off the real historical world, while struggling for meaning, it strove to create a negative distance between itself and the world of mass-readers in order to prevent its being instantly consumable. But, ironically enough, as Terry Eagleton brilliantly points out, the modernist work escapes from one form of commodification to fall prey to another, in that:

> if it avoids the humiliation of becoming an abstract, serialized, instantly exchangeable thing, it does so only by virtue of reproducing that other side of the commodity which is its fetishism. The autonomous, self-regarding, impenetrable modernist artefact, in all its isolated splendour, is the commodity as fetish resisting the commodity as exchange, its solution to reification part of that very problem.
>
> (Eagleton 1985:67)

In short, modernism, in its dominant form, as the term itself clearly states, represents the ideological climax of the historicist poetics which have dominated modernity. With modernism and its diegetic refusal, its opaque texture, the 'cult of the new' reaches its peak, by reaching, at the same time, the furthest distance from the 'cult of the same', that is to say, from the family ghost's cellar.

Most of the debate on postmodernism since the 1980s has been dedicated to the highly vexed continuity/discontinuity issue. Of course, the question is so controversial because historicising the present is too ambitious a project. Nevertheless, there are some secure points from which to start: firstly, we are still in the capitalist system, where the commodification process is increasingly pervasive and the commodification of art ends up as the aestheticisation of commodity (aesthetics as commodity and commodity as aesthetics); secondly, there has been a prodigious broadening of the literate public since the postwar period; thirdly we are witnesses to a reaction against the negative aesthetics of modernism, through the adoption of that which it repressed: mass culture, popular genres, narrativity.

As early as 1965, during a conference on 'the experimental novel' in Palermo, the avantgardist *Gruppo 63* realised that, with the new Robbe-Grillet (the passage from the *nouveau roman* to the *nouveau nouveau roman*) and with authors like Pynchon and Barth, the plot was no longer forbidden to the experimentalist. Furthermore, they realised that 'l'avanguardia stava diventando tradizione. . . . L'inaccettabilità del messaggio non era più criterio principe per una narrativa (e per qualsiasi arte) sperimentale, visto che l'inaccettabile era ormai codificato come piacevole' (Eco 1988:527).[2] The exhaustion of the avantgarde, then, can be linked with the return of the plot, of narrativity, the most

2 'the avant-garde was becoming the traditional . . . the unacceptable message was no more the prime criterion for an experimental fiction (or whatever art), since it was by then codified as acceptable'.

exchangeable items on the literary market. Roughly, if modernism is allied to *ethos* (search for meaning), postmodernism is allied to *mythos* (search for action, if for different action). In America the key year was 1967, when John Barth announced the 'exhaustion of literature' or, rather, 'the usedupness of certain forms or exhaustion of certain possibilities' (Barth 1975:19). The example was Borges, but, as he made clear some years later, he meant the exhaustion of the aesthetics of high modernism, which by that time had completed its programme, clearing the way for the 'replenishment of literature', that is, for the birth of the anti-aristocratic literature of postmodernism: 'a fiction more democratic in its appeal than such late-modernist marvels' as Beckett's or Nabokov's novels (Barth 1980:70). His counter-examples were Calvino's science-fiction-like *Cosmicomics* (1965) and García Márquez's *One Hundred Years of Solitude* (1967): two works which conflate fantasy and reality, straightforwardness and artifice, finally, 'high' and 'low'. In short, they would seem to apply Fiedler's slogan 'Cross the border, fill the gap' (Fiedler 1971), through the cross-pollination of premodernist writing and experimental writing, popular genres and sophisticated fiction.

What postmodernism seems to do is to accept (how mindlessly is the question!) the reality of commodification: ultimately, if in the capitalist society a work of art is a commodity, then, there is no way out of it: aesthetic autonomy is just an illusion. It is not autonomy but isolation. Therefore, following Eagleton's argument, the modernist reification of art as an isolated fetish (commodity as fetish) is supplanted with the postmodernist reification of art as mechanically reproducible exchange (commodity as exchange), in so far as 'only that which is already a commodity can resist commodification' (Eagleton 1985:68). Hereupon, the slogan of the postmodernist positive aesthetics might be the Brechtian one of 'starting from the bad new things, rather than from the good old ones', provided that this means: only by intruding upon the present industrialised and standardised society can one can have a say against it. Unfortunately, it is not that simple. But before approaching this complexity, before entering the textual core of our discourse on the resumption and dissolution of popular genres and on the high/low osmotic process in general, let us have a closer look at the structure and the meaning of this aesthetic strategy.

Mass Literature: the Literature of 'Newness' and 'Infinite Sameness'

To Tzvetan Todorov, the main feature of mass literature, in particular of detective fiction, lies in its strict respect of genre rules: 'faire "mieux" qu'elles ne le demandent, c'est en même temps faire moins bien . . . qui veut "embellir" le roman policier, fait de la "littérature", non du roman policier"[3] (Todorov 1977:56). In short, mass literary works belong to that happy realm where there is no contradiction between the work and its genre; a confrontation which, for Todorov, is the engine of great literature. Now, by taking this structural-historicist model of the *écart* from the norm, of innovation, into account, let us see what it tells us when applied to a postmodernist work which integrates popular genres and 'high' aesthetics. The first thing to note is that the dialectical action Todorov talks about does not take place between the work and its own genre, but between itself and an aesthetic foreign genre, that is to say, between two aesthetic cores which have historically been poles apart. If it is so then we cannot help registering a novelty, surely a novelty concerning our century. In fact, if it is true, in a way, that high modernist works, as Jameson observes, had to do with popular culture and art, postmodernist works 'no longer "quote" such

3 'doing better than they demand, it is at the same time doing worse . . . those who want to embellish detective fiction, make "literature", not detective fiction'.

"texts" as a Joyce might have done, or a Mahler; they incorporate them, to the point where the line between high art and commercial forms seems increasingly difficult to draw' (Jameson 1990:112).[4] As a result, the so-called 'mainstream', or 'great literature', in order to perpetuate its propulsive dialectics, to innovate its tradition, turns to someone else's rules, that is, to their breaking (double infraction), by drawing on forms and themes of strictly-codified fiction.

If this is so, we should speak less of *écart* than of *dissipation* of the norm, that is, 'production by dissipation'.[5] It is a literary production which is not manufactured via a swerve inside the genre system, but by way of a turbulence introduced from outside. In this light, the parody (in its etymologically ambivalent meaning) of detective fiction and science fiction, the more or less serious resumption of the sensationalist and pornographic novel, etc., brings about a structural distortion of these genres. They are *dissipated*, accelerating their consumption and giving birth to a new genre, an experimental *supergenre*. This is the way postmodernist literature pays its tribute to the monster rambling in the modernist prison/cellar, setting it free. At the same time, popular genre authors turn to the techniques of experimental fiction for innovation, violating

---

4 On the one hand, Joyce's *Ulysses* can be considered popular in that its characters represent mass individuals and their daily life. On the other hand, however, it can hardly be considered popular because its avantgarde techniques, its opacity, resist mass reading: a person like Bloom could never have read Joyce's masterpiece. In *Ulysses*, mass culture and avantgarde techniques lie side by side only to produce irony, that is, distance between the highbrow reader (and author) and the lowbrow mass man.

5 This term derives from the concept of Ilya Prigogine's *dissipative structures*, which contradicts the second principle of thermodynamics and of entropy. The concept is paradoxical, where 'mentre un sistema va *dissipando* energia, la dissipazione, invece di condurre verso l'entropia, conduce alla formazione di un nuovo ordine, cioè di nuove struture. Di regola, le strutture dissipative si producono in un sistema in cui sia stata introdotta instabilità . . .' ('while a system is *dissipating* energy, the dissipation, instead of leading towards entropy, leads towards the formation of a new order, that is, new structures. Normally, dissipative structures are produced in a system where instability is introduced . . .'; Calabrese 1992:153).

their genre code and thus completing the literary osmotic process between the heretofore separate domains. In fact, many novelists begin as genre authors and end up in the mainstream. Two outstanding examples are Kurt Vonnegut and Daniel Pennac, whose first works were respectively listed by publishers as science fiction and *noire* but were then given a more 'literary' profile. Consequently, it is hard to draw the line between dissipation (external parodical intrusion) and innovation (internal deviation from the norm). However, if the *écart* and *dissipation* structural principles tell us 'how' postmodernist aesthetics works, they do not explain to us the reason 'why' it is so.

One way to answer this question is to go back to Alexis de Tocqueville, whose analysis of the newly-born democratic American society serves our purpose. Tocqueville, in his attempt to understand the functioning of democratic society, realised the importance of the new, of the unexpected, in the production and consumption of bourgeois literature. While aristocratic readers, for obvious reasons, were for a rigorous and a traditional aesthetics, and against radical novelties, the readers of new times, oppressed as they were by monotonous work, looked for new, pleasant and accessible pastimes that could be instantly enjoyed. As a consequence of this, bourgeois authors generally tried to shock their readers rather than create art, complicitly yielding to the new system, where writers created according to consumers' needs like any other producer. But the most interesting point in Tocqueville's analysis, is that the dialectic novelty/ tradition, innovation/repetition is not only an instrument to understand the passage from aristocratic to democratic art (diachronic level), but also an instrument with which to comprehend the functioning of the new system itself (synchronic level). He registers the importance of novelty for bourgeois literature, but at the same time he stresses also that the *new* is to be *accessible*, somehow already known. In this way, the instances of the new and of the old, of the diverse and of the same, are not in opposition, but two sides of the same coin, that is, two moments of the same entity: mass culture.

It is particularly with reference to fashion that the two 'opposite' terms are naturally joined. On the one hand, fashion provides a social model of aggregation which is abstract enough to fulfil everybody's needs; on the other hand and by the same token, it satisfies everybody's need for diversity, for change, for individual features in a society tremendously homogenising. Therefore, the two moments (sameness-abstraction *versus* newness-individualisation) are organic and the only real purpose of this circular process is its own reproduction, novelty serving only to start the process of repeatability. This quality makes mass-culture production, either fashion or literature, homological to commodity production. In short, if on the capitalist marketplace the exchange-value (abstract form) of goods is separate from their use-value (practical content), which is precisely what makes a good commodity, in mass literature the new forms of works are likewise separate from their content: 'The novelty is a quality which does not depend on the use-value of the commodity. [...The] illusion of novelty is reflected, like one mirror in another, in the illusion of infinite sameness [*das immerwiedergleiche*]' (Benjamin 1973:172). If it is the same for literature, the implication is highly significant, since what matters for a novel is not its content but its successful form, the right formula which helps the mass cultural system to survive, irrespective of any truth content. The apparently new, then, is intrinsically also the permanently same, as it happens in all classic detective stories, where accidents and unforeseen events merely enable the iteration of the same scheme, the same delightful delay of the *dénouement*. The newness of the case serves only to foster the eternal return of the same solution.

These are the 'bad new things' postmodernism has before itself. At this point, the postmodernist writer can either decide that the bad contains the good or that the bad *is* good. In the latter case – when postmodernism rhymes with poststructuralism – the author merely perpetuates the 'diabolic' process of mass culture, falling blissfully prey to commodification. In the former case, the author accepts the bad but, at the same time, extrapolates the good from it, disambiguating his or her populist gesture of high/low integration. The argument is as follows: if in the age of culture-industry the work of art is really a commodity, the fact might just as well be admitted. If aesthetic autonomy is more and more an illusion or the price to be paid is isolation, then the only way out is to reverse the internal dialectics of the mass literature process, to use sameness to trigger real newness. The same should only be 'apparent' and should serve the rise of the genuinely new. In this light, popular genres, that is, strictly codified fiction, are produced and used only in order to be upset, deconstructed, 'estranged', so that the new, the diverse, may be produced and transmitted. In Marxist terms, it can be said that postmodernism yields to exchange-value (the trendy formula) only to restore use-value truth content, the actual complexity of reality. In this way the struggle for meaning does not take place outside, avantgarde-like and unproductively, but inside the machinery of the culture industry or, better still, 'in the interstices between modernism and mass culture' (Huyssen 1993:43). Even Adorno and Horkheimer, from their apocalyptic perspective, do not seem to overestimate the possibility for human beings to constitute, as subjects, the limit of reification, seeing in 'the hopeless effort of repetition . . . the only trace of hope that the repetition may be futile, that human beings cannot be totally controlled' (cited in Huyssen 1993:26). The alternative aesthetic strategy we have just outlined tries to see mass readers as subjects and uses the endless (and hopeless) series of repetitions not to renew mass culture's hold over them, but to shake them out of that sort of trance they fall into under the monotonous and hypnotic rhythm of the culture-industry's drums. It introduces a sort of shock treatment in order to break the chain of repetitions, so that form is not separate from its content and does not merely reproduce itself as commodity, perpetuating the reification process. This seems, to me, the actual strategy of several contemporary authors, who revert to popular genres to experiment with new fictional paths.

Detective Fiction and Science Fiction in Postmodernism: Beyond Masscult and Midcult Towards Hybridisation

Here I would like to take the case of detective fiction and science fiction: two historical genres which were born as literature *tout-court* and then abandoned to mass culture's hands with the appearance of the Great Divide. At present this fiction, whose progenitors were Mary Shelly and Edgar Allan Poe and its successors Jules Verne and Conan Doyle, Isaac Asimov and Agatha Christie, is again being embraced by what is now called mainstream. Indeed, they are considered, when suitably transformed, to be exemplary postmodern genres, in that they intrinsically express the postmodern condition (see Spanos 1972 and McHale 1987).

The paradigmatical example of this postmodern strategy, as far as detective fiction is concerned, might be Eco's *Il nome della rosa* (1980), a novel which conflates several genres (allegory, medieval chronicle, etc.), including detective fiction. But, as the author himself points out, it is a novel which, though it announces mysteries from the very beginning, 'continua a illudere il lettore ingenuo, sino alla fine, così che il lettore ingenuo può anche non accorgersi che si tratta di un giallo dove si scopre assai poco, e il detective viene sconfitto' (Eco 1988:524).[6] In fact, Guglielmo da Baskerville and his novice Adso da Melk (the parody of the popular pair of Doyle's stories), even though they fortuitously

6 'goes on deceiving the naïve reader up to the end, so that the naïve reader may not realise that it is a detective novel where very little is detected, and the detective is beaten'.

detect the abbey killer, do not succeed in preventing the destruction of the abbey, and finally only doubts and questions about the divine order and the universal truth are left. In Pynchon's cult-book *The Crying of Lot 49* (1966), Oedipa plays the part of the private eye to sort out her ex-lover's mysterious legacy. But the result of her quest through California disappoints the reader because her paranoid search (full of 'either' and 'or') is truncated. As the heroine is about to discover, perhaps, the truth, the story ends, and when the story ends the real mystery begins. With Martin Amis's apocalyptic *London Fields* (1989), the paradoxical use of detective fiction reaches its climax, while fulfilling the needs of postmodern literary self-consciousness. Here, the ambiguous figure of the author-narrator of the story is the killer and an even more ambiguous bizarre *femme fatale* the victim. But from the creative viewpoint the real victim is the persona of the author-narrator and the real author of the story is the victim: 'She outwrote me. Her story worked. And mine didn't' declares the author-narrator (Amis 1989:466).[7] The classical 'whodunit' is substituted by the postmodern 'whydoit', which serves less the referentiality of the *story* than the metafictionality of the *discourse*. Pennac's *noir* saga[8] is not as affected as Amis's fiction, in the same way that Pennac's Paris is not Amis's apocalyptic London. It is a mysterious Sue-like Paris, but, unlike Sue's, Malaussène's hyperbolic world (Pennac's anti-hero) is not Manichean and the culprits are never really or simply guilty. Guilt is, so to speak, diffused and inundates the entire society. The disruption of detective-fiction conventions is here achieved through overdetermination. Roland

7 As regards this hybrid narratorial figure, see my 'Hard Metafiction and the Return of the Author Subject: The Decline of Postmodernism?', *Postmodern Subjects/ Postmodern Texts*, eds. Jane Dowson and Steven Earnshaw (Amsterdam: Rodopi 1995).

8 Pennac's novels are: *Au bonheur des ogres* (1985), *La fée carabine* (1987), *La petite marchande de prose* (1990), *Monsieur Malaussène* (1995).

Barthes (1973) considers the repetitions of mass literature *hors-jouissance*, but, he adds, if they are made explicit, overdone, they become eccentric, uncovering their erotic potential. Similarly, in Pennac's stories, strange murders, odd investigations, as well as bizarre detections, proliferate. Every case is solved, every puzzle given a solution. But it is too much. The fact is that hyper-mysteries demand hyper-solutions, but a hyper-solution trivialises the solution itself: the hyper-solution dissolves 'les seductions du dénouement', against which instead the narrator alerts us. This is the way the erotic flower of the new can sprout from beneath the fertile manure of the same.

As far as science fiction is concerned, these flowers can take the colourful forms of Calvino's *Cosmicomiche* (1965) and *Ti con zero* (1967): Barth's prime example of postmodern, replenished literature (after high modernist exhaustion), and defined as 'space-age fables', where 'along with the nebulae and the black holes and the lyricism, there is a nourishing supply of pasta, bambini, and good-looking women sharply glimpsed and gone forever' (Barth 1980:70). Here, cosmic (high) and comic (low) form a fiction where 'sacred' themes are handled with a lightness of (self) irony and parody. But further to the conflation of cosmic and everyday space, there is also the compression of the primordial past (quasars and dinosaurs) and of the (post)modern present (semiotics and plastic). In short, it is a sort of reversed science fiction: *cognitive estrangement* (Suvin 1979) is secured not by bringing near to our reality what is far (science-fictional *novum*), but driving away what is near, our familiar reality, to the far away distance of mythical origins. Kurt Vonnegut's multi-layered novel (autobiographical, historical, fantastic, parodical) *Slaughterhouse 5* (1969), which tells of the fire-bombing of Dresden during the Second World War 'in the telegraphic schizophrenic manner of tales of the planet Tralfamadore' (Vonnegut 1991:subtitle), is the price science fiction has to pay for the process of innovation/dissipation. In this novel the genre is parodically *mise en abyme* through the alien science-fiction writer Kilgore Trout. Its conventions are laid bare by subverting its transparent language of mimesis and believability through a self-reflexive discourse (performed by an over-intrusive author-narrator) aware of its aesthetic status. If conventional science fiction can be defined as 'a realistic unreality', since it helps 'the willing suspension of disbelief', Vonnegut's science fiction, on the contrary, aligning itself with the postmodern cult of metafictionality, helps 'the willing suspension of *belief*'. If Vonnegut's fiction can ultimately be considered meta-science fiction, comic science fiction seems the proper name for Stefano Benni's *Terra!* (1983) and *Elianto* (1996), where the extreme hybridisation process brings about a joyful blend of allegory, science fiction, fantasy, comics, cartoons, etc. Benni's comic rewriting of classical stories like *Moby Dick* and *Orlando Furioso* as well as mass culture products like *Star Wars* and *Star Trek*, along with the political satire of contemporary Italian and Western (televisual) society, are the typical features of his unaffected fiction. But science fiction, and its close relative (negative) utopia, can serve a rather different purpose, as in feminist discourse. Angela Carter's *Heroes and Villains* (1969) or *The Passion of New Eve* (1977) seem to reinvigorate the science-fiction/utopian genre tradition through their feminist themes and rewriting of the patriarchal cultural tradition.

From Populist Aesthetics to Mass Politics

This is the way the 'infinite same', the 'endless repetitions' of detective fiction and science fiction can be broken with to enable the new to come through, without falling, simultaneously, into the midcult trap. What is new are the existential (Eco, Pynchon), literary (Amis) or social (Pennac, Pynchon) quests performed by these texts through their plots and characters; particularly through the estrangement of the conventional structure of detective fiction based precisely on the *dénouement*, therefore turning to (generic) dissolution. The new is the real *novum* Calvino's fables and Carter's dystopias succeed in extracting from the mass-produced *novum* (the endless same), calling into question established norms of thinking; or the real *novum* of Vonnegut's and Benni's meta/comic science fiction, which through extreme parody and satire dissipate both science, science fiction, and above all our stereotyped society. Only in this way can literature flee the apparent unavoidable choice between 'fetish' and 'exchange', between museum and market. In the age of mass culture and consumer society, the novel can resist commodification only through commodification. It can restore its use-value (its 'truth') only through the 'bad new thing' of exchange-value.

The less formal the postmodern populist aesthetic is, the less ambiguous it is. In order to totally disambiguate his or her gesture, the postmodern novelist, as the poet and polemicist Franco Fortini reminds us, should make the historical and political choice to set his writing 'in un habitat piuttosto che in un altro, fa[re] riferimento non ad un indefinito sociale ma ad uno specifico sociale'.[9] In short, s/he should not be a follower of the mindless pluralism of 'anything goes'. None of this is to say that literature is revolutionary. Revolution is a question of politics rather than literature. A 'revolutionary' literature is such only if it is rooted in a revolutionary political movement and this movement does not fail. Otherwise, it will be appropriated like the most 'revolutionary' avantgardes of this century, whose scandals have been turned into successes. 'How idealist to imagine that *art*, all by itself, could resist incorporation. The question of appropriation has to do with politics, not with culture; it is a question of who is winning at any

9 'in one habitat rather than another, to refer not to an indefinite social group but to a specific one' (Fortini 1986:79).

particular time' (Eagleton 1990:372). Since in the 1990s the winner is still the same winner as in 1848 and popular culture has not advanced hand in hand with its own social promoters, in order to exist it has to pay the price of commodification or of highbrow incorporation at the expense of genuine value.

Unfortunately, 'il libro non ha ucciso la cattedrale e dobbiamo smetterla di pensare che il libro la ucciderà, cioè che il leggere sia un valore, che leggere buoni libri sia un valore. Questa è una mitologia . . . che va radicalmente distrutta'.[10] The positive aesthetics of *this* postmodernism may be really positive only if it is aware that the question of integration cannot simply be a formal gesture but must have real truth content, nor can it be a question of mere literary destiny but of the destiny of a mass political movement.

Luigi CAZZATO
University of Bari

10 'the book has not killed the cathedral and we have to give up thinking the book will do it, that is, give up thinking that reading has value, that reading good books is valuable. This is a myth . . . which must be radically destroyed' (Fortini 1986:87).

Works Cited

Amis, Martin. *London Fields*. (1989). Harmondsworth: Penguin, 1990.

Barth, John. 'The Literature of Replenishment: Postmodernist Fiction'. *The Atlantic* 245 (1980): 65-71.

---. (1967). 'The Literature of Exhaustion'. *Surfiction Now . . . and Tomorrow*. Ed. R. Federman. Chicago: The Swallow Press, 1975: 19-33.

Barthes, Roland. *Le plaisir du texte*. Paris: Editions du Seuil, 1973.

Benjamin, Walter. (1955). *Charles Baudelaire: A Lyric Poet in the Era of High Capitalism*. London: New Left Books, 1973.

Benni, Stefano. *Elianto*. Milano: Feltrinelli, 1996.

---. *Terra!* Milano: Feltrinelli, 1983.

Calabrese, Omar. (1987). *L'età neobarocca*. Bari: Laterza, 1992.

Calinescu, Mattei. *Five Faces of Modernity: Modernism, Avant-Garde, Decadence, Kitsch, Postmodernism*. Durham: Duke University Press, 1987.

Calvino, Italo. *Ti con zero*. (1967). Milano: Garzanti, 1988.

---. (1965). *Cosmicomiche*. Milano: Mondadori, 1993.

Carey, John. 'Revolted by the Masses'. *Times Literary Supplement*, 12 January 1990: 34/44-5.

Carter, Angela. (1977). *The Passion of New Eve*. London: Virago Press, 1993.

---. *Heroes and Villains*. (1969). Harmondsworth: Penguin, 1981.

Cazzato, Luigi. 'Hard Metafiction and the Return of the Author Subject: The Decline of Postmodernism?' *Postmodern Subjects/Postmodern Texts*. Eds. Jane Dowson and Steven Earnshaw. Amsterdam: Rodopi, 1995. 25-41.

Eagleton, Terry. *The Ideology of the Aesthetic*. Oxford: Basil Blackwell, 1990.

---. 'Capitalism, Modernism, Postmodernism'. *New Left Review* 152 (1985): 60-73.

Eco, Umberto. (1983). 'Postille a *Il nome della rosa*'. *Il nome della rosa*. Milano: Bompiani, 1988. 507-33.

---. (1980). *Il nome della rosa*. Milano: Bompiani, 1988.

Fiedler, Leslie. (1970). 'Cross the Border, Fill the Gap'. *Collected Essays*. New York: Stein and Day, 1971. 461-85.

Fortini, Franco. 'Tra valore e disvalore. Conversazione con Franco Fortini'. *Il superlibro. Conversazioni sul romanzo di successo*. (1983). Eds. Alberto Cadioli and Giovanni Peresson. Ancona: Il lavoro editoriale, 1986. 77-91.

Gramsci, Antonio. *Quaderni dal carcere. Letteratura e vita nazionale*. Roma: Editori Riuniti, 1991.

Hall, Stuart and Paddy Whannel. *Popular Arts*. London: Hutchinson Educational, 1964.

Huyssen, Andreas. (1986). *After the Great Divide: Modernism, Mass Culture, Postmodernism*. London: Macmillan, 1993.

Jameson, Fredric. (1983). 'Postmodernism and Consumer Society'. *Postmodern Culture*. Ed. Hal Foster. London: Pluto Press, 1990: 111-25.

Marquez, Gabriel Garcia. (1967). *One Hundred Years of Solitude*. London: Picador, 1978.

McHale, Brian. *Postmodernist Fiction*. London: Routledge, 1987.

Parrinder, Patrick. *Science Fiction: Its Criticism and Teaching*. London: Methuen, 1980.

Pennac, Daniel. *Monsieur Malaussène*. Paris: Gallimard, 1995.

---. *La fée carabine*. Paris: Gallimard, 1987.

---. *La petite marchande de prose*. Paris: Gallimard, 1985.

---. *Au bonheur des ogres*. Paris: Gallimard, 1985.

Pynchon, Thomas. (1966). *The Crying of Lot 49*. London: Picador, 1979.

Spanos, William V. 'The Detective and the Boundary: Some Notes on the Postmodern Literary Imagination'. *Boundary* 2.1 (1972): 147-68.

Suvin, Darko. *Metamorphoses of Science-Fiction. On the Poetics and History of a Literary Genre*. New Haven: Yale University Press, 1979.

Tocqueville, Alexis de. *Democracy in America*. New York: Collins/Fontana, 1996.

Todorov, Tzvetan. (1966). 'Typologie du roman policier'. *Poétique de la prose*. Paris: Edition du Seuil, 1971. 55-64.

Vonnegut, Kurt. (1969). *Slaughterhouse 5*. London: Vintage, 1991.

Woolf, Virginia. (1919). 'Modern Fiction'. *The Common Reader 1*. London: The Hogarth Press, 1984: 146-54.

Wordsworth, William. 'Prefaces'. *The Poetical Works of Wordsworth*. Ed. Thomas Hutchinson. London: Oxford University Press, 1961.

Zabel, Morton Dauwen. (1951). *The Portable Henry James*. Harmondsworth: Penguin Books, 1979.

The Postmodern Revival of the Historical Novel in Italy: Aesthetic and Cultural Implications

The last thirty years have seen an increase in the use of history as the subject matter of narrative. This phenomenon, by now well recognised not only in Italy but internationally as well, has brought about a veritable revival of historical fiction. Much of Italian literary criticism, however, denies the traditional definition of the genre and has proposed many alternate terms. Those most widely used are the 'neo-historical novel', the 'antihistorical novel', or even the 'pseudo-historical novel'. The terminology used by critics in the English speaking world intentionally avoids the designation 'novel' and in its place uses either the term 'narrative' or 'fiction'. Regardless of the term one uses, it is nonetheless certain that this new genre has assumed important proportions and is today, along with science fiction, one of the most used by postmodernist prose.

As mentioned, the new historical narrative first began to appear internationally in the early 1970s. In Italy, however, some years earlier, we can locate the exceptional but isolated success of Tomasi di Lampedusa's *Il Gattopardo* (1957), the first bestseller of the Italian market. While Elsa

Morante's *La Storia* had outstanding success in 1974 the true, large scale explosion of novels dedicated to the narration of history took place only in the 1980s, a decade which began with the resounding success of Umberto Eco's *Il nome della rosa* and ended with the remarkable proliferation of the genre. Among the many novels written during this decade, we can cite the following examples: *Retablo* and *Il sorriso dell'ignoto marinaio* by Vincenzo Consolo, Luigi Malerba's *Il fuoco greco*, *La chimera* by Sebastiano Vassalli, Dacia Maraini's *La lunga vita di Marianna Ucrìa*, Rosetta Loy's *Le strade di polvere*, Raffaele Nigro's *I fuochi del Basento* and *La baronessa dell'Olivento*, Vincenzo Cerami's *La lepre*, Fulvio Tomizza's *L'ereditiera veneziana*, Athos Bigongiali's *Una città proletaria*, and Maria Rosa Cutrufelli's *La briganta*. The writing of such novels has continued into the 1990s. The return of literature which is, in Manzoni's terms, 'a mixture of history and invention', is a phenomenon difficult enough to define since it places first-time novelists alongside established writers, affects literary prizes and academic debates, embraces both large scale publishers and alternative presses, and includes purely commercial novels as well as those with intellectual aspirations. Any comprehensive evaluation is consequently difficult. One thing, however, is certain: we are not simply dealing with a literary fashion. It is in no doubt due to recent changes in the book market that the genre has experienced such a great success. During the early 1980s the unprecedented sales of *Il nome della rosa*, made possible for the large part by new and aggressive marketing strategies, clearly showed the already established industrial restructuring of Italian publishing. It is highly likely that the literary success of the historical novel was made possible by the editorial necessity to acquire an ever larger reading public. The historical novel, by virtue of the fact that it is a genre open to an almost infinite number of narrative possibilities, is capable of responding to the public's various expectations.

Novels in which we find an elegant and innovative recuperation of the historical model can not simply be defined as historical. Neo-historical novels present a 'multi-genred' character, that is to say, the co-existence of many literary models within a single text. In fact, the most interesting of neo-historical novels show not only a plurality of types but the characteristics of many literary genres. The mixing of genres results, however, in the weakening of typical connotations associated with each adopted model and as a consequence produces a disorienting effect which makes narrative structure appear poor, open, and hardly cohesive when compared to the traditional co-ordinates of reading. An ever more frequent interweaving of literary models results in an elastic, free and varied use of paradigms. This does not mean, however, as many have maintained, that the postmodern signals the end of genre, nor does it mean that contemporary novels cannot be linked to determinate aesthetic and formal traditions. On the contrary, it is to the very interplay of destructuring and innovation of narrative models undertaken by postmodernist literature that we owe the re-birth of theoretical interest regarding genre. With postmodernism the concept *genre* undergoes an epistemological revolution which renders its reconceptualisation necessary. Such reconceptualisation must begin with a fundamental assertion – namely: that genres today operate as open models; they are interactive 'modes' within variegated, plurivocal texts. The fact that many neo-historical novels assume a characteristic 'multi-genre' form does not exclude them from being read according to the individual genres that they employ. One can consider a novel as historical even if it presents, beyond the stylistic and expressive figures peculiar to this genre, traits typical of other genres. What matters is that we reflect upon the consequences that the co-existence of different *fabula* have on novelistic configuration. The literary repertory of the postmodern obliges us to employ new and more pliable forms of analysis aimed at revealing how genre is intricately elaborated within novels that can be classified, beyond being historical, as pulp, romance, adventure, allegorical, political or philosophical. Clearly, the aesthetic evaluation of works must respect the individuality of each particular novel. In addition, this new mode of narrative must be studied in its totality, that is to say, as a sociological phenomenon. Such a perspective is indispensable for the definition of the neo-historical novel's constitution. Regarding the organisation of narrative, the neo-historical novel develops its own rhetorical and structural modalities by way of a dialectical relation with other genres. In addition, we should pay attention to purely commercial novels, while being careful, however, to avoid over-estimating them.

From this perspective it should be noted that the diffusion of the historical novel in Italy was influenced, especially in the last decade, by market trends set by such international best-selling authors as Ken Follet and Colleen McCullough. In Italy we can presently find an extensive group of writers who draw inspiration from an emulation of such models. In the Anglo-American novel there now exists a bifurcation between writing which is closely connected to the needs of literary consumption and novels which are more refined and intellectually demanding. Such novels have been exhaustively studied by theorists of the postmodern and are the subject of a copious critical bibliography. Due to the widespread theory that radical destructuring has nearly cancelled genres altogether, a large part of postmodernist criticism, as stated earlier, does not accept the term 'historical novel' and in its place prefers 'historical fiction'. In the critical study of the postmodern the term *genre* assumes a multiplicity of meanings. For example, Linda Hutcheon holds that historiography and literature are genres, while maintaining, however, that even such macro-genres are lacking in theoretical stature. She states that the recent 'problematizing of the nature of historical knowledge' has upset the differentiations between the old 'disciplines' to the point that every theoretical distinction between literary and historical writing is rendered impossible. The fictional narration of history undertaken by a novel is brought analogously close to historiography's 'true' narration. It seems that what we can call 'truth content' is not a sufficient parameter for distinguishing these two rhetorical practices. By being so extreme, this thesis does, however, bring to light an aspect of the postmodern, that is to say, its profound reassessment, on the level of social perception at least, of the historical relations which exist between the present, the past and the future. This helps to explain why the category of 'historical narrative' has become, in the form of a heuristic metaphor symbolising the self-consciousness of history, one of the central epistemological paradigms in contemporary theory and has assumed prominence in thought that describes the postmodern as a reality marked by an absence of a historical dimension. According to many contemporary theorists, such as Fredric Jameson, Remo Ceserani and Giulio Ferroni, what the neo-historical novel expresses is the very need to explore the modalities and extent of this new spatial and temporal perception, paradoxically defined 'a-historical'.

Such an exploration, however, is anything but systematic. Beyond the fact that they are all set in the past, neo-historical novels often have very little in common. The choice of historical period and situation, as well as style and mode of representation, differ radically. With respect to the question of history, understood both in its ideological outline and the manner in which it is hermeneutically approached, the aspect of the historical novel most open to change is the level of difficulty. In certain novels the reconstruction of the past is purely a pretext. History is treated as a store-house of materials to be used without philological rigour. In others, by contrast, and such novels are indeed numerous, we can see a high degree of philosophical awareness and a remarkable capacity for the problematising of historical content. In novels of the first kind, the reconstruction of the past is stereotypical and aimed purely at the creation of a spectacular and exotic atmosphere. In effect, they sweeten the past, a phenomenon clearly evident even in the cinematic versions of certain contemporary novels.

The fact that the neo-historical novel is not simply a commercial trend is confirmed by the fact that some of Italy's most significant novelists write using this genre. Such 'hyper-literary' writers as Vincenzo Consolo, Luigi Malerba and Sebastiano Vassalli, writers who not only emerge from the neo-avant-garde and experimentalism of the 1960s but are anything but commercial, have participated in the recuperation of the genre. It is therefore necessary to question the critical commonplace that considers the neo-historical novel as a minor genre aimed only at satisfying market demands. With regard to the marketplace, experimental writers have not simply passed from a critical position to one that is more economically accommodating, as some critics would maintain. To allege that the narrative re-visitation of the past is a sign of self-censorship and escape from the present is unfounded, as is the position that holds that the historical novel is a regressive genre characterised by a conservative cultural restoration of the *status quo*. The fact that the 'culture industry' has positively exploited this line of argument in order to gratify the expectations of a traditional reading public, does not signify, however, a correspondence with the truth. During the 1980s – a decade that we can call the Craxi years – a period, in short, characterised by a certain hedonism and consumerism – the reading of neo-historical novels was often emblematically identified with pure diversion and escapism, what a popular slogan of the time referred to as a 'return to pleasure'. In many cases we can see that the *Zeitgeist* of this period is clearly visible even from within certain novels. In the following passage from the introduction to *Il nome della rosa* Eco subtly and ironically expresses the sheer pleasure associated with storytelling when it is freed from the pre-occupations of political commitment:

> I transcribe without worrying about the present. The notion going around at the time when I found Abbot Vallet's text [1968] was that one should only write with a commitment to the present and in order to change the world. Now, ten years later, the consolation of the man of letters (restored to his lofty dignity) is that he can write for the pure love of writing. So now I feel free to tell, for the simple pleasure of storytelling, the story of Adso da Melk. Now that the awakening of reason has chased away the monsters once generated by its sleep, I am comforted and consoled to find the story so incommensurably distant in time, so gloriously free of any relation with our time, timelessly foreign to our hopes and certainties. (Eco 1986:15)

It is clear, however, that the author of *Il nome della rosa* does not write for the 'simple pleasure of storytelling' and that with respect to the present the story narrated is anything but 'incommensurably distant' and 'timelessly foreign'. The emphasising of distances, aimed at creating an almost fable-like narrative *aura*, is an ironic mask whose purpose is that of gaining the reader's confidence. While Eco's novel tends toward an exaggerated complexity and multiplicity of senses, such intricacies of content are always tied to a formal style which is more or less responding to the new expectations of a mass society's reading public. In fact, the neo-historical novel during the 1980s did not employ an elevated language. For the most part, writers of neo-historical novels intentionally address non-academic readers, a gesture which is, in-and-of-itself, not culturally conservative, given that the historical novel has always been a popular and didactic genre. Accusations which speak of a return to the *status quo* and literary traditionalism are not always accurate since they fail to consider the innovations advanced by certain novels. Such criticism is more often than not linked to a frustration which stems from the success made possible by a non-specialist public.

A fundamental distinction must therefore be made between conservative and highly stereotyped neo-historical novels and novels that represent history after an innovative and allegorical fashion, such as Luigi Malerba's *Il fuoco greco*, Vincenzo Cerami's *La lepre*, as well as Vincenzo Consolo's *Retablo* and his *Il soriso del ignoto marinaio*. It is only in this particular sector of contemporary literary production that we can distinguish a continuity with the historical novel in its nineteenth-century form.

Such a thesis does not imply, however, that postmodern narrative constitutes an imitation of nineteenth-century prose. One cause for reflection in the debate surrounding the re-birth of the historical novel is the resistance with which criticism refuses to accept the traditional name of the genre. In fact, various neologisms have been invented in an attempt to avoid every possible resemblance to the nineteenth-century model, the most extreme example being that of Giuseppe Petronio who defined work in this genre as 'novels based upon themes from the past'. Petronio begins with the assumption that the genre attained well-defined characteristics during the Romantic and Risorgimento period which make it a closed and irreproducible model. We can see that this position can not be supported when we examine the arguments used in order to sustain it. In effect, according to Petronio, the quality which would most precisely define the genre is what he calls a 'strong and organic conception of history'. This conception, in turn, is linked to the formation of what he calls a 'popular historical consciousness' and the 'spreading of the concept nation' (Petronio 1992:41). There is no doubt that the nineteenth-century historical novel developed within processes relating to national constitution. This does not mean, however, that a positivistic, apologetic and triumphalistic vision of history is necessarily intrinsic to the genre. One must only think of Manzoni, that is to say, of the most significant novel in Italian literature. In addition, regarding *content* as opposed to *form*, an ideology of history alone cannot sufficiently define the constitution of a genre. Whomever maintains the contrary operates within a normative rather than pragmatic approach to literary genres. According to Petronio there is a certain instability in contemporary literature, as far as narrative themes are concerned. He adds that present-day narrators change themes and genre models with great facility; such concerns, argues Petronio, are no longer of interest. He holds that the recuperation of so-called popular genres by hyper-literary writers may in part be a response to their desire for a larger reading public but, he adds, that it is also tied to the desire to educate the reading public and hence participate in the construction of a wide-spread cultural consciousness, what Petronio himself defines as a 'mass avant-garde'.

Beyond uncertainties having to do with the definition of the genre's constitution, the neo-historical novel, even when considered aesthetically, is subject to conflicting positions which are, however, reducible to two opposing tendencies. The first is composed of essentially positive readings undertaken by post-modernist criticism. Neo-historical novels are here seen as the ideal terrain for the study of the 'anthropological mutations' brought about by the postmodern itself. The second tendency is composed of negative positions advanced by those who consider the literary levelling of the distance between the present and the historical past as a banalisation of writing brought about by market demands. Giulio Ferroni, for example, maintains that for the most part postmodern literature is the result of a literary fashion.

By virtue of the fact that he does not see the literary success of the genre as an expression of latent or manifest cultural needs, for Ferroni the revival of the historical novel is not a significant phenomenon. He maintains that it is simply the consequence of market mechanisms. I would suggest, however, that behind the vagaries of literary fashion we can often distinguish a series of social and cultural needs. In any case, it is undeniable that commercial success or failure are factors that condition the formation of reading habits and that the demand as well as the fashion for neo-historical novels has persisted over a long period of time. It should be added that Ferroni's position does not correspond to a prejudiced underestimation of the neo-historical novel since he recognises a noteworthy potential in the genre as such. The problem revolves around a distinction between what he calls 'a commemorative literature' which celebrates 'fixed values' in order to produce a 'nostalgia for the fashions of the past'; and a 'posthumous' literature intent upon deepening, as do the novels by Vincenzo Consolo, 'the alterity of the past through a critical understanding of both the present as well as the past'. 'Commemorative' literature is seen as lacking the profundity of historical memory. It is only in novels considered to be 'posthumous' that the perspective of historical depth is preserved, even if such depth is achieved by diverse modalities and styles. The 'posthumous' category can in fact be applied to divergent literary experiences that are linked, however, in their resistance to the market place.

In one of the most extensive and well-researched studies of the neo-historical novel in the United States, Elisabeth Wesseling maintains, in opposition to a large part of American criticism, that the genre should be considered as the most recent version of the traditional historical novel. Her thesis – what she provocatively announces as the *Postmodernist Innovations of the Historical Novel*, the sub-title of her book – is sustained by a well-argued theoretical position which defines the genre as a 'historically variable social institution'. The existence of a continuous line running from the Romantic and Risorgimento period through what Wesseling calls the 'modernist experiments' and into the present is confirmed by an exhaustive historiographical reconstruction of the first part of the nineteenth-century and of the Scottish novel. For the most part, Wesseling concentrates upon numerous examples from contemporary neo-historical fiction, which she divides into three typologies and analyses according to the hermeneutic key of self-reflexivity. The three typologies are: 'time traveling', 'nostalgic science-fiction' and the 'parahistorical'. Present-day developments in the neo-historical novel are held to be the consequence of a gradual process that Wesseling calls the 'subjectification' of historical consciousness: a trend that we can find already underway in the modern. By making room for the memorial mechanisms of consciousness rather than objectively reconstructing events, modernist novelists, maintains Wesseling, have brought about a fundamental modification of the Romantic model. It consists of a re-orientation of the visual axis away from the external and social toward the subjective spaces of interiority. The result is what she terms the 'objectification' of history.

In twentieth-century historical novels, as opposed to those of the nineteenth-century, history is no longer understood to be the field of truth in relation to which the fantastic inventions of writers are compared and contrasted. What is lost in this new conception of history is a certain faith in the documentability of truth. In its place we find an effort to achieve memorial self-consciousness. In the postmodern historical novel speculation regarding 'self-reflexive conjecture' is made all the more acute but no longer revolves around subjectivity since the integrity of subjective consciousness appears fragmented. The mechanisms of memory take on the dissociated form of a collective thought which is not socially determined by class but is the result of a 'self-reflexivity without subjects'. The acquisition of historical consciousness is thus made problematic and is further complicated when considered hermeneutically. Where the modern novel foregrounded the conjectural modalities of interpretation, the postmodern novel immediately highlights the crisis of consciousness and its intrinsically ideological nature. The problem is no longer whether history is intelligible or not, but that of the partiality, arbitrariness and interchangeability of historical interpretations, all of which are considered to be ideological positions linked to political power. With this in mind, we can clearly discern the affinity between the postmodern novel and the development of certain tendencies in present-day philosophy. It is not simply a coincidence that the virtual explosion of historical narrative has taken place in the very moment in which reflection upon the nature of history has assumed both theoretical and historiographical importance.

During the last fifteen years numerous trends in contemporary theory have come into conflict or arrived at a consensus in debates having to do with how history is to be written and if indeed history *can* be written. On the one side we find the international theoretical debate regarding the postmodern; and on the other we have the Italian debate over the new literary historiography. Over and above such contentions, however, scholars agree that the postmodern is a period of 'anthropological mutation' wherein cognitive models have undergone radical transformations. What we can call the 'culture of information' has brought about a gradual but unstoppable fragmentation of individual consciousness, weakening, as such, the role of the subject as the co-ordinating agent of time and space. The loss of historical consciousness is a direct result of the difficulty with which the new spatial and temporal relations are to be negotiated on the individual and collective level. The ability to discern the distance between the present and the past fades as the distance between cultural and geographic differences diminishes. History, in effect, loses its density and is flattened out onto the present. The past is understood according to its superficial and stereotypical aspects and is perceived only by way of aesthetic connotations. The active re-elaboration of memory is today made difficult, or perhaps even impossible, by the passivity required for the reception of information which is often beyond the control of the individual subject. Any depth once associated with knowledge has been replaced by the superficiality of sheer information; active experience has given way to passive reception. Self-reflexivity, in short, has taken the place of interaction. As Jameson argues, the disappearance of the 'radical past' is inevitable. Regardless of the fact, however, that history can no longer be reconstructed in literature, since the images of history that we possess are all cliché and citations, the 'historical narrative' of the neo-historical novel assumes importance because it becomes an allegory of what Jameson calls 'impossible desire' – that is to say, the desire to organise space and time according to cognitive frames that the postmodern has invalidated. On the one hand, this desire corresponds to the need to react against the loss of historical distance; on the other, it signals the necessity to re-invent ways of co-ordinating the relation between the past, present and future. The popularity of the neo-historical novel can be considered the result of the social need for 'historical narrative', a need which, beyond being simply metaphorical, corresponds to the necessity to elaborate interpretations of the rapid social, economic, and cultural transformations specific to our time and place. It may be that by way of this genre literature can establish a critical niche from which to express a voice against the so-called death of history.

The present brief survey of contemporary theory should sufficiently present us with the need not only to re-think history but to re-establish the categories of historical inquiry. We can call this need a cultural phenomenon. We are faced with the need for critical perspectives capable of giving sense to history. Such a need can be seen as one of the main reasons for the flowering of the neo-historical novel, even if the literary construction of sense in history is often tragically negative and violently characterised by a past imagined as degraded or by apocalyptic visions of the future.

Margherita GANERI
University of Calabria

Works Cited

Eco, Umberto. *Il nome della rosa*. Milano: Bompiani, 1986.

Di Lampedusa, Giuseppe. *Il Gattopardo*. Milano: Feltrinelli, 1958.

Ferroni, Giulio. 'Qualche distinzione sul postmoderno nella letterature'. *Lettera dall'Italia* 33 (1994): 35-6.

Hutcheon, Linda. '"The Pastime of Past Time": Fiction, History, Historiographic Metafiction'. *Postmodern Genres*. Ed. Marjorie Perloff. Norma: University of Oklahoma Press, 1989.

Jameson, Fredric. *Postmodernism, or the Cultural Logic of Late Capitalism*. Durham: Duke University Press, 1991.

Manzoni, Alessandro. 'Del romanzo storico e in generale dei componimenti misti di storia e di invenzione'. *Opere varie*. Vol. II. Ed. M. Barbi and F. Ghisalberti. Milano: Casa del Manzoni, 1943.

Morante, Elsa. *La Storia*. Torino: Einaudi, 1974.

Petronio, Giuseppe. 'Cinque domande sul ritorno al passato'. *Tirature '91*. Ed. Vittorio Spinazzola. Torino: Einaudi, 1991. 41-2.

Wesseling, Elisabeth. *Writing History as a Prophet. Postmodernist Innovations of the Historical Novel*. Amsterdam: J. Benjamins, 1991.

Postmodern Cinema?:

Or, La Cinéma Postmoderne Expliquée Aux Enfants

Many of the theorisations of postmodern culture have readily pointed to cinema as furnishing prime examples of the postmodern. Oddly though, the term 'postmodernism' has never been systematically utilised by established film scholars. While in the zone of cultural studies the term has great currency, it is almost unknown in the specialised area of film studies. This is a symptom of the discipline's investment in other paradigms. Postmodern approaches such as micro-archival techniques and the hyper-historicism of the new film history (revisionist history) abound, while aesthetic considerations of postmodernism and cinema are rare. In fact, in some quarters of film scholarship, the merest use of the term 'postmodernism' has become a problem.[1] This is underlined by the major theorisations of cinema and postmodernism coming from other disciplines, for example, Fredric Jameson and Jim Collins from literature and Scott Lash and Norman Denzin from sociology. Film theorist Warren Buckland points out that, despite theorising early cinema, Fredric Jameson fails to cite any research carried out on early cinema:

---

1 At film studies conferences, the word 'postmodernism' is hardly used. At the University of Kent at Canterbury conference, 'Hollywood Since the 1950s', the term 'post-classical' (meaning Hollywood and mainstream cinema since about 1960) was, at times, used in much the same way that 'postmodern' could have been used.

> many of Jameson's insights have been made, with far more historical accuracy and theoretical systematicity, within film studies itself. . . . *Signatures of the Visible* is not so much a work of film theory but seems more like the testament of a well-known 'outsider' who has become caught up in the imaginary pleasures of film and film theory.
>
> (Buckland 1992:170)

While such flagrant academic tourism tends to delegitimise Jameson and some other writers, I contend that postmodernism is a valuable term for film studies, precisely as an aesthetic theory, and this essay will discuss certain modes of contemporary cinema in the light of postmodern culture. First, I will sum up prevalent attitudes to postmodern cinema, after which I will go about providing a perspective on postmodern characteristics which regale contemporary cinema, as it seems to me that in order for postmodernism to be accepted by film scholarship, it must be reduced in scope and identified as problematic at certain points. As far as I can see, this perspective is fruitful, allowing insights that are unavailable to the dominant paradigms in film scholarship.

The introduction to the special postmodernism issue of *Screen* sums up the failed assimilation of postmodernism into film scholarship: 'Despite their enthusiasm for succeeding waves of theory in the '70s, British academics were notably inhospitable to postmodernism in the '80s . . . [which] reflected the substantial institutional investment in dominant paradigms' (Hayward and Kerr 1987:4). Postmodernism began to gain currency at a time when film scholarship was least receptive to new theoretical currents. During the 1970s, film studies had established its credentials through what is sometimes known as 'Screen theory', a heroic and self-important articulation of the king-discourses of the time: Lacanian psychoanalysis and Althusserian Marxism. The following decade saw a reaction to Screen theory's seeming orthodoxy and lack of engagement with history. So a significant degree of scholarly work in the discipline turned from high theory to film history and areas such as investigations of precise representations rather than the nature of representation generally. This strand of film academia was unwilling to engage with a new theoretical impetus, while the Screen theory strand was entrenched in the theoretical paradigms that had been so important in shaping the discipline.

Yet these very theoretical paradigms have been largely unsuccessful in their dealings with contemporary cinema, certainly less successful than they had been in elucidating classical cinema. How can the term 'postmodernism' help explain contemporary cinema? Some film scholars may argue that the terms and strategies associated with postmodernism are already available to analysis in other discourses or critical paradigms used to explain films. This misses the point. It ignores postmodernism as an all-embracing development that has recontextualised not only the products of the film industry (and the film industry itself), but the approach to cinema that the academy has taken. This is like a quantum leap for film perception, to a situation involving a high level of film literacy and historical knowledge in audiences that have, at times, been theorised by film scholars as virtual dupes, and from film history as an esoteric scholarly activity to it being incorporated into films as part of the public domain and, as Lyotard pointed out, as fodder for quiz shows (Lyotard 1984:76).

I would like to see film studies attempt to apply the most modern theoretical approaches to modern cinema, rather than persist in using 'universal' theories that appear to uncover universal truths in the analysis of films as diverse as classical Hollywood and contemporary Hollywood and all else as well. If cinema as an institution and as a body of films has changed since the heyday of the studio system, and many commentators appear to think that there have been significant developments in cinema since the Second World War, then surely we need to institute some strategies of understanding for the cinema that were not developed for the almost exclusive application to films from the 1930s and 1940s. 'There was . . . the arrival of forms of cultural production which appeared to require analyses not premised on established modernist perspectives. . . . The heyday of the modernist film had faded' (Hayward and Kerr 1987:3). Cinema has certainly changed in some dramatic ways over the past twenty or more years. Since the 1960s, film production has been marked by its integration within larger media industries run by international entertainment corporations. Films are no longer simply produced for distribution and exhibition at cinemas, but have a larger focus placed on their longer shelf life through video sales and television broadcast. Another significant effect on films is that they are part and parcel of other industries, so films will include tied-in products such as music and will become a saturation marketing exercise, as witnessed by *Jurassic Park* (1993) and the three *Batman* films.

In cinema, modernism has been identified most strongly with European art cinema and the avant-garde. This is premised upon the seeming elitism of these films and their regular dismissal of the popular, so they are seen rather simplistically as an aesthetic and ideological opposition to Hollywood's films. But these theorisations are very Amerocentric, denying the popularity that some art cinema has in its home country. For example, David Bordwell has no hesitation in slipping *Alfie* (1966) into his chapter on art cinema alongside films of European auteurs such as Ingmar Bergman and Andrei Tarkovsky (Bordwell 1985:207). The avant-gardes had always manifested the cutting edge of cinema, both politically and aesthetically, but have been marked by their almost total disappearance.

While many branches of modernist art became the establishment, in the case of films, the critical acclaim accorded to European art cinema and avant-garde cinema led to their canonisation in film schools and universities. This has guaranteed their influence in the USA, but the lack of a solid tradition of art cinema has led to the development of a strain of highly cineliterate film making within the mainstream. A recent book on modernism and film, oddly by another non-specialist, Neil Orr, misses the point about postmodernism. He points out that many of the techniques associated with postmodernism have been used in modernist films (Orr 1993:3). Precisely, but what he misses is that the context of their use has changed, to a point where these are not experiments or ground-breaking techniques, but part of the established language of cinema. Or would he simply equate Dziga Vertov's *Man with a Movie Camera* (1929) with a pop video on MTV that used the same devices? Sometimes it even seems hard to talk about films as a distinct object at all. Television has become the principal outlet for films, making theatrical release secondary to television broadcast and the increasingly dominant video sell-through. By the late 1950s television became regarded as another exhibition outlet for films (Gomery 1984:83), while by the 1980s television companies were heavily involved in film production, like Channel Four in the UK. The involvement of television in film production has arguably led to a more episodic form, one that would easily facilitate broadcast in sections and with numerous commercial breaks.

In addition to this, postmodernism in cinema is the pulling of the institution of cinema into line with the larger scale multimedia industries, with the specificity of cinema lost in favour of an integration with other culture industries. Obvious examples of this are the tied-in songs that grace most mainstream products coming out of Hollywood. The three Batman films were produced by multimedia conglomerate Time-Warner. *Batman* (1989), *Batman Returns* (1992) and *Batman Forever* (1995) all have soundtrack LPs (three films, five LPs) available on Warner Brothers music label as a complement to the films' production and distribution by Warners' film aspects. Indeed, the Batman films were a prime example of the intersection of filmic products with the wider field of products sold on the back of cultural events. Children's toys were the most prevalent tie-in with these films, with a number of moveable figures and objects such as miniature Batmobiles being made available. By the time of *Batman Forever*, the nexus of product relations had encompassed an animated television show as well as 'Legends of the Batman' which had inspired related toys. Stickers showing stills from the film were also available, as were cards for the first Batman film six years earlier. Over that period of time, the concentration of marketing on the children's market was surely the main impetus behind *Batman Forever* being targeted at children more directly than its predecessors.

The new site for this postmodern cinema is the multiplex, where, in a similar manner to television, the visitor has a choice of channels rather than having to see the single latest big movie. What's more, you can have your own equivalent of a TV-dinner in the form of the prescribed cinema foods (popcorn tubs, hot dogs), and if that's not enough there's usually an eaterie of some sort integrated with the design of the multiplex. As new semi-urban spaces, multiplexes reflect the geographical impetus of the construction of mini-communities in big sheds on the edges of urban areas, often accessible only by automobile and simultaneously diffusing the cultural urban-centrism as well as underlining the centrality of private transport in new modes of leisure.

Baudrillard's *In the Shadow of the Silent Majorities* points to there being no second guessing audiences. (After all, in the land of market research the British election of 1992 was won by the Labour party.) His book additionally deals in postmodernity as the implosion of the social (matching Margaret Thatcher's no society), marking the end of cinema as a social institution, to be replaced by the virtual community of television. Rapidly declining cinema attendance since the Second World War removed cinema from its status as a mass art, which has only been stabilised by its industrial reorganisation inserting it as a subset of television. The advent of audience research (a dusted down and recycled 1950s methodology) in film studies has marked a removal from earlier film theory that dealt with an abstract model of film viewers. Audience research is concerned with particularity, the reality of people watching cinema, deconstructing the monumental universal 'spectator' of 1970s Screen theory. Spectator theory was primarily associated with the British film journal *Screen*, and the 'spectator' was formed by a confluence of Althusserian Marxism (which interpellated or hailed the film watcher as a film watcher) and Lacanian psychoanalysis. *Screen* marked out a space (a modernist arena) for heroic theory which although it allowed a large amount of polemic and debate, also led to some 'radical' if ridiculous hypotheses. For example, one of the most famous and highly-regarded articles to emerge from *Screen* in the mid-1970s was Laura Mulvey's 'Visual Pleasure and Narrative Cinema'. While it is still an impressive and thought-provoking article (and still firmly within the theoretical canon of film studies), Mulvey could postulate that as classical cinema was built wholly around male views, both on screen and as constructed spectator, women could only enjoy cinema masochistically. I will reiterate what I stated earlier, that while psychoanalysis appeared to be fruitful for analysis of classical cinema, it has proved less effective when applied to contemporary cinema, further undermining the Marx-Freud axis of Screen theory.

One response, audience research, is a hyper-empirical response to the seeming excesses of film theory in the 1970s. As a reconstituted discipline, it has had to accept that its horizons are limited to providing microscopic snapshots of the realities of filmgoing. (Although some have more heroic pretensions of universalism, vestigial to the discipline's origin as a guarantee of truth). It is necessary that this form of inquiry remains aware of its limitations, particularly as postmodernity has seen a wholesale reconstitution of the terrain upon which identity is negotiated and renegotiated.

Cinema has been a fruitful ground for those seeking metaphors for 'the human condition' – whatever that universal may mean these days. For example, the replicants of *Blade Runner* (1982) represent humanity with false (media) memories and no real roots. In fact, cinema and life have become fully entwined. Film characters can lack any solid identity, manifesting postmodern schizophrenia absolutely like the killer in the Clint Eastwood film *The Dead Pool* (1988), who, as we are told by a psychoanalyst, has no personality of his own, but has just cobbled together a succession of excerpts of characters from films, books and television. Contemporary identities are overwhelmed by electronic audiovisual culture, which means that audiences tend to be very visually literate, and the bombardment appears to get faster and faster.

Tom Gunning has referred to early cinema as 'the cinema of attractions' and additionally posited a re-engagement with this centring of fairground excitement: 'recent spectacle cinema has reaffirmed its roots in stimulus and carnival rides, in what might be called the Spielberg-Lucas-Coppola cinema of effects' (Gunning 1990:61) while Linda Williams identifies Hitchcock's *Psycho* (1960) as a significant point of fundamental change in the modes of cinema (Williams 1994:15). She points to the film's theatricality and viscerality at the expense of pure concentration on the merits of story development. Not only were the conditions of the film's distribution and exhibition controlled as part of the whole experience, but the film itself is premised more upon the aesthetic of the fairground ride. This 'rollercoaster' as she calls it has developed into a staple of contemporary mainstream cinema, although it bears remarkable similarities with early cinema and marginal forms that have not been seen as part of the narrative film tradition. Horror films like *The Exorcist* (1973) and action pictures like *Star Wars* (1977) demonstrated a new form of spectacle where the technology of special effects began to present brand new images in a direct and visceral fashion, a process which has continued and has a recent manifestation in *Jurassic Park* (1993).

In contemporary cinema, it is essential that the film as product is differentiated from that offered by television, which leads to a concentration on technological spectacle and taboo. This has ushered in the disintegration of narrative as the organising principle of the film, a key notion of postmodernism in the cinema. Stanley Solomon points to recent cinema as a prime example of the disintegration of classic narrative in the Aristotelian sense. Referring to films such as *Star Wars* and *Raiders of the Lost Ark* (1981), he writes: 'The narrative elements in such films are chronologically arranged incidents that, given the premises, could happen but have no tragic or comic necessity for happening – the causes stemming not from story but from an available mixed bag of general emotions, special effects, and faith in production values' (Solomon 1989:65). He suggests that narrative may have lost its determining role in films. While it may have retained its role as principal unifying agent it can no longer be seen as the central organising process of mainstream films. Many contemporary films have a thin veneer of narrative that unifies action and provides continuity for the audience, yet both *Star Wars* and *Raiders of the Lost Ark* were perceived at the time of release as returning to the adventure films and stories of the pre-War period. The narratives of the films were revivals of a past type of narrative, but with its status altered within the films. Solomon goes on to point out:

> plot is being replaced by texture. By texture I mean incident or event or conversation – as distinct from structured action that has beginning, middle and end. An incident is not sustaining in itself, but many incidents and many conversations strung together may resemble something like a

> traditional narrative. Texture includes tone and spectacle, and if it is consistently applied it is another principle of organizing narrative art.
> (Solomon 1989:76)

The status and, as Solomon sees it, the nature of narratives has changed between much present cinema and the cinema of classical Hollywood, which has primarily been theorised as being narrative-led.

Along similar lines, Scott Lash's theorisation of postmodernism in cinema as a regime of signification declares that the figural, image and other elements, have replaced the concentration on narrative that has been a characteristic of classical cinema. He declares: 'In films of recent years spectacle . . . does not any longer become subordinate to narrative. That is, there has been a shift from a realist to a postmodernist cinema, in which spectacle comes heavily to dominate narrative' (Lash 1988:325). Many contemporary films seem to build a narrative to fit between their scenes of special effects and other set pieces. Perhaps the best examples are films from the contemporary action genre, where, in films such as *Double Impact* (1991) and *The Punisher* (1990), the narrative just seems to vaguely unify a succession of violent set pieces.

While the disintegration of narrative, or certainly its demotion from legislator of the film's processes, can be linked to notions of the decentred subject, the schizophrenic postmodern subject's bombardment with a diverse selection of images has meant a high level of cineliteracy. This entails the recognition of forms, strategies and elements from the past and present of visual culture, the past having been decidedly pulled into the present by films and TV.

The overwhelming use of pastiche as an aesthetic strategy, what Fredric Jameson has referred to as 'talking in a dead language' (Jameson 1991:17) is one of the central defining aspects of postmodern culture. This involves the utilisation of signifiers, often in formations, that belong to an outdated and specific form.

Jameson characterises pastiche as a 'neutral' form that does not comment upon the form itself but purely uses it as a vehicle (thus unlike parody). Additionally, postmodern pastiches do not use specific genre languages, for example costume drama, unless that genre is perceived generally to be a historical item, to be dead in terms of contemporary culture, although whatever makes a recognisable form can be used as a 'readymade' signification unit which has instant denotations and connotations for the cineliterate audience.

Examples abound: for instance, since the American cycle of film noirs of the 1940s and 1950s, we have seen a number of films that attempt to re-engage with the thematic interest of this cycle through an articulation of their highly specific film style. *Chinatown* (1974) is an early example, followed by *Body Heat* (1981), *Angel Heart* (1987) and the remakes of noir classics *The Postman Always Rings Twice* (1981) and *DOA* (1988). While these remade and updated the originals to include more explicit sex and pop-video kinesis respectively, the collapse of the distinction between past and present was manifested in the comedy *Dead Men Don't Wear Plaid* (1982). Here, excerpts from a number of film noirs were intercut with contemporary footage to build a story revolving around hard-boiled detective Steve Martin and including a cast of the long-dead such as Humphrey Bogart and James Cagney.[2] *Dead Men Don't Wear Plaid* recasts the culture of the past, converting it into a contemporary commodity, through the processes of assemblage, hybridity and recontextualisation.

Film noir has resurfaced in *Blade Runner* (1982), which seems to have been regularly cited as the postmodern film par excellence, and appropriates some of the film style of film noir, especially in the characteristic voice-over narration. This is recontextualised into a science fiction film where the design of

2 This technique was used on a Holsten Pils advertisement, taking excerpts from famous films, while its first cinematic appearance was in *The Last Remake of Beau Geste* (1977).

the future is an amalgam of elements, many from the present. While the original film is not considered to be a film noir, Scorsese's *Cape Fear* (1991) is self-conscious in its wielding of the thriller format. As an exercise in Hitchcockian suspense, Scorsese's film is ironically a recasting of the original film, 'fitted' to Bernard Herrmann's music from the original film.

The film musical, as it was in the heyday of classical Hollywood, is a moribund form ripe for being pastiched by postmodern cinema. Scorsese's *New York, New York* (1989) rebuilds the form to some degree, while Coppola's *One From the Heart* (1982) and *Absolute Beginners* (1986) attempt to reformulate the film musical, but with a high degree of reference to the styles of classical musicals, especially the large-scale production number. Other persuasive examples of distinct forms having been pastiched include *The Company of Wolves*'s (1984) articulation of classic gothic horror film iconography (while the film itself is 'not real' but 'about narratives'), while the classic Hollywood western film becomes the central image repertory and source of humour for *Back to the Future III* (1990), where jokes include Marty McFly (Michael J. Fox) calling himself 'Clint Eastwood'.

Alongside this concern with older cinema, there has also been a turning away from the modern, an atavistic return to the styles of earlier cinema, in some cases *to* early cinema. The use of black and white photography has become something of a marker for the dissatisfaction with technological modernism. Wim Wenders's *Wings of Desire* (1987) related black and white with transcendent reality in much the same way as *A Matter of Life and Death* (aka *Stairway to Heaven*, 1946) had nearly forty years earlier. Black and white photography has become the flip side of the colourisation that attempted to convert old black and white films into new, TV-friendly products. Yet colourisation as a policy was undermined by the sheer volume of black and white films that graced television sets in the western world, while black and white photography quickly became a major stylistic strategy for that new zone of visual impetus: pop video. Jim Jarmusch's *Stranger than Paradise* (1984) was not only in black and white, but seemingly used an aesthetic inherited from early film language from about eighty years previously, with a predominance of static tableaux and little in the way of built-up space or close ups.

Postmodernism has meant that film language is no longer simply functional, it has become part of the film's surface design. So the use of 'expressionistic' lighting or dutch-tilted camera is no longer the signifier of extreme emotional dislocation that it was in films like *The Third Man* (1949) or film noirs. Instead, it has become a surface manifestation which reminds the audience of cinema's previous uses of the devices. This can be accounted for by the unprecedented growth in visual literacy and film history in the western world. Audiences are generally used to seeing old films on television as well as seeing them referred to continually in more recent films. So the context for viewing is one where what was once the cutting edge of film language is now the tired cliche that cannot be utilised unless it is precisely as a cliche.

If modernism in the cinema can be premised upon a language, then postmodernism in the cinema can be seen as the assimilation and death of the impact of that language and its use value. Since the *Nouvelle Vague*, certain techniques have been associated with a cinema of modernism, specifically techniques that foreground subjectivity and personal vision and techniques that lay bare the mechanisms of the film itself. Postmodern culture has recuperated these techniques into the mainstream en masse. Of course, there has always been an assimilation of some of the language of the avant garde into the mainstream of the time, for example, certain surrealist and expressionist techniques were easily integrated into Hollywood dream sequences. Yet the totality of the integration in recent years marks it out as profoundly different from this gradual and selective broadening of language by the mainstream. In addition to this, if art cinema and the avant garde have functioned for the mainstream of the past as precisely an avant garde, a cutting edge of film language that has been more syntactically advanced than the mainstream which has assimilated slowly in its wake, then recent cinema exhibits a radically different relationship between the two entities. Since the 1960s, broadly speaking, the cinematic avant garde has become less and less tenable as a linguistically progressive body (filmwise) and has ceded technical innovation to the mainstream and films at the edges of the mainstream. This has to be seen as a primary movement identified as postmodern culture, with the motor for this change being the proliferation of visual culture on television and more specifically the possibilities opened for a complex film language by television advertisements and their younger sibling pop videos. The pressures for saturation sales that have been one of the hallmarks of consumer capitalism's development have allowed a space for what would have been considered earlier to be experiment and obfuscation, all in the name of product differentiation, of trying to have their product identified as distinct from others. Of course, this superficially seems to lead to a situation where many advertisements look similar: an example is the proliferation in recent times of the shot that Hitchcock used in the tower sequence in *Vertigo* (1956) to express shock or amazement.[3] Generally, however, we can speak of a mainstream that has usurped the avant garde's traditional function of being the cutting edge of visual culture.

That the language of the avant garde has been recuperated by mainstream culture is demonstrated by the use of the principal spatial strategy of the avant garde film *The Riddles Of The Sphinx* (1976), the use of a continuous pan by a static camera which establishes film space through continual revolution, in the

3 This is a depth of space effect, where the background to a static figure is made to elongate while the figure remains in the same position.

pop video for 'Destroy The Heart' by The House Of Love (1987). The arena of advertisements and pop videos has assimilated the language of the avant garde to the point where it is unable to continue its revolution of the language of cinema as the cutting edge of visual culture has been taken by expensively-made pop videos and adverts.

This may make the avant garde untenable as the revolutionary force (certainly in terms of film language) that was one of its central historical roles, and yet it still has a continued existence. What remains is a focus on content as the primary identification of a self-consciously marginal cinema. From a position of 'saying something new in a new language' it has become 'saying something'. This is why much of the remains of the avant garde and modernist cinema (counter cinema, experimental cinema and the mini-capitalist mainstream of art cinema) have to be seen as firmly a part of modernist culture as their continued survival as distinct entities requires an elitist or minority audience.

Films such as *Performance* (1970), which marked an interface between modernist cinema and popular culture, accelerated the collapse of the avant garde as they offered a space where its modes could be seen by larger audiences, but it did so by simultaneously sacrificing something in the way of effect. Thus the avant garde of the 1970s in Britain became increasingly esoteric, in a quest to negate the possibility of larger audiences for such films. Films such as Laura Mulvey and Peter Wollen's *Riddles of the Sphinx* (1976) aimed, through the use of direct address by the one of the film's directors, and through the use of a regular revolving camera, to break up the syntax of traditional and mainstream cinema. The net effect was to procure an extremely small audience for avant garde films, yet, by the 1980s, one of the great white hopes of the young avant gardists, John Maybury, jumped ship and immersed himself in making pop videos. Arguably, postmodernism marks the avant garde impulse being absorbed by commercial culture – and this suggests that patronage was more available from commercial sources than from state bodies which had largely funded the avant garde during the 1970s. Apart from Maybury, the Quay brothers (identical twins Timothy and Stephen) had been involved in cutting-edge pop videos (Peter Gabriel's *Sledgehammer*), as well as television advertisements (Ronseal wood treatment), in both cases retaining a high degree of their individual style. The Quay brothers' films, such as *The Cabinet of Jan Svankmajer* (1984) and *The Street of Crocodiles* (1986), demonstrate very clearly the self-conscious use of an avant garde film language. The brothers are American, but living in the UK. They use an alien and historical language, that of middle Europe with the implication of the pre-World War Two period. *The Street of Crocodiles*, for example, uses an iconography of animated Victorian dolls, dusty Victorian machines and middle-European writing as a concession to Bruno Schulz's source text. The work of the Quay brothers suggests that the avant garde has continued by reusing a historical and dead language, much like the equivalent of speaking Latin, yet it is the audience's ability to recognise, on no matter how simple a scale, 'readymades', almost fully-developed discourses that allows a system of signification such as this.

One of the most striking aspects of contemporary Hollywood cinema, a characteristic regularly identified with postmodernism, is the all-embracing intertextuality of many films. Hardly a film goes by without its allusion to at least one other film or television show. This hyperreferentiality is usually dealt with under the aegis of pastiche or postmodern pastiche, and has a tendency towards the articulation of 'readymades' from other sources. This situation has been allowed by the tremendous level of visual literacy (or rather audiovisual literacy) attained by the populations of the media-saturated first world. Perhaps the best examples of this type of cinema are the films directed by Quentin Tarantino, where film genres, television shows and music all allude to culture outside of the film. *Reservoir Dogs* (1992) has a substantial section of dialogue devoted to an obscure television show from the 1970s. This has no narrative importance, it is a dead end in terms of the film's internal development, yet gives an example of the film text as referring outwards, away from itself, that is a characteristic of postmodernism in films. Another prime example in the same film is the seemingly parallel text of the 1970s music radio station, 'K-Billy Super Sounds of the Seventies'. This provides a number of songs that intersect with the film rather than integrate themselves, while the film's posing of the radio station gives them a seeming point of unity. The songs cohere as a soundtrack LP that is, like the radio station, half inside and half outside of the film.

This is undoubtedly a change from the dominant modes of Hollywood until the 1960s, and had only really became a dominant form by the 1980s, yet there have been few convincing attempts to deal with this cinema of connections and references – or, at least, the attempts that have been made do not seem to get us very far. This situation seems to add credence to the notion that there has been a paradigm shift, displacing the major ways that we have tried to make sense of culture and the world, knocking them off centre while newer (or older but not dominant) paradigms have started to contest that space. The most fruitful theoretical context for appraising contemporary Hollywood as an aesthetic is Baudrillard's theory of simulation and the Simulacrum. This suggests that there has been a collapse of culture into reality, leading to an amalgam of the two: reality is imbricated with cultural modes, but further, we are no longer able to differentiate the real and the representational any more. This not only has dramatic ramifications for the relationship of filmtext to audience, but for the relationship of film scholar to filmtext.

Simulation has incorporated discourses of criticism into the cultural object, another example being the concern with history as construct related by *Forrest Gump* (1994), and, more precisely, in *Bill and Ted's Excellent Adventure* (1989). This film is a virtual treatise on history, with the eponymous heroes having to give an end of term history presentation, getting into a time machine and collecting well-known historical figures to parade in front of their class. The lecturing academic (much like Laura Mulvey in *Riddles of the Sphinx*) has also been assimilated: in David Cronenberg's *Videodrome* (1983), Dr. Brian O'Blivion pontificates about television while appearing only on a television set, while what he says bears an uncanny resemblance to Baudrillard!

It is reassuring to think that academic concerns, and especially film studies concerns have reached out into a wider context – a situation where criticism has collapsed into the object. Much has been made of the influence of film schools on the movie brat generation, but Zucker, Abrahams and Zucker, the producers/directors of the *Naked Gun* series of films were instructed under David Bordwell and Kristin Thompson at the University of Wisconsin Madison, probably the English-speaking world's centre of film scholarship. Indeed, their films reflect a theoretical approach to cinema, and I have often thought that they would be a good point from which to start teaching film. *Hot Shots! Part Deux* (1991) has a sequence that no film scholar can forget, where a scene from *Apocalypse Now* (1979) is reconstructed with Charlie Sheen replacing his father in a boat going up the river. In the opposite direction another boat appears, carrying Martin Sheen; when they meet, each says, 'Loved you in *Wall Street*!' This dense network of film references requires a high degree of film literacy, and evinces a profoundly different relationship between audience and texts from that of even twenty years ago. It seems to me that to persist blindly in using old paradigms would be like trying to attempt to account for the scene I described without knowledge or reference to *Apocalypse Now* or *Wall Street* (1987)

This situation, a network of interconnecting micro-narratives, has been allowed by the development of a hypertext mentality in film and television audiences, where they are more concerned with decentred connections like Internet than with any unitary discourse of the film. This accounts for the downgrading of classical narrative, into sheen and micro-narratives, in this overall shift from a concern with the syntagmatic in classical Hollywood to a focus on the paradigmatic in recent cinema. For example, the conclusion of *Wild at Heart* (1990), where the film's fraught references to *The Wizard of Oz* (1939) culminate in the appearance of the good witch, who tells Sailor (Nicholas Cage) what to do. He then runs after Lula and they have a reunion that is like something out of a romance novel, to the tune of Richard Strauss's Late Romantic tone poem *Im Abendrot*, after which Sailor stands on top of the car and sings 'Love Me Tender' in the style of Elvis. *Wild at Heart* is not a musical, but what it does is continually reference the outside of the text, juxtaposing two radically different traditions of music and a generic parody with references to one of Hollywood's most famous films.[4] In terms of the recycling of popular culture, and its consequent reassessment, postmodernism seems to be an aesthetic return of the repressed to match the theoretical return of the repressed.

Audience members do not perceive things the same way: many intertexts may be lost on many viewers, and also many intertexts will be made that were never part of the film's intentions. For, indeed, an audience member that watches

[4] Most of these aspects I have been describing can be found in classical cinema, but not in the Official Version. The concern with spectacle, margins and references to other films appear on the side of cinema that film history has ignored or tried to repress: singing cowboy films (like Roy Rogers), musical shorts (which have existed since the first decade of the century), pornography (which film historians seem to totally deny) and low comedy, such as *The Three Stooges*.

ten hours of television per day will obviously perceive a film differently from someone who watches none, the first will have an infinite number of coordinate points against which to map the film they are watching. The postmodern cinema constitutes a highly fragmentary experience, due to films constantly referring outwards to other films and consequently being heavily episodic.

As already stated, the concept of postmodernism has not really had much effect in the field of film studies. Despite the raised voices that declare its transitory status, film studies is arguably well within the grip of postmodern philosophies: revisionism, historicism, archiving, interest in marginal cinema, backlashes against master discourses, etc. This is the questioning, philosophical version of postmodernism, but postmodernism can illuminate things that other theories fail to trace, and provide approaches which are not a part of the film studies orthodoxy, and yet perhaps should be. Stanley Solomon pointed out that classical narrative, narrative as it has been theorised in the academy, is virtually absent from much recent cinema. The dictatorship of narrative drive has gone from cinema, overarching developmental classical narrative as the central raison d'être of cultural production has broken down to be replaced by fragmentary and episodic micro-narratives. In cinema, these are often autonomous spectacles (car chases, shoot outs, love and sex scenes, conversations, special effect sequences, etc.). The assimilation of cinema into the highly flexible corporate leisure industries – into the very heart of simulated modern life itself – has helped to change the nature of films that are produced by Hollywood and other mainstream cinemas. Perhaps the key characteristic of postmodern cinema is the referentiality of films, enabled and encouraged by the cineliteracy of audiences who (in the western world, anyway) are used to consuming audiovisual products in vast amounts. There is a fundamentally altered economic situation from the heyday of classical Hollywood, even from twenty years ago, and this has produced a cinema that has developed significantly over that time. So it seems a rather uncomplicated theoretical route to imagine that universal truths can be gleaned from films today using the same approaches as for the films of fifty, or even one hundred years ago.

K. J. DONNELLY
University of East Anglia

Works Cited

Baudrillard, Jean. *In the Shadow of the Silent Majorities*. New York: Semiotext(e): 1983.

Buckland, Warren. 'Fredric on Film Theory'. *New Formations* 16 (1992): 163-70.

Bordwell, David. *Narration in the Fiction Film*. London: Routledge, 1985.

Gomery, Douglas. 'Hollywood's Hold on the New Television Technology'. *Screen* 29.2 (1988): 82-90.

Gunning, Tom. 'The Cinema of Attractions: Early Film, Its Spectator and the Avant Garde'. *Early Cinema: Space Frame Narrative*. Eds. Thomas Elsaesser and Adam Barker. London: BFI, 1990. 56-62.

Hayward, Philip and Paul Kerr. Introduction to 'Postmodern Screen' (special issue) *Screen* 28.2 (1987): 2-8 .

Jameson, Fredric. *The Geopolitical Aesthetic: Cinema and Space in the World System*. London: BFI, 1992.

---. *Postmodernism; Or the Logic of Late Capitalism*. London: Verso, 1991.

Lash, Scott. 'Discourse or Figure? Postmodernism as Regime of Signification'. *Theory, Culture and Society* 5.2-3 (1988): 311-36.

Lyotard, Jean-François. *The Postmodern Condition: A Report on Knowledge*. Manchester: Manchester University Press, 1984.

Mulvey, Laura. 'Visual Pleasure and Narrative Cinema'. *Screen* 16.3 (1975): 6-18.

Orr, John. *Cinema and Modernity*. London: Polity Press, 1993.

Solomon, Stanley. 'Aristotle in Twilight: American Film Narrative in the 1980s'. *The Cinematic Text*. Ed. R. Barton Palmer. New York: AMS, 1989. 63-80.

Williams, Linda. 'Learning to Scream'. *Sight and Sound* 4.12 (1994): 14-17.

Desire and Delusion:

Amateur and Postmodern Heterosexuality

Described as an inter-generic 'absurdist romantic thriller', the recent film *Amateur* (Dir: Hal Hartley, 1994) embodies several key instabilities which have been held to characterise a cinema of the postmodern. Its emergence out of a variously configured collaboration between UCG, American Playhouse Theatrical Films and Channel Four Films places the film beyond categorisation as either mainstream or purely art house. Such commercial hybridity in terms of production also extends to the indeterminacy of audiences brought to it through a consumption pattern of distribution and exhibition which typifies the contemporary 'cult' feature: the film enjoyed a brief period of intense metropolitan box office success before a slower though longer exposure to audiences through both High Street video rental and the 'independent' cinema circuit. Further, the film is indicative of profound shifts in the meaning of the concept of Auteur which, as Tim Corrigan has cogently argued, must be assessed in relation to any definition of postmodern cinema. This is not the place to rehearse intricate arguments left in the wake of formalist, structuralist and poststructuralist critiques of the Death of the Author but it is clear that a contemporary notion of the Auteur has a complex filiation to outdated but nonetheless intransigent Romantic conceptions of film maker as unique expressive artist. The latest in a series of feature-length films – *The Unbelievable Truth* (1989), *Trust* (1990) and *Simple Men* (1992) – *Amateur* contributes to a corpus of works in relation to which the figure of the director functions as guarantor for a specific kind of film in which 'classical' Hollywood and European modes of film styles are conjoined: generic conventions drawn from standard thriller-chase plots and the romantic tragedy provide a conventional hermeneutic while the visual style enjoys a degree of autonomy from simple narrative demands in its use of anti-naturalistic lighting, self-conscious use of frame composition and a frequently protracted scene duration produced by non-action orientated editing. *Amateur* is further defined by a mode of dialogue patterning often typifying Western European cinema – significant silences, address off-camera, ellipses, extended verbal interchanges which seem hardly to require the presence of listeners. This dialogical dimension is further borne out in the extra filmic discourses which contribute to the circulation of meanings around the signifier 'Hal Hartley'. From an interview included in the Faber screenplay, Hartley combines a view of himself as an Intending Consciousness (defined by personal 'integrity', 'sincerity' and 'rigorousness') with a postmodernist aesthetic of intertextuality which militates against this: 'A lot of the situations in this movie strike me as standard cop show stuff, but with the information different. A TV cop show made by someone who doesn't know how to make TV cop shows.' Such self-conscious 'amateurism' instantiates a specific configuration of the territory left for a postmodern auteur who cannot claim a pure space of 'alternative' critique outside of the cultural ubiquity of dominant Hollywood narrative forms but offers instead to collapse the older modernist ideological binaries that pitched a cinema of the intellect – Europe/art-house/personal vision/visual style/film maker against a cinema of visual pleasure – Hollywood/mainstream/formulaic plot/factory production/director. If *Amateur* is a text organised around 'speaking' the cinematic languages of Europe and America simultaneously, what does such dialogism actually effect in terms of reading? Arguing that postmodern cinema, and postmodern culture more generally, is by definition at worst a-political and at best politically ambivalent has become something of a critical shibboleth. Filmic eclecticism, stylistic contradiction, intertextual referencing and a promiscuous intermixing of genres are either symptomatic of an exhausted and aesthetically bankrupted culture industry, or they represent a democratised avant-gardism fully adapted to the political realities of visually literate audiences for whom adversarial counter-cultural politics have no force or function. However, the terms for debating the political effect of textual practices within the aesthetics of the postmodern are radically different if approached from the point of view of feminist analysis. Feminist film theories are chiefly concerned to analyse gendered roles within visual texts so, my question is, what does the use of discrete film forms imply for an analysis of gender, sexuality and power? Does the presentation of coexistent cinema histories offer a critique of dominant codes for signifying female sexuality, or merely duplicate them? In answer, my reading of *Amateur* suggests that double-coded films confront the limits of both positions, provoking a definitively postmodern indeterminacy by necessarily participating in the very structures it purports to question. This indicates once again that there is no easy assimilation of feminist concerns within the visual texts of postmodern culture. However, *Amateur* does explicitly foreground meanings of identity and selfhood which makes it fertile ground for exploring the consequences for a feminist analysis of thinking the relations between 'self', gender and sexuality within a postmodernist or, better, post-structuralist framework. In short, I want to approach the age-old query – what is the nature of female desire? – in relation to the sexual identities signified within the film (as 'characters') and to assess what these imply for the patterns of identification available to the film audience.

A pale, plain and undernourished woman named Isabelle (Isabelle Huppert) is sitting in a cafe attempting to write pornography on a laptop when an injured man with amnesia stumbles in: the opening shot had previously shown him lying in the street overlooked by a terrified dark-haired women who, assuming his injuries are fatal, runs away to leave him for dead. Later the identities of these initial characters are revealed as Sofia (Elina Lowensohn) and Thomas (Martin Donovan) but the first enigma posed by the film is the identity of the man who does not even know his own name. Isabelle takes Thomas home and reveals that she has recently left a convent after fifteen years because of visits from the Virgin Mary urging her to enter the world so that she may intervene in an as yet unknown destiny. The plot proceeds to enmesh Isabelle and Thomas with Sofia, a celebrated porn star who Isabelle recognises from a rented video as the one she has been ordained to help. A wholly self-conscious and parodic thriller narrative is set in motion when some computer floppy disks (which contain enough information to blackmail Jacques, the head of a foreign governmental organisation) fall in Sofia's possession. Jacques sends two corporate killers to retrieve them at all costs. Ironically, as Isabelle's fascination with Sofia impels her to enlist Thomas to help find and protect her, Sofia knows Thomas as her husband, a violent and sadistic pornographer, and it is from him that she is attempting to escape. This sets up a complex interplay between the three characters since the narrative does not prioritise any one of them as its organising centre. They are each in different ways engaged in a pursuit for identity: Thomas's amnesia figures the question 'Who am I?' literally, Isabelle has no past or personal history having only recently joined the social world, while Sofia is attempting to escape from a corrupted self. From a feminist point of view, the interest of the film lies in the way in which the enigmas around 'identity' are simultaneously explored as enigmas around sexual identity.

Isabelle

From her unadorned appearance and pallid skin, her frail body which is rarely fed, the Catholic iconography and religious visions, Isabelle signifies one half of the enduring patriarchal binary which constructs female identity in terms of an asexual, virginal purity that transcends the demands of desire and the claims of the corporeal. Isabelle, though, is consumed with the fantasy of becoming a woman where truly to be a women is to be a sexual women: hence her comically ingenue attempts to refigure herself in the form of a sexually knowing and experienced woman firstly as a literary pornographer and then as a nymphomaniac: 'Have you ever *had* sex?' Thomas asks. 'No'. 'How can you be a nymphomaniac and never had sex?' 'I'm choosy'. At the heart of Isabelle's identity there is a perception of lack, and it is a specifically *sexual* identity that is marked as absent from her self-definition as a woman 'in the world'. Her desire for sexual encounters, her 'amateur's' pursuit of a sexual persona, provides a point of view for the film to manifest how far what is taken to be natural about female sexuality is actually the work of historical and cultural processes. As social construct theorists of sexuality have argued, heterosexuality does not come naturally. While sexual desire and passion might feel personal and private, individual experiences are to a large degree governed by cultural 'scripts' which determine *a priori* the – gendered – roles that each may take up. A humorous effect is produced by Isabelle's lack of shared understanding about what these might be. For instance, on a date at the cinema arranged through a 'hot phone-sex party line', a perfunctory grope leads Isabelle to ask 'What are you doing?' to which her date replies 'I'm molesting you.' 'Am I supposed to like it?' she asks. 'You could beg me to stop'. 'And would you?'. 'No', he answers, and she leaves. At a more profound level, though, I would suggest that the question of identity as it is proposed by Isabelle exemplifies the difficulty for women of splitting epistemological concerns (Who am I?) from ontological ones (What am I?). This is not due to some inherent or essential fault in women's capacity to reason but, rather, to indicate that her question – 'how can I have access to female sexuality?' is in some ways a philosophical delusion which conceals the power effects of a gendered economy of identity formation by positing a neutral and non-specific 'I' outside of it. To negate this problem, it is worth returning to Jacques Lacan's insistence that *desire* is the motor force of identity formation. For Lacan, identity is never a matter of essence but, rather, a misrecognition of the subject formed in its splitting – but this is not of the same order of division by which Isabelle is internally polarised: What does Isabelle want? To be a woman. How will she become a woman? By being desirable. At the broadest level, this works to confirm the cultural assumption that there is no female identity aside from female sexuality. More specifically, Isabelle has immersed herself in the male-defined visual and written discourses of pornography and it is from 'Gang Rape' and the sadistic scenarios of written porn that she has learned the 'script' of what that female sexuality might be. For Isabelle to achieve a sexuality, the film suggests, she must reinvent herself to the order of male desire which requires her inscription by/into the culturally dominant commodified forms of heterosexuality. Isabelle seeks to refigure herself into a fantasy form of what she *believes* men want. This is made explicit in a scene which marks her movement towards the porn sexuality embodied by Sofia. In a classic instance of fetishistic transformation, Isabelle dresses in Sofia's sexy lingerie, black stockings, leather skirt and shiny high heels. Thomas is aroused enough to begin to make love to her only when she has assumed this image which opens up another way to interpret the function of his missing identity – as a 'structuring absence' into which the male spectator can project his controlling gaze. This would configure the film as a fantasy scenario highly redolent of Freud's theories on male adult heterosexuality.

In the 'Contributions to the Psychology of Love', Freud suggests that the passage through the Oedipus complex (in which tabooed active sexual feelings towards the mother are repressed and sublimated) produces a split in which tenderness and sexual desire are rendered incompatible: where hostility accompanies sexual arousal, there is evidence of a psychical struggle which is projected outwards to create two kinds of relations with women: either asexual adoration or debased sex relations. As Elizabeth Grosz notes, either position is a position formed out of ambivalent feelings produced in the man's pre-Oedipal relation to his mother.

> She is both virginal, pure, noble, sexless (as a consequence of his repression of his own sexual wishes about her), and a whore, the result of his realisation that, long before his birth, the mother has already been unfaithful to him (with the father). If she is a sexual being, she has betrayed him by being desired by others, like his fantasy of the prostitute.
> (Grosz 1990:129)

It hardly needs demonstrating that, between them, Isabelle and Sofia represent the terms of this psychical polarity. However, the film is 'knowing' in its contemporary use of virgin/whore iconography: Sofia's dark eyes, heavy make-up, jewellery, dyed black hair and 'provocative' clothing signifying the sexualised woman while images are composed to frame Isabelle against a Madonna & Child museum poster, or to counterpoint her 'difference' from the images of women in porno magazines. Further, the film stretches the cliche beyond credibility (by proposing that the only other sexual identity open to a chaste virgin is its 'opposite', the nymphomaniac pornographer) so that one must assume the intention is to subvert the Freudian orthodoxy. Indeed, there are several scenes which work with a certain level of awareness of feminist debates concerning female sexuality and its commodification in which the signalled 'knowingness' performs self-reflexively to forestall criticism. For instance, in a typical postmodernist intermingling of incongruous registers, one of the assassins – Kurt – sets about preparing to torture information out of Sofia:

> Kurt: Do you resent your position as a woman in the motion picture industry? I'm sorry. I find you attractive, and I'm interested in commodities.
> Sofia: What are you talking about?
> Kurt: A commodity is an article of trade.
> Sofia: What has this got to do with me?
> Kurt: You're a product.
> Sofia: I am?
> Kurt: You're a commodity. Thomas tendered your body in exchange for money.
> Sofia: So I'm an article of trade?
> Kurt: Yes. A useful thing, in terms of classic capitalism. I studied economics. I know what I'm talking about.

My feelings, however, are that the virgin/whore dichotomy is not, and cannot, be subverted so easily since the audience is still being offered visual pleasure on the basis that at least one women functions as an erotic spectacle. Despite their 'differences', Isabelle and Sofia come to occupy the space that many feminist film theorists have argued is the only one available to the screen woman: she is there only as an absence, an absence into which male castration fears and fantasies can be projected – she is what she is for a man and therefore literally 'is' not. That there is no 'authentic' female sexuality rests on the view that female identity itself is negatively defined as 'other than', or 'not-male'. There is a danger here, though, of assuming from this model that if female sexual identity 'is not', then male sexual identity somehow 'is'. This, I think, is the source of many feminists' impatience with the 'phallocentrism' of psychoanalytical theories of the acquisition of sexual identities. To explain – the standard formulation of Lacanian theory is succinctly expressed as follows 'Sexual difference can only be the consequence of a division; without this division it would cease to exist. But it must exist because no human being can become a subject outside the division into two sexes. One must take up a position as either a man or a woman' (Mitchell and Rose 1982:2). But this implies that once sexual differentiation has taken place through the castration/Oedipus complex sexual identities for both sexes are a) coherent/stable and b) fixed/permanent which, as Jacqueline Rose argues so persuasively, neutralises any radical or critical potential of Lacan's understanding of sexuality. That potential is made apparent by shifting the meaning of heterosexuality away from a model founded on a notion of complementary, stable, sexed identities (active/masculine/fetishistic; passive/feminine/narcissistic) to an insistence on the non-foundational character of sexual subjectivity. The latter model dispenses with the idea of a unified subject who 'has' an independent sexual identity and stresses instead that identity is produced only in relation to others: sexual subjectivity is a temporary (though psychically intense) effect produced by desire. For Lacan, desire is always the sign of a lack or incompleteness produced in the formation of the self; as the very constitution of identity is founded on the fiction of one's wholeness known only in the vacillating subject/object relations with an other, 'consciousness desires the desire of another to constitute itself as self-conscious' (Grosz 1990:65). Regardless of its path to satisfaction, desire is never directly for the other but for the desire *of* an other, for the recognition of self that the other's desire confirms. In other words, identity is only provisionally confirmed intersubjectively in relations to others. However, Lacan's theoretical schema rests on the *gendered* sexualities that are produced in the circulations of the 'desire for the desire of the other'. It is important to observe that *both* sexes are defined by their differentiating relations to the phallus. The phallus is, variously, that which marks the originating split in the subject and the loss of unity in the relation to the mother occasioned by recognition that she desires another for, if she desires, she must lack: 'Castration means first of all this – that the child's desire for the mother does not refer to her but beyond her, to an object, the phallus, whose status is first imaginary (the object presumed to satisfy her desire) and then symbolic (recognition that desire cannot be satisfied)' (Rose 1989:62). The phallus is therefore the signifier of a desire which actuates the primary division within subjectivity itself. This is enough to undermine any presumed essential link between sexuality and gender by pointing to the fact that sexual differentiation is brought about by the phallus. So what does the 'desire of the other' mean for a *male* sexual subject? Primarily, the male is affirmed as phallic *only* through the other who desires him: that a woman desires him is interpreted as a sign that she lacks something, or wants something which she lacks and he 'has', thus confirming his superior and powerful status over her. And what does the 'desire of the other' mean for a *female* sexual subject? Lacking the penis (the possession of which the male mistakenly assumes is the real condition for the exercise of sexual dominance), a female also lacks the means for occupying the position of the subject who can 'have' the phallus. Two consequences ensue. Firstly, male desire for a woman is locked into a solipsistic circuit in which he seeks her desire for him only to confirm his relation to the phallus: 'he desires his "possession" of the phallus be affirmed through the woman's desire for his penis, which is (symbolically) detachable from him and capable of being "given" to her'

(Grosz 1990:135). Secondly, what she cannot 'have', she must instead be content to 'be': 'she desires access to the phallus he "owns"' so female desire is to occupy temporarily the position of 'being' the Phallus, to be the object of male desire. In view of this, Isabelle conforms to this scenario in which female sexuality is in the gift of men: she asks Thomas to have sex with her in the belief that this will grant access to the phallic sexual identity she seeks. The structures of visual objectification frequently criticised in pornography are, then, only an intensified form of the heterosexual relation in general: sexuality for the woman is always sexuality for the man. But I would suggest that Isabelle's desire raises a far more interesting set of issues. Too often psychoanalytical accounts of female sexuality conclude with the scenario I have outlined: women are psychical screens for the projection of male fantasies of domination. As in a looking-glass, where female sexual fantasies are held simply to mirror the image of the male psyche, 'typically' female fantasies are passive: to be seduced, to be raped, to be tied up and beaten, even in fantasy to 'be' for the male. While I cannot dispute that those fantasies frequently take a fetishistic form, I would, however, suggest that the Lacanian scenario of heterosexual desire is of limited value in accounting for *women's* investment in *men* as sites of fantasy. For there is something 'left over' in Isabelle's sexual subjectivity which cannot be accounted for in this schema: her desire for Thomas is a desire for what?

Thomas

Pursuing the notion that the three figures in the film function intersubjectively, it is clear that the meanings of each are formed through a complex triangulated pattern of identifications. Who is Thomas *for* Isabelle? Who is Thomas *for* Sofia? For Isabelle, he is a romantic figure who represents her sexual awakening while for Sofia he represents her sexual debasement in the porn industry. For the female spectator, this offers a highly ambivalent mode of identification which splits Thomas into both good and bad Object. Again, the monolithic Mulveyan model of female spectatorship in which women in the audience are supposed to identify with their screen 'like' (as *objects* of the look) seems inadequate to the structure of possible identifications. The film constantly defers confirmation of his past identity which sets up an oscillation between identifying with Isabelle (the romance plot which 'must' end in the narrative pleasure of union in sexual consummation) and identifying with Sofia (the escape/revenge plot which 'must' end in his accountability for past crimes). This introduces a simultaneous structure of identification which culminates in a highly equivocal scene – Isabelle and Thomas begin to make love in the flat at the point at which it becomes evident to the spectator that he may after all be connected with Polaroids of a mutilated porn actress/prostitute slashed across the face with a knife. I would suggest from this that Thomas's absence of self and of agency is significant in that it opens a space which, unusually in cinema, allows him to be positioned as object of desire – three times she lays claim to his identity in saying 'I am with you now. It doesn't matter who you were'. In other words, his lack of identity facilitates his location within Isabelle's fantasy structure in which Isabelle is instituted as an active agent of her own sexual desire. Her investment in him is clearly expressed as an erotic but, importantly, romantic fantasy. Stevi Jackson, who has recently addressed female investment in romantic idealisation, demonstrates the primary importance of psychical construction to erotic attachment: 'the other we pursue so compulsively is frequently our own creation, the 'real' person we think we love may be no more than a pretext around which our fantasies are woven' (Jackson 1995:53). Isabelle's pursuit of a sexual union (which I previously located in the register of the phallic) can be relocated within the scenario of union and completeness that is the essence of the heterosexual fantasy of romance. The film narrative, though, frustrates this by interrupting Isabelle's tentative initiations and they do not consummate before he is shot dead by the police (in a case of mistaken identity!). From the point of view of spectatorial expectation set in train by Isabelle's desire, this is clearly a melancholic culmination but from the perspective of Lacan's theory of the origins of heterosexual difference it is perhaps the inevitable symbolisation of his pronouncement that 'there is no sexual relation'. As desire itself is produced in the splitting from the original plenitude of the maternal dyad, 'desire for the other's desire' must always re-enact the impossibility of the return to Oneness: completion in heterosexual union is a delusion because 'in the sexual relationship, one loves narcissistically, because love is always narcissistic in so far as it is a desire for an unreachable unity' (Benvenuto and Kennedy 1986:190). In the path towards merging, loss of self, of trying to overcome the meaning of sexual difference, the myth of romance is finally one of self-completion. But the male sexual subject is forever alienated from self-completion by his relation to the mark of difference, the phallus. In this, there is room for recasting the romance fantasy as one for the *female* subject who stands in a different relationship to the cancelling of the meaning of sexual difference. Instead of staging the scene of desire for woman's completion in the phallus, it could be argued that the romance returns the female subject to a pre-Oedipal self-completion in undifferentiation from the maternal body, a pleasure assured by neither having a penis, nor needing one. Yet this would be to suggest a possibility for female pleasure which is outside of the heterosexual economy, and it is this possibility which is 'left over' in Isabelle's subjectivity. I want to conclude with some remarks on the potential for situating the figure of Sofia who, it can be said, signifies a surplus flow of desire in the identification between two women.

Sofia

As several theorists of lesbian subjectivity have contended, the task of formulating female desire as *active* desire is hard enough within the heterosexual model of psychosexuality but to approach active female desire in homosexual terms almost impossible. For Isabelle, Sofia as well as Thomas is an object of desire in the sense that it is Sofia who sets in motion Isabelle's narrative movement and is situated as 'that which is sought for'. Though not explicitly marked as 'lesbian', this nonetheless introduces a spectatorial position which may offer pleasure connected, in Jackie Stacey's phrase, with 'women's active desire and the sexual aims of women in the audience in relationship to the female protagonist on the screen' (Stacey 1987:49). Cutting across the other currents of desire in the film, then, there seems to be a space for envisaging how a lesbian spectator might be solicited by the film's address. The pivotal moment arrives when Isabelle is transfixed by the image of Sofia in a porn video which she freeze-frames and then touches as if to make a physical connection. In Hartley's account, this single image functions for Isabelle as 'the sign she has been waiting for. She doesn't recognise it as a coincidence. She recognises it as an image not simply representing knowledge, but containing it' (Hartley 1994:xxxiii). Sofia, then, physically *embodies* the resolution to Isabelle's epistemological search for the meaning of her identity. Nonetheless, as Teresa de Lauretis' critique of Stacey's account of 'specifically homosexual pleasures of female spectatorship' makes clear, identification *with* the image of another woman is by no means of the same order as sexual desire *for* that woman. In fact, in strictly Freudian terms 'identification with' one's 'like' is actually a symptom of the swerving of a sexual aim or, better, a process in which the object is 'desexualised'. Isabelle's fascination with Sofia, thus, might more adequately be considered to exemplify both the female-female identifications positioned in the visual register of narcissism: 'one woman – the younger or more "childlike" of each pair – wishes to be like, to become or literally to impersonate the other, either in order to take her place in the world . . . or to replace her as the desire of both her husband and the audience . . . or in order to acquire her image as a woman liberated, free and "saturated with sexuality"' (de Lauretis 1991:259). As 'both are terminal cases of identification, the first with an oedipal mother/rival image, the second with a feminine ego ideal' (259), conditions of desire between woman are placed back firmly within the heterosexual order and there referred, ultimately, to the male order. In sum, the terms for either representing a directly lesbian sexual subjectivity or a lesbian spectatorial position are severely limited. In short, *Amateur* invokes the narrative of female-female desire but, I would suggest, to the effect only of exposing the delusion of transcending the heterosexual presumption which sets the scene of desire.

And yet, it is highly significant that Hartley explicitly modelled the freeze-framed image of Sofia caught in the throes of orgasm on Bernini's statue of religious mystic St Teresa which famously for Lacan stands as the very cipher of female sexual pleasure or jouissance: 'just as with St Teresa – you only have to go to look at the Bernini statue in Rome to understand immediately she's coming, no doubt about it. And what is she enjoying, coming from? It's clear the essential testimony of the mystics is that of saying they experience it but know nothing about it' (Lacan: Seminar XX in Mitchell and Rose 1982:147). This brings analysis to the terminal point of many theories of female sexuality – if the terms of sexual enjoyment are phallic ('enjoyment of mastery, of the ego's imaginary bodily compactness and mental coherence' (Benvenuto and Kennedy 1986:192) – what of women's enjoyment? In St Teresa's orgasmic communion with God, both Hartley and Lacan see the image of an '*en plus*' or 'more' figured in the face of a woman frozen in the ecstasy of sexual bliss with something beyond desire (outside of language, outside of culture and outside of the work of the phallus). Not all of female sexuality is accounted for in the 'desire for the desire of the Other' for there is something in women's sexual pleasure which exceeds phallic determination. While it is evident that such thinking simply repeats the terms which make female sexuality the mystical 'dark continent', the notion of female 'ecstasy' clearly contains within it a hazard: taken literally, from the Greek, as ex-stasis ('to move out of oneself'), female ecstasy represents an instability at the heart of the gendered identities around which heterosexual sexuality circulates since the woman is 'elsewhere'.

It would be pleasing to conclude that *Amateur* accomplishes this unsettling. However, I must be left unsatisfied. For, despite the offer of space of/for women outside of the power structures of heterosexuality, the potential disruption that the precariousness of female sexuality may hold must be balanced against its significance within a specific visual economy. The film's image of Sofia's ecstasy is produced within the context of video pornography, framed as voyeuristic spectacle and addressed to male spectators for whom her orgasm is the visible sign of the pleasure 'given' to her. Is this, then, a critique of the specularisation of female sexuality as the film's 'knowingness' seems to imply? Or, does the image on-screen of Sofia on video effortlessly collapse the two moments of consumption (private video porn, public independent cinema) and, even after all the twists and turns of desire, confirm the male spectator's place of mastery and control? The answer, of course, depends on where you are sitting.

Esther SONNET
Southampton Institute

Works Cited

Benvenuto, Bice and Roger Kennedy. *The Works of Jacques Lacan*. London: Free Association Books, 1986.

Corrigan, Tim. *A Cinema Without Walls: Movies and Culture After Vietnam*. London: Routledge, 1994.

De Lauretis, Teresa. 'Film and the Visible'. *How Do I Look? Queer Film and Video*. Seattle: Bay Press, 1991. 223-64.

Freud, Sigmund. *On Sexuality*. Harmondsworth: Penguin, 1977.

Grosz, E. *Jacques Lacan: A Feminist Introduction*. London: Routledge, 1990.

Hartley, Hal. *Interview/Screenplay – Amateur*. London: Faber and Faber, 1994.

Jackson, Stevi. 'Women and Heterosexual Love: Complicity, Resistance and Change'. *Romance Revisited*. Eds. Lynne Pearce and Jackie Stacey. London: Lawrence and Wishart, 1995. 49-62.

Mitchell, Juliet and Jacqueline Rose. Eds. *Jacques Lacan and the École Freudienne*.

Rose, Jacqueline. *Sexuality in the Field of Vision*. London: Verso, 1989.

Stacey, Jackie. 'Desperately Seeking Difference'. *Screen* 28.1 (1987): 48-61.

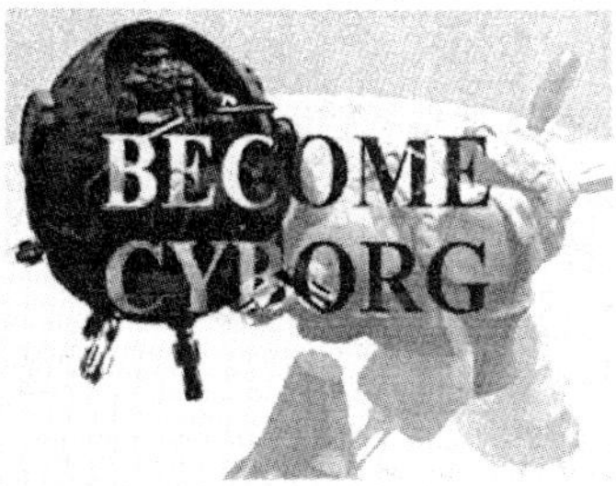

fig.1

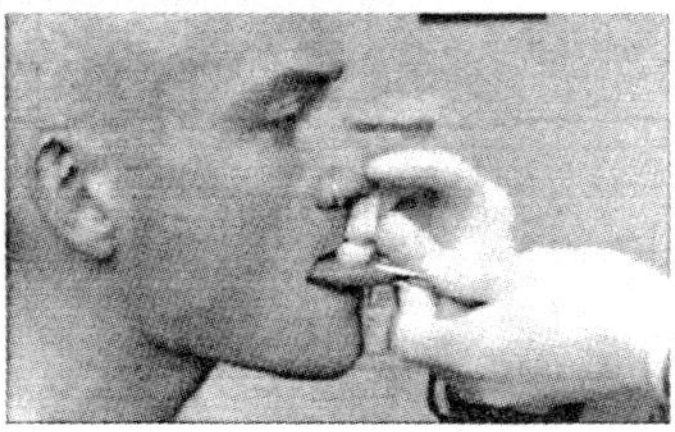

fig.2

'Your mistake', Ng says, 'is that you think that all mechanically assisted organisms – like me – are pathetic cripples. In fact, we are better than we were before'. (Stephenson 1995:231)

Technology must cease to evolve with the goal of getting humans out of the loop, and aim instead at forming with humans a higher level, synergistic machine. (De Landa 1991:217)

[The next generation of our technology] will enter every home and office and intercede between us and much of the information and experience we receive. The design of such intimate technology is an aesthetic issue as much as an engineering one. We must recognise this if we are to understand and choose what we become as a result of what we have made. (Myron Kruger, 'Responsive Environments' quoted in Rheingold 1992:113)

Introduction[1]

The second most often asked question of those with pierced bodies (after, 'Didn't that hurt?') is 'Why (on Earth!) did you do that?' There are as many possible answers to this question, however, as there are body-parts to pierce. Yet there seems to be a growing part of 'the scene' that wishes to call itself 'Modern Primitive', thereby structuring its response to this question of 'Why . . . ?' within a (borrowed) system of ritual and belief. (This desire to reinscribe an ancient,

1 I must thank Ruth Adams (University of Lancaster) for a preview copy of her dissertation, 'Conceptual Problems of Body Modification: "Modern Primitives" and New Age religion'; and Tim Sanderson (Central St Martins College of Art and Design) for his, '*Two* + *Two* = *Elephants*: Evolution and Art', as both were very helpful in directing the mutation of this piece.

spiritual dimension within contemporary life is common in many current lifestyle choices and even political actions. For example, some aspects of rave culture borrow much of their iconography and spirituality from Hinduism; note especially the London clubs, *Escape from Samsara, Institute of Goa, Return to the Source, Megatripolis*. . . . And many roads protest groups – who are strongly allied with free party networks – graft their environmentalism onto Ancient Celtic spiritualism and even modern Astrology.) What does it mean, then, to be a 'Modern Primitive'?

Fakir Musafar, celebrated Body Modifier, performer, shaman and editor/publisher of 'Body Play and Modern Primitives Quarterly', coined the term 'Modern Primitive' (also used by Vale and Juno in their collection of the same name) to describe the subjective stance that he (and those on whom he practices) occupies. Increasingly disaffected with the fragmentation and lack of spiritual direction offered by contemporary (Western) culture, the 'Modern Primitives' look to the cultures of others (often marginalised by the mainstream and idealised by the underground) to offer their lives structure. In the editorial to 'Body Play', entitled 'Worship Through The Body', Fakir writes:

> I was in Malaysia this August on a specific mission: to investigate the possibility of participating in their Thaipusam in January 1995 . . . I waited 52 years to connect with the 'source' of my inspiration for 'worship through the body'. . . . I had real insight during my August trip – an insight about the value of offering one's body as a gift to deities, revered ones and ancestors. One has choices in life. You can believe in an invisible world or not. And if you feel there are beings besides the ones you can see and touch, you can either ignore them or reach out and honor them. Your active worship of invisible beings, if they are real to you, will then come back as real gifts and blessings. (Musafar 1994b:3)

This Editorial then documents in words and photographs Musafar's involvement in three different piercing rituals: the Tamil Hindu Thaipusam Festival in Malaysia; the 'Sun Dance' ritual of North American Sioux culture (extensively detailed in Issue 9); and the Sufi Dervishes of the Rufiah culture. How PoMo can you get? At a time when meaning is constantly undermined by hypertextual anarchy and when spirituality has been usurped by technology, the 'Modern Primitive' is in desperate need for a 'Return to the Source' of Being.

This all seems rather obsessional to me. Remember how Kant articulated the rigid construction of the subject in his first *Critique* and the way that his aesthetic theory at first dissolved this rigidity and then reconstrained it, in his third *Critique*?[2] Much the same is happening with certain Body Modifiers wishing to reinscribe their practices within ancient cultural formations. What is this Primitive apart from an idealised reconstruction of something that was absorbed, surpassed, chewed-up and spat-out by the Capitalist Machine long ago? Just as the obsessive reinscribes its body (and all the possibilities for its body) within an ideal rigid structure of ritualised cleansing, organisation, movement, chanting or whatever, so too does the 'Modern Primitive' ritualise its body-changes within a similar Ideal organisation. *But it doesn't have to be this way*. There is a way to disrupt this obsessive organisation of the 'Modern Primitive' and for this we need to take the line of flight of the Cyborg. Maybe one day – the same day that De Landa's robot historian comes to write the history of its race (along the lines of *War in the Age of Intelligent Machines* [1991]) – a Cyborg historian will think with affection of its own idealised primitives, the Body Modifiers of today.

The project of this piece, then, is to articulate 'Becoming-Cyborg' in such a way that those Body Modifiers among us can steer away from the theological restrictions of the 'Modern Primitive'. Let us first, then, introduce some ideas about 'Becoming'.

2 See Kant 1933:B133 and B277; Kant 1952:175–7; see also, Brassett 1991 and Brassett in Earnshaw 1994, for a more detailed discussion of Kant's methods of subjectification.

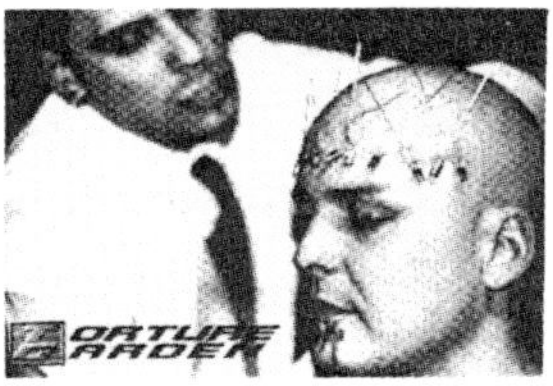

fig. 3

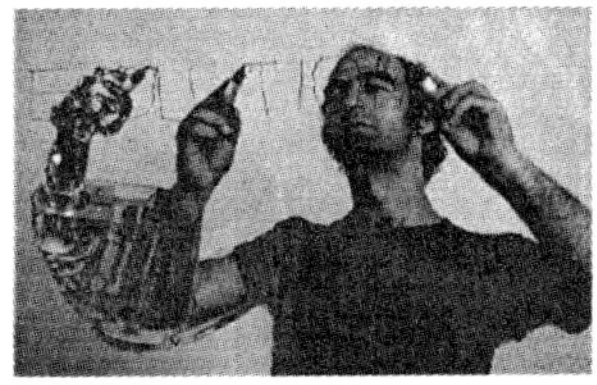

fig. 4

Becoming and bits of bodies

Apparently, PoMo really knows where it is when it comes to Becoming and its traditional adversary, Being. In his detailed and well-traced outline of the ways of Modernism and PoMo (*The Condition of Postmodernity* [1990]), David Harvey clearly identifies (and rigidifies) the location of this age-old distinction. His guide leads us as follows: Being = stasis, the aesthetics of place and the politics of the fascist, and can be thought of as PoMo; Becoming = ethics of time and space, and the politics of change, and can be broadly painted as Modernist. With this simple formulation we can easily orientate ourselves in this book. Which is made even easier as Harvey places a big arrow with the legend 'I am here' at the point where Modernist = Becoming: 'There are some who would have us return to classicism and others who seek to tread the path of the moderns. From the standpoint of the latter, every age is judged to attain "the fullness of time, not by being but by becoming". I could not agree more' (Harvey 1990:359).

On the face of it, Harvey's account of (and preference for) Becoming over Being seems laudable to me; but I can't help being put off by his desire to bind it in the shackles of a nostalgia for Modernism. The Modernism = Becoming beloved by Harvey, is that which provides a unified response to a world experienced as fragmentary and disintegrating;[3] and as Harvey makes clear throughout his book, the Modernist response to fragmentation (whether articulated through philosophy, literature or architecture) is to impose upon it an ever more sturdy rational system.[4] The critic and theorist Fredric Jameson unwittingly provides a perfect commentary upon the relationship between Harvey's longing for a lost Modernism and the 'Modern Primitive's' desire for a return to spiritual perfection, in his *Fables of Aggression. Wyndham Lewis, the Modernist as Fascist* (1979). He writes (in one of his characteristically huge sentences, which I have truncated):

> The modernist gesture is thus ideological and Utopian all at once: perpetuating the increasing subjectivisation of individual experience . . . , it also embodies a will to overcome the commodification of late nineteenth-century capitalism, and to substitute for the mouldering and overstuffed bazaar of late Victorian life the mystique and promise of some intense and heightened, more authentic experience. (Jameson 1979:39)

We can see that Harvey's Modernist = Becoming and Fakir Musafar's Body Modifiers = Modern Primitives operate along the same organisational lines. Both demand allegiance to an authenticity that once was but is now no more. A definition of Becoming which nostalgically looks backward and hopes for the recovery of a paradise now lost.

My own cartography of Becoming, however, follows the vectors announced by Deleuze and Guattari in their 'Capitalism and Schizophrenia'

---

3 In the Preface to the 1909 edition of his novel *What Maisie Knew* [1897], Henry James wrote: 'The one presented register of the whole complexity would be the play of the child's confused and obscure notion of it, and yet the whole, as I say, should be unmistakably, should be honourably there, seen through the faint intelligence, or at least attested by the imponderable presence, and still advertising its sense' (James 1966:9). While this provides a perfect description of the literary modernist's writing practice, it also shows the way in which Modernism as a whole embraced the notion of structure at a time when the certainties of Victorian life were believed to be crumbling.

4 Once again this movement is reminiscent of Kant's restratification of the anarchic aesthetic experience under the diktat of Reason, in his *Critique of Judgement*. See also fn.2.

volumes: *Anti-Oedipus* (1984) and *A Thousand Plateaus* (1987). In the second of these books, they explain:

> Becoming is a rhizome, not a classificatory or genealogical tree. Becoming is certainly not imitating or identifying with something; neither is it regressing-progressing; neither is it corresponding, establishing corresponding relations; neither is it producing, producing a filiation, or producing through filiation. Becoming is a verb with a consistency all its own; it does not reduce to, or lead back to, 'appearing', 'being', 'equalling', or 'producing'. (Deleuze and Guattari 1987:239)

For Deleuze and Guattari Becoming renounces all attempts at organisation and actively seeks to destroy not only the structures of rational authority, but also the moral high-ground that Harvey wants occupied by no-one but the *avant-garde*. For Harvey, Becoming is synonymous with Progress; the Progress revered by Hegel and his followers as Dialectic. But, as the quotation from *A Thousand Plateaus* (1987) above shows, progress (and, 'Modern Primitives' should note, regress) has nothing to do with their sense of Becoming.[5] In *A Thousand Plateaus* (1987), they write: 'A line of becoming is not defined by the points that it connects, or by the points that compose it; on the contrary, it passes *between* points, it comes up through the middle, it runs perpendicular to the points first perceived, transversally to the localisable relation to distant or contiguous points' (Deleuze and Guattari 1987:293). Unlike the conception favoured by Harvey, this Becoming is not so easy to pin down. Becoming as Progress (or even a *Return* to Progress) has very definite points of origin and aim, and although it may designate movement over stagnation, it is a movement which is allowed only a very limited range of options. Here, however, Deleuze and Guattari describe a Becoming that doesn't work on this 'join-the-dots' principle. This Becoming is

5 In the works produced by Deleuze and Guattari – not only their 'Capitalism and Schizophrenia' volumes, but their *Qu'est-ce que la philosophie?* (1991) too – Becoming is wrapped up with many of their favourite terms: deterritorialisation, rhizomes, smooth space and nomads, to name only a few.

not goal-orientated, it is not a teleology; rather, it dissipates a stratified system of goals – arranged like points in Cartesian geometry – by ensuring that any point is passed through. We are left with Becoming that is not a hierarchy of goals, but is 'a verb with a consistency all its own'. For Deleuze and Guattari, Becoming is what swarms do, it is how Nomads relate to smooth space[6] and how rhizomes erupt . . . and it has an intense relationship with the Body without Organs. Before the concept of Becoming is fleshed out, I will mention Bodies without Organs, as they will also be useful in understanding Cyborgs.

As they first disrupt the organised body/mind, subject/object dualities, Deleuze and Guattari focus upon Artaud's creation of the Body without Organs (BwO). The BwO produces nothing; it is nothing more than a collection of machinic interfaces upon a general plane of desirous fluctuations. It has no organisation and no purpose. The BwO is recognised only as a machinic amalgam; not an organism; not the organised, systematised body with all its parts allocated a specific role; but an agglomeration defined by the desires it couples. In 'plateau' 6 of their *A Thousand Plateaus* (1987), designated as 'November 8, 1947: How Do You Make Yourself a Body Without Organs?'[7] Deleuze and Guattari write:

> The BwO is opposed to . . . the organism, the organic organisation of the organs. The *judgement of God*, the system of the judgement of God, the theological system, is precisely the operation of He who makes an organism, an organisation of the organs called the organism, because He cannot bear the BwO, because He pursues it and rips it apart so He can be first, and have the organism be first. (Deleuze and Guattari 1988:158-9)

6 This is further allied to the notion of 'Cartography' not only in the joint works of Deleuze and Guattari already mentioned, but also in Guattari's *Cartographies Schizoanalytiques* (1989); for a discussion of this see Brassett 1994; see also fn.11.

7 The first English translation of this appeared as 'How to Make Yourself a Body Without Organs' in Peraldi 1981:265-270.

The BwO is not averse to organs, as such, but to their hierarchisation into the organism. 'Modern Primitives' should be afraid of the BwO. To the 'Modern Primitive' the BwO acts as a wind blowing away the spirits congregating on the organised body leaving it without a system of meaning with which to Be. Each metallic insertion, each wounding inscription, each painful overcoding of a ruptured Body as the 'Being-Organised' of the 'Modern Primitive' (Fakir Musafar's 'Worship Through The Body'[8]), talismanically wards off the BwO.

As the Body Modifier disturbs the surface structure of its body with marks or objects, *it can't help but become a BwO*, disorganising that which the dominant culture demands should be whole or perfect. The tongue, for example, once pierced, ceases to be merely an organ with which one speaks, eats, licks. . . . The pierced-tongue begins to work according to its own desires, flicking, poking, tapping, twisting and pulsating – the ordinary organisations in which the tongue works have become disrupted with a needle and 3cm long barbell. 'Rite of Passage'? 'Expression of Self'? Don't make me laugh – a pierced body-part has disengaged from the accepted codings of (whatever) culture it worked itself into. To overlay 'ritual' or 'individuation' upon an act of piercing is a gross act of bodily oppression, or self-delusion. That the BwO, in certain hands, then reterritorialises[9] upon the idea of the Primitive, is an unfortunate outcome. In discussing Artaud (who else?) once more, in their *Qu'est-ce que la philosophie?*

---

8 'But what is the value of a gift to a deity? Certainly love, intent and adoration count a lot. But is there more that one can offer? In cultures that worship through the body, the extra something is often the body itself' (Musafar 1994b:4).

9 This is an important term in the works of Deleuze and Guattari. In their 'Capitalism and Schizophrenia' volumes they identify three processes for the organisation (or otherwise) of flows. These are: territorialisation, deterritorialisation and reterritorialisation. The production of a Territory – a territorialisation – comes about when flows on the Plane of Consistency are organised into a whole hierarchical system. Deterritorialisation, quite simply, describes the dissolution of these territorial growths, reinvigorating the plane of consistency. Similarly, reterritorialisation describes the turning back of a deterritorialised flow to the uniformity of a territory. These terms are used and explained in great detail in the fourth chapter of Deleuze and Guattari 1991, entitled '*Géophilosophie*', pp.83-108.

(1991), Deleuze and Guattari write:

> Artaud said: write *for* illiterates – speak for aphasics, think for acephalics. But what does this 'for' mean? It isn't 'with the intention of . . . ', or even 'in the place of . . . ', it is 'before' [*devant*]. It is a question of becoming [*devenir*]. The thinker isn't acephalic, aphasic or illiterate, but becomes it. He becomes Indian not to finish becoming, rather 'in order that' the Indian (who is Indian) becomes something else and tears himself away from his agony. (Deleuze and Guattari 1991:105)

Becoming, they write here, is always a double action: a becoming some*thing*, and an allowing of that *thing* to become something *else*. Thus they get away from the Idealisation of the thing towards which Becoming moves, according to which the progressive Modernist Becoming – so missed by Harvey – is defined. And the 'Modern Primitive's' regressive approach to Becoming is circumvented too; for what else does their 'becoming-Indian' (for example) denote other than a situating of the place of that Indian (Idealisation)? Thus Becoming should not be regarded as a teleology but a *process*: a process which operates on multiple vectors in the promotion of a smooth space.[10] The implication of all this is that – in the terms favoured by Deleuze and Guattari – the practice of Body Modification is one of deterritorialisation.

In order to examine this claim further, we need to take the line of flight of the Cyborg: for once we have seen the Cyborg disorganise the hierarchical territory of the body (and its organs), we shall be able to see the relationship it has with Body Modification and deterritorialisation.

---

10 Deleuze and Guattari detail three distinctions between smooth and striated space, the third of which runs as follows: 'Finally, there is a third difference, concerning the surface or space. In striated space, one closes off a surface and "allocates" it according to determinate intervals, assigned breaks; in the smooth, one "distributes" oneself in an open space, according to frequencies and in the course of one's crossings (*logos* and *nomos*)' (Deleuze and Guattari 1987:481). The relationship with the concepts of territorialisation etc. (see fn.10) should be noted.

Cyborgs and subjectivities

> In the wake of the data-processing and robotics revolutions, the rise of genetic engineering, and the globalisation of markets, neither human work nor the natural habitat can return, even to their state of being a few decades ago. . . . The proper way to deal with what we have to acknowledge as a *de facto* situation is to reorientate it – which implies a redefinition in terms of *contemporary conditions* of the objectives and methods of each and every form of movement of the social. (Guattari 1989b:135)

For Guattari, the programme for this reorientation runs in terms of social, mental and environmental ecologies (what he also terms – as I have, following him – cartographies). What comes out of this process but the Cyborg? The question of subjectivity becomes more forcibly posed, Guattari argues, the further 'machines of production of signs, images, syntax and artificial intelligence' are developed (Guattari 1989b:134). In 'The Three Ecologies' the method of cartography involves critique and the articulation of new possibilities.[11] It is clear, he argues (along with many others) that technological innovations have resonances far exceeding the particular domains in which they occur. Such innovations are not intrinsically transgressive, however. The genesis of much new technology is in the laboratories of the Capitalist Machine. If De Landa's book shows us anything, it is the proximity of Cyborg production and the Capitalist War Machine. But the ways of territorialisation, reterritorialisation and deterritorialisation are interwoven with extreme complexity. The Capitalist Machine's ideal techno-subjective innovation would be an Artificial Intelligence (AI): a thinking, individual, slave machine – a reterritorialisation of deterritorialised techno-flows. The Cyborg has a different Becoming altogether.

[11] 'By their very essence, analytical cartographies reach far beyond the existential territories to which they are assigned. Like artists and writers, the cartographers of subjectivity should seek, then, with each concrete performance, to develop and innovate, to create new perspectives . . . ' (Guattari 1989b:133).

The techno-flows of the Cyborg should be left to deterritorialise . . . but how?

Both De Landa and Kelly (in his *Out of Control* [1994]), view Cyborg production very differently to the making of an AI. One of the most striking claims made by De Landa is that research into AI is somewhat misguided. Why bother trying to *replicate* human intelligence in a machine, the closing sections of his book ask, when the possibilities of *adding to* human intelligence appear to be so much more exciting? One of the prime movers of research into AI, De Landa explains, was the US Defense Department's need to remove humans from the decision-making loop in the 'playing' of war games. (Whatever the scenario, human players just could not instigate all-out nuclear war; so in order for those in charge of Military strategy, tactics and logistics to prepare for its eventuality, humans had to be replaced by intelligent machines, which would have no such compunction for avoiding Armageddon.)

The trouble is, as the need for increased machine intelligence is required – to remove 'soft' humans from each rung of the military decision making process (until the ideal is reached: a mechanised soldier with the ability to identify and destroy enemies on its own) – the most fundamental problems arise. De Landa describes some human functions that neither software nor hardware can (yet) imitate: these are photoanalysis and cryptanalysis – which, for the civilian, means the ability to make sense of three-dimensional space and the ability to translate from one language into another. Any form of working machine vision or translation needs to interface, somewhere along the data-processing loop, with what William Gibson's console jockeys call 'meat'.[12] That is, in order to create machines which operate intelligently, the best thing is to create a new construct out of the interface of human and computer. And so we have what Dr Fred Brooks of the University of North Carolina, terms Intelligence Augmentation

[12] See Gibson 1986.

(IA)[13] . . . the making of the cybernetic organism.

Cyborgs trickled onto the cultural scene via an article written by Manfred E. Clynes and Nathan S. Kline for *Aeronautics* (September 1960), called 'Cyborgs and Space'. This article explains that if space travel is to become a future possibility, then the production of Cyborgs will be a necessity. The epigraph states: 'Altering man's bodily functions to meet the requirements of extraterrestrial environments would be more logical than providing an earthly environment for him in space . . . Artefact-organism systems which would extend man's unconscious, self-regulatory controls are one possibility' (Gray 1995:29). After much technical discussion (of items such as the Rose osmotic pump,[14] and its insertion into laboratory mice) the authors conclude: 'Solving the many technological problems involved in manned space flight by adapting man to his environment, rather than vice versa, will not only mark a significant step forward in man's scientific progress, but may well provide a new and larger dimension for man's spirit as well' (Gray 1995:33). Even at their conception, the wider psychological, social and cultural significance of Cyborg production was recognised. The question remains, in whose hands would such productions be trusted? Writers like Joseba Gabilondo – in his 'Postcolonial Cyborgs. Subjectivity in the Age of Cybernetic Reproduction' – regard Cyborgs as, at best, figures of a dreamed Utopia, or, at worst, 'the hegemonic subject position that [capitalism's] ideology privileges' (Gray 1995:424). This response is understandable, insofar as it goes: once the Cyborg has been found a convenient place in which to be pigeonholed, the writer leaves, clapping the dust from his

[13] 'In the AI community, the objective is to replace the human mind by the machine and its database. In the IA community, the objective is to build systems that amplify the human mind by providing it with computer-based auxiliaries that do the things that the mind has trouble doing' (Rheingold 1992:37).

[14] '[F]or continuous slow injections of biochemically active substances at a biological rate' (Gray 1995:31).

hands after a fit-up job well done. *Of course* the Cyborg is borne from the myriad flows of capital through various military and industrial complexes, but like many other technological innovations funded by – what Guattari in 'The Three Ecologies' calls – 'Integrated World Capitalism' (Guattari 1989b: *passim*), once generated the 'product' seems to have a life of its own, like a socio-cultural virus.[15] This discussion, however, anticipates one which follows concerning the relationship between the production of schizos and BwOs.

Much work has been done over the past decade on the production and cultural significance of Cyborgs, by Donna Haraway,[16] A. R. Stone[17] and other writers in the Feminist tradition. For Haraway, the production of Cyborgs necessarily dissolves the subjective and bodily boundaries cherished by the History of Occidental Philosophy and Science. Haraway's aim is to provide for a writing of the body which disorganises the structure placed upon it by traditional scientific and philosophical discourses. She dismisses the traditional limits between Human and Animal, Human and Machine, and the Physical and the Non-Physical, in order to create an entity that is essentially transgressive. Haraway writes:

> The cyborg is a creature in a post-gender world; it has no truck with bisexuality, Pre-Oedipal symbiosis, unalienated labor, or other seductions to organic wholeness through final appropriation of all the powers of the parts into a higher unity. In a sense, the cyborg has no origin story in the Western sense; a 'final' irony since the cyborg is also the awful apocalyptic *telos* of the 'West's' escalating dominations of abstract individuation, an ultimate self untied at last from all dependency, a man in space. . . . The cyborg is resolutely committed to partiality, irony, intimacy, and perversity. (Haraway 1985:67)

15 Such a cultural virulence can be seen happening with the genesis of personal computers via the Hacker parasites in the 70s, or the dissemination of LSD from the CIA via the psychedelic underground in the 60s.

16 Particularly since Haraway 1985.

17 See Stone 1991 and 'Split Subjects...' in Gray 1995.

On the whole this seems quite appealing. Haraway muddies the boundaries between bodies (and everything else) and describes the resulting existential soup in terms of 'biotic' information processing systems. We see the tantalising presence of 'perversity', 'irony' and a certain amount of desire. But this seems to be counterbalanced by such gestures towards the tradition of organisation as '*telos*', 'individuation' and 'self'. With Cyborgs like this, is it any wonder that Gabilondo cannot see anything other than the influence of capitalist hegemony?

Which brings us up to schizos and back to BwOs. For many commentators – Gabilondo and Harvey alike – the schizo is one of the most pernicious creations of PoMo thought. Harvey writes:

> Deleuze and Guattari . . . , in their supposedly playful exposition *Anti-Oedipus*, hypothesise a relationship between schizophrenia and capitalism that prevails 'at the deepest level of one and the same economy, one and the same production process', concluding that 'our society produces schizos the same way that it produces Prell shampoo or Ford cars, the only difference being that schizos are not saleable.' [*Anti-Oedipus*, p.245] (Harvey 1990:53)

and Gabilondo: 'Claims for the Schizophrenic logic of the postmodern 'Subject' try to incorporate the modern Subject into postmodernism through the logic of nostalgia, which tries to reincorporate cultural logics and elements from the past into the present – history as nostalgic device' (Gray 1995:429). The most in-depth account of the productive relationship between capitalism and schizophrenia is given in Chapter 3 of Deleuze and Guattari's *Anti-Oedipus* (1984) (particularly sections 9 and 10). This is a notoriously difficult and long chapter and a brief map should be made here of this relationship.

Capitalism refers to a particular way of corresponding to the general flow of capital. On the whole, Capitalism tries to slow down this flow, these flows, in order to agglomerate, congeal, organise capital in the hope of maximising, or realising, its own ends. The Capitalist Machine converges with the Schizophrenic insofar as it deterritorialises the hierarchisations performed by other machines (what they call the Primitive Territorial Machine and the Barbarian Despotic Machine), decoding their formations and smoothing out their stratifications. This, however, is only part of the story. If it wasn't, then Harvey, for example, would be correct in saying that Schizophrenia and Capitalism were commensurate with each other. The Capitalist Machine may have deterritorialised the flows of Capital across the entire face of the planet, it may have co-opted the speedy, Nomadic War Machine, but each of these processes has been subject to an even greater organisation by the Capitalist Machine: what Deleuze and Guattari call an axiomatisation and reterritorialisation. They write:

> The flows are decoded *and* axiomatised by capitalism at the same time. Hence schizophrenia is not the identity of capitalism, but on the contrary its difference, its divergence, and its death. . . . Hence one can say that schizophrenia is the *exterior* limit of capitalism itself or the conclusion of its deepest tendency, but that capitalism only functions on condition that it inhibit this tendency, or that it push back or displace this limit, by substituting for it its own *immanent* relative limits, which continually reproduces on a wider scale. It axiomatises with one hand what it decodes with the other. (Deleuze and Guattari 1984:246)

The schizophrenic processes, used so successfully by Capitalism to deterritorialise, thus lurk at its perimeters like wild animals outside an encampment. The schizo, then, is no mere playful image tweaked by Deleuze and Guattari into an intricate system of metaphorics: it is the dangerous limit, 'tendency' and product of the Capitalist Machine.[18] Thus Schizoanalysis (the critique of the limits of the movement of the Capitalist Machine) and cartography coincide. Both are interested in deterritorialisation, both emphasise Becoming over Being, both map the process by which contemporary subjectification

[18] We should note – as, indeed, Harvey does (Harvey 1990:53), although he later forgets this in order to deride the work of Deleuze and Guattari (Harvey 1990:352) – that the schizo is not the clinical schizophrenic, subjectified by psychiatry.

operates.[19] The Cyborg was, for Haraway, the West's 'awful apocalyptic *telos*'; following the processes of Schizo formations under Capitalism described above, I would rather characterise it as both its 'dangerous limit' and 'tendency'. Therefore, the Schizo and the Cyborg – which are both subjective constructs of the Capitalist Machine (De Landa shows that Cyborgs are the material products at the cutting edge of military technology) – should be of interest to anyone involved in critique. This is compounded by the fact that they both describe subjective processes which are necessarily transgressive of the boundaries laid down by Capitalism (hence its desire to tightly constrain them as Institutional Beings or Artificial Intelligences).

I doubt if Fakir Musafar would be pleased with my identification of his 'Modern Primitive' practice with the stratifications of contemporary Capitalism. But, after everything that has gone before, can his practice be seen as anything other than overcoding, axiomatisation or reterritorialisation? Once again, this presupposes that the act of Body Modification is irrevocably bound up with processes that deterritorialise.

Final Remarks

Harvey has nothing but contempt for Deleuze and Guattari's works. For him they epitomise the PoMo approach to, and analysis of, subjectivity under contemporary capitalism. All those schizos and nomads! But on even the most superficial of glances, we can see that Deleuze and Guattari don't easily fit onto Harvey's map of contemporary philosophy and politics. Deleuze and Guattari advocate Schizoanalysis and smooth space, Becoming and the BwO, cartography

19 See Guattari 1989a.

and critique. Becoming has nothing to do with points, points of view or supposedly PoMo Being; and nothing to do with progress, the primacy of the *avant-garde* that Harvey pinpoints as Modernist Becoming. In true nomad style, Deleuze and Guattari's philosophy swarms across the boundaries of Harvey's outline of Modernism and PoMo. Where does this leave us with respect to Cyborgs and Body Modification?

The cyber-artist and performer Stelarc has moved in his 'shows' from piercing the body to extending it. After 'the three films of the inside of the stomach, lungs and colon/the 25 body suspensions [by large meathooks high above city streets]' (Stelarc 1995:93) he now amplifies diverse aspects of his bodily functions with a variety of sensors and transducers. Stelarc's desire is the emptying of the body of organs, replacing their functions with much more durable techno versions on the surface of the skin, in the hope (similarly expressed by Clynes and Kline in their 'Cyborgs and Space' article) that new environments (extraterrestrial or informational) can be more accessible. Stelarc's body modifications are diametrically opposite to those of Fakir Musafar – even if, physically, they seem quite similar. If Body Modifiers were not easily seen as 'primitive' Cyborgs, then Stelarc's example proves it.

We should remember, however, that Body Modification is not just about piercing. Body Modifiers have tattoos, scars, prostheses, spectacles and contact lenses, cars and bicycles, and a different outfit for every occasion. In all of these cases we can see the flowering of the cyborg, the making of the BwO, with all manner of what Lotringer calls 'technophilic intensity' (Lotringer 1981:274). That these intensities can be turned back onto the stratifications of Capitalism (even when they are done in the name of alterity – witness the 'Modern Primitive') is important insofar as such reterritorialisations can be avoided.

In the closing article of the SEMIOTEXT(E) collection *Polysexuality*, Sylvère Lotringer writes: 'Technophilic intensity (speed and fusion) automatically *liberates all the other potentialities of becoming* (Becoming-animal, or plant, or thing) that are closely closeted in what the culture keeps calling – God knows why – the free individual' (Lotringer 1981:274). This is the project of Stelarc's performances and the result of Deleuze and Guattari's Schizoanalyses. This is also what articulates Tetsuo – the Iron Man. Tetsuo is shown in some of the film's early scenes inserting pieces of grimy metal into his body. After an accident – in which a speeding car smashes into his newly cyborged leg – his body develops strange powers, growing metallic prostheses and amalgamating bits of junk until, by the film's conclusion, he has Become Cyborg. Tetsuo is the archetypal Body Modifier: he *needs* the metal he crams into it. His organised body just isn't good enough. And, once he has coalesced with the salaryman responsible for his accident, they head off to cyborgise the world.

For De Landa, to Become Cyborg involves 'establishing a "partnership" with computers and on allowing the evolutionary paths of both humans and machines to enter into a symbiotic relationship' (De Landa 1991:10). As I intimated above, this doesn't just involve computers: the driver of a car has extended the limits, form and function of her body in new and different ways; similarly with the player of electronic games. The Doctor who confronts the anxious salaryman, in *Tetsuo. The Iron Man*, remarks, 'There's a piece of metal stuck in your brain! I can't believe you're still alive! . . . You'll die if it's removed. Think of it as a piece of jewelry.' So, until nanobots, hardware/software/wetware interfaces, or intelligent prostheses become readily available, I'll have to make do with these bits of surgical steel jewellery.

Jamie BRASSETT
Camberwell College of Arts
Central Saint Martins College of Art & Design

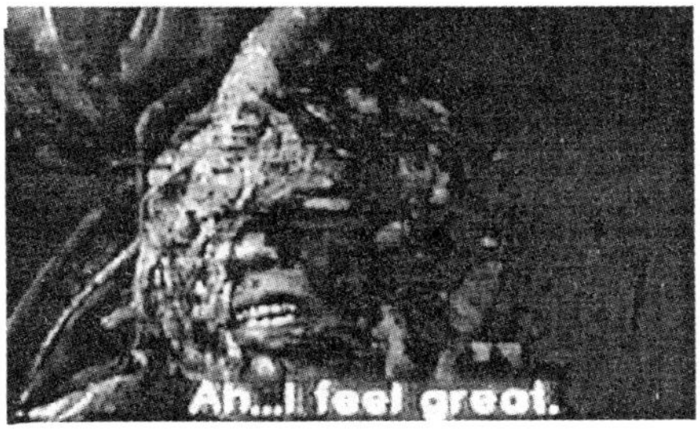

fig. 5

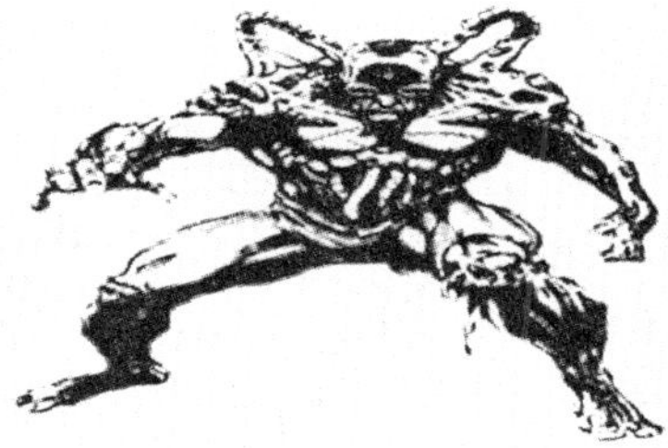

fig.6

Illustrations

All original work is reprinted with the kind permission of the individuals and organisations concerned.

figs. 1 & 6 Images created and mutated by Kurt (artist, game designer and computer animator) of AURA VISUAL (London 1996).

fig. 2 Author has his tongue pierced. (Still from the television documentary, 'Pins and Needles' [Harris 1995 (original in colour)].)

fig. 3 Photograph of Ron Athey (by Jeremy Cadaver), *Torture Garden* flyer, Saturday 5th October, 1996; also in Wood 1996:63.

fig. 4 Stelarc with Third Arm (by K. Oki [original in colour]) in Stelarc 1995:92.

fig. 5 The salaryman expresses his feelings after having mutated and coalesced with the Tetsuo cyborg. (Still from *Tetsuo. The Iron Man* [Tsukamoto 1993].)

Works Cited

Brassett, Jamie. 'Space, Postmodernism and Cartographies'. *Postmodern Surroundings*. Ed. Steven Earnshaw. Amsterdam: Rodopi, 1994. 7-22.

—. 'Kant Within the Limits of Judgement Alone'. *Pli* 3.2 (Spring 1991): 16-9.

Clynes, Manfred E. and Kline, Nathan S. 'Cyborgs and Space' in Gray. 29-33.

De Landa, Manuel. *War in the Age of Intelligent Machines.* New York: Zone Books, 1991.

Deleuze, Gilles and Guattari, Félix. *Qu'est-ce que la philosophie?* Paris: Editions de Minuit, 1991.

—. *A Thousand Plateaus.* London: The Athlone Press, 1987.

—. *Anti-Oedipus.* London: The Athlone Press, 1984.

Gabilondo, Joseba. 'Postcolonial Cyborgs. Subjectivity in the Age of Cybernetic Reproduction' in Gray. 423-32.

Gibson, William. *Neuromancer.* London: Grafton Books, 1986.

Gray, Charles Hables, ed. *The Cyborg Handbook.* New York: Routledge, 1995.

Guattari, Félix. (a) *Cartographies Schizoanalytiques.* Paris: Editions Galilée, 1989.

—. (b) 'The Three Ecologies'. *New Formations* 8 (1989): 131-47.

Haraway, Donna. 'A Manifesto for Cyborgs: Science, Technology and Socialist Feminism in the 1980s'. *Socialist Review* 15.2 (1985): 131-47.

Harris, Neil, dir. *Pins and Needles.* dancing fleas productions ltd. Anglia Television, Oct. 1995.

Harvey, David. *The Condition of Postmodernity.* London: Basil Blackwell, 1990.

James, Henry. *What Maisie Knew.* Harmondsworth: Penguin, 1966.

Jameson, Fredric. *Fables of Aggression. Wyndham Lewis, the Modernist as Fascist.* Berkeley: The University of California Press, 1979.

Kant, Immanuel. *The Critique of Judgement.* Oxford: Clarendon Press, 1952.

—. *The Critique of Pure Reason.* 2nd Impression. London: Macmillan, 1933.

Kelly, Kevin. *Out of Control. The New Biology of Machines.* London: Fourth Estate Ltd., 1994.

Lotringer, Sylvère. 'Defunkt Sex' in Peraldi. 271-97.

Musafar, Fakir. (a) 'Worship Through The Body'. *Body Play and Modern Primitives Quarterly* 10 (Spring 1994): 3-6.

—. (b) 'Sun Dance'. *Body Play and Modern Primitives Quarterly* 9 (Spring/Summer 1994): 7-12.

Peraldi, François, ed. *Polysexuality*. New York: SEMIOTEXT(E), 1981.

Rheingold, Howard. *Virtual Reality*. London: Mandarin Paperbacks, 1992.

Stelarc. 'Towards the Post-Human. From Psycho-body to Cyber-system'. *Architectural Design*. 'Architects in Cyberspace' (Profile No.118). London: Academy Group Ltd., 1995. 90-6.

Stephenson, Neal. *Snow Crash*. London: Penguin Books, 1993.

Stone, Allucquere Roseanne. 'Split Subjects, Not Atoms; or, How I Fell in Love with My Prosthesis' in Gray. 393-406.

—. 'Will the Real Body Please Stand Up? Boundary Stories about Virtual Cultures'.*Cyberspace: First Steps*. Ed. Michael Benedikt. Cambridge, Mass.: MIT Press, 1991. 81-118.

Tsukamoto, Shinya, dir. *Tetsuo. The Iron Man*. ICA Projects, 1993.

Wood, David, ed. *Torture Garden: From Bodyshocks to Cybersex*. London: Creation Books, 1996.

Vale, V. and Juno, Andrea. *Modern Primitives*. San Francisco: Re/Search Publications, 1989.

DAVID T. LLOYD

Writing on the Edge

Interviews with Writers and Editors of Wales

Amsterdam/Atlanta, GA 1997. 155 pp.
(Costerus NS 112)
ISBN: 90-420-0248-4 Hfl. 50,-/US-$ 26.-

Complex and controversial issues have accompanied the development of English-language literature in Wales, generating a continuing debate over the nature of Welsh writing in English. The main issues include the claim of some Welsh-language writers to represent the only authentic literature of Wales, the question of whether or not an extended literary tradition in English has existed in Wales, the absence (until fairly recently) of a publishing apparatus for English-language writers, the rise of a Welsh nationalism committed to preserving the Welsh language, and the question of whether English-language literature in Wales can be distinguished from English literature proper. The primary impulse for the interviews with the thirteen writers and editors in *Writing on the Edge* was to explore these and other issues relating to the literary and cultural identity in Wales in the last decade. The book's title reflects these ongoing debates about the nature and direction of contemporary Welsh literature in English, which is often perceived as peripheral both to Welsh-speaking Wales and to the literary culture of England. As one of the contributors to the volumes says "This is what it is to be Welsh ... It's an edge. There's no moment of life in Wales that hasn't got that edge, unless you decide you're not Welsh."

HANS R. RUNTE

Writing Acadia
The Emergence of Acadian Literature 1970-1990

Amsterdam/Atlanta, GA 1997. 243 pp.
(Chiasma 6)
ISBN: 90-420-0237-9 Hfl. 75,-/US-$ 39.-

The phenomenal development of writing and literary creation among the francophone communities of eastern Canada has gone largely unnoticed and unprobed outside the fragmented land of Acadia. *Writing Acadia* attempts for the first time to observe from a distance the invention of literature in oral Acadia, and to interpret, assess and order the manifold manifestations of the transition from epic story-telling to writing as a means of nation-building. Having begun to write, modern Acadia has truly (re)written herself into existence, an existence now threatened by postmodern un-writing of literature.

Destined not only for specialists but also and especially for readers with a general interest in literature, including students of all levels, *Writing Acadia* presents generous samples of Acadian poetry, drama and prose, with accompanying English translations.

EDITIONS RODOPI B.V.

USA / Canada:
2015 South Park Place
Atlanta, GA 30339
Phone (770) 933-0027 / **Fax** 933-9644
Call toll-free (U.S.only) 1-800-225-3998

All Other Countries:
Keizersgracht 302-304
1016 EX Amsterdam, The Netherlands
Tel. ++ 31 (0)20 622 75 07
Fax ++ 31 (0)20 638 09 48

e-mail: orders-queries@rodopi.nl — http://www.rodopi.nl

TRANSLATING SENSITIVE TEXTS: LINGUISTIC ASPECTS

Ed. by Karl Simms

Amsterdam/Atlanta, GA 1997. 342 pp.
(Approaches to Translation Studies 14)
ISBN: 90-420-0270-0 Bound Hfl. 175,-/US-$ 92.-
ISBN: 90-420-0260-3 Paper Hfl. 50,-/US-$ 26.-

This volume brings together twenty-two of the world's leading translation and interpreting theorists, to address the issue of sensitivity in translation. Whether in novels or legal documents, the Bible or travel brochures, in translating ancient texts or providing simultaneous interpretation, sensitive subject-matter, contentious modes of expression and the sensibilities of the target audience are the biggest obstacles to acceptance of the translator's work. The contributors bring to bear a wide variety of approaches - generative, cognitive, lexical and functional - in confronting this problem, and in negotiating the competing claims of source cultures and target cultures in the areas of cultural, political, religious and sexual sensitivity. All of the articles are presented here for the first time, and in his Introduction Karl Simms gives an overview of the philosophical and linguistic questions which have motivated translators of sensitive texts through the ages. This book will be of interest to all working translators and interpreters, and to teachers of translation theory and practice.

EDITIONS RODOPI B.V.

USA / Canada:
2015 South Park Place
Atlanta, GA 30339
Phone (770) 933-0027 / **Fax** 933-9644
Call toll-free (U.S.only) 1-800-225-3998

All Other Countries:
Keizersgracht 302-304
1016 EX Amsterdam, The Netherlands
Tel. ++ 31 (0)20 622 75 07
Fax ++ 31 (0)20 638 09 48

e-mail: orders-queries@rodopi.nl — http://www.rodopi.nl